THE IRON BARONS

Recent Titles in
Contributions in Economics and Economic History
Series Editor: Robert Sobel

Business Depressions and Financial Panics: Collected Essays in American Business and Economic History
Samuel Rezneck

Towards an Integrated Society: Reflections on Planning, Social Policy, and Rural Institutions
Tarlok Singh

The Age of Giant Corporations: A Microeconomic History of American Business, 1914-1970
Robert Sobel

Samuel Gompers and the Origins of the American Federation of Labor, 1848-1896
Stuart Bruce Kaufman

Statistical View of the Trusts: A Manual of Large American Industrial and Mining Corporations Active Around 1900
David Bunting

State and Regional Patterns in American Manufacturing, 1860-1900
Albert W. Niemi, Jr.

The American Banking Community and New Deal Banking Reforms, 1933-1935
Helen M. Burns

Gold Is Money
Hans F. Sennholz, editor

The Drive to Industrial Maturity: The U. S. Economy, 1860-1914
Harold G. Vatter

Individual Freedom: Selected Works of William H. Hutt
Svetozar Pejovich and David Klingaman, editors

Friedrich A. Sorge's *Labor Movement in the United States:* A History of the American Working Class from Colonial Times to 1890
Philip S. Foner and Brewster Chamberlin, editors

Essays in Southern Labor History: Selected Papers, Southern Labor History Conference, 1976
Gary M Fink and Merle E. Reed, editors

THE IRON BARONS

A Social Analysis of an American Urban Elite, 1874-1965

Contributions in Economics and Economic History, Number 18

John N. Ingham

Greenwood Press
Westport, Connecticut London, England

Library of Congress Cataloging in Publication Data

Ingham, John N
The iron barons.

(Contributions in economics and economic history ; no. 18)
Bibliography: p.
Includes index.
1. Steel industry and trade—United States—History. 2. Social classes—United States—History.
I. Title.
HD9515.15 301.44'92 77-84761
ISBN 0-8371-9891-7

Library of Congress Catalog Card Number: 77-84761
ISBN: 0-8371-9891-7
ISSN: 0084-9235

First published in 1978

Greenwood Press, Inc.
51 Riverside Avenue, Westport, Connecticut 06880

Printed in the United States of America

10 9 8 7 6 5 4 3 2 1

FOR BILLY INGHAM, 1971-1974

Contents

Tables

Acknowledgments

The author of any book incurs a number of debts to others during the years of research, writing and publishing. This endeavor is no exception. My principal intellectual debt is to Samuel P. Hays of the University of Pittsburgh. The idea for this project first surfaced as a seminar paper during my initial year of graduate study, and Professor Hays continued to guide it through several important phases.

For financial support, I would like to thank the State University of New York and its Research Foundation, which provided me with two successive summer stipends to finish the research and write the manuscript. I am also indebted to the staffs of many libraries for their assistance: the Carnegie Public Library of Pittsburgh; the Pennsylvania Historical Society; the Ohio Historical Society; the Western Reserve Historical Society; Cleveland Public Library; Youngstown Public Library and Wheeling Public Library.

I also wish to extend my profound thanks to Brenda Kingman, who patiently and expertly typed several drafts of the manuscript. In addition, I wish to thank my colleagues at the State College at Brockport, especially Owen S. Ireland, W. Bruce Leslie and Kenneth P. O'Brien. I have also benefited from seminar contact and friendship with several graduate students at Brockport: Elizabeth Phelps Brengle, Thomas Dugan, Richard and Susan Graziano, Richard Habeeb, Sheila Izzo, Daniel Karin and Carolyn Vitale.

Finally, I wish to thank my wife, Gwynne, and children, John, Jim and Susan, for their encouragement over these years, and particularly for never allowing me to take myself too seriously.

Preface

The years from 1874 to 1900 represent a seminal period in the iron and steel industry in America; they stand as distinct from the earlier and later epochs. In 1874, the industry was dominated by a large number of small firms, and a handful which had attained medium size, with production of about 25,000 tons of iron per year. Although Bessemer converters had been introduced into America several years before, there was still little manufacture of steel. Thus a relatively stable and prosperous iron industry was on the brink of a great Bessemer steel revolution which would engulf it during the next quarter century. This revolution would profoundly alter the size of many firms in the industry and would lead to large, integrated corporations. Then, in a great merger movement, hundreds of these firms would be absorbed into huge, new holding companies controlled largely by investment bankers.

The period from 1874 to 1900, then, was one of both substantial stability and revolutionary change, a period distinctly different from the era after the turn of the century and the era before the Civil War. The iron and steel entrepreneurs of the period from 1874 to 1900 form an important transition group from an older, almost preindustrial system to the mature economy of the 1920s. In order to more clearly perceive their role, it is necessary to look more closely at the evolution of the iron and steel industry during these years.

The American iron and steel industry had its beginnings in the seventeenth century, when a blast furnace was built at Saugus, Massachusetts, in 1645. Throughout the seventeenth and eighteenth centuries, a small and widely dispersed industry produced castings for stoves, household utensils, nails, sheet iron and farming implements, and produced iron for shipbuilding. After 1800, however, the industry expanded substantially, with hundreds of individual entrepreneurs entering into production. These tiny firms were short-lived; they "rose and fluttered and fell like May flies."[2]

Prior to the 1830s, all iron production was based upon the use of charcoal fuel in smelting local iron ores. The use of wood fuel made smelting development dependent upon extensive use of the land; and in many respects the industry was more analogous to agriculture than to the iron and steel firms of the late nineteenth century. The wide-scale introduction of anthracite coal as a blast furnace fuel in the 1840s removed the limitations which charcoal fuel had placed upon the iron industry, since the furnaces no longer needed to be located near the source of wood fuel. Thus, local dispersion became less characteristic, and iron plants began to concentrate in several areas of the Northeast—particularly in eastern Pennsylvania, where large deposits of anthracite were located.

By the time of the Civil War, the American iron industry was large and well established, with furnaces located in twenty-six states. It was engaged in producing pig iron , iron blooms, and bar, sheet and railroad iron, as well as iron wire, iron forgings, car wheels, and iron castings. Yet its very size and relative dispersion also pointed to the fundamental lack of integration of these facilities. Most of the leading rolling mills and finished-iron producers were not connected with the blast furnaces which provided their pig iron. The industry was still segmented rather than integrated. There was virtually no steel industry in existence in the years prior to the Civil War. Most of the steel produced was blister steel, and only after the 1850s did small quantities of higher-quality crucible steel begin to be manufactured. Generally, steel was still too expensive to be a factor in the marketplace, with only about 12,000 tons being produced in the entire country.

Two major developments in the years after the Civil War fundamentally altered the nature of the industry, and lent a unique industrial and technological atmosphere to the late nineteenth century. The first of these was the development of coke—made from bituminous coal—as a substitute for anthracite. This, along with the introduction of iron ore from the Mesabi range in Minnesota, moved the center of iron and steel production to western Pennsylvania and Ohio, especially to Pittsburgh. The second major innovation was the introduction and eventual widespread adoption of Bessemer steel.

A principal reason for the rise of the western Pennsylvania area to predominence in the iron and steel industry was the shift to bituminous coal and coke after 1870, which rapidly replaced anthracite as the leading fuel. Since large veins of bituminous coal were found in the Connellsville region near Pittsburgh, this spurred the shift to that area; and by 1880 the western part of the state had passed the east in its product value of iron and steel goods ($65.4 million to $70.2 million). The east, however, still produced a greater amount of pig iron.

The trend of the industry to center in Allegheny County was clear even by 1875, when the county produced nearly 25 percent of all the rolled iron manufactured in the United States. The dominance of western Pennsylvania and eastern Ohio in the iron and steel industry continued well into the twentieth century. By 1900, Pennsylvania produced 47 percent of all pig iron in the United States, 80 percent of the open hearth steel, 52 percent of the Bessemer steel, and 56 percent of the finished rolled iron and steel products. Ohio ranked second with 18 percent of the aggregate iron and steel output. Of significance, however, was the fact that Illinois ranked third, with 10 percent. During the twentieth century, the industry continued moving west until its center was in Chicago, surpassing Allegheny county's production in the 1920s.

The shift to Bessemer steel production had an even more dramatic impact upon the industry, as seen in the rise of basic productivity and in the changes in plant and corporate structure which accompanied it. In 1874 American pig iron production was only 41 percent of Great Britain's; but in the next twenty years the industry experienced such phenomenal growth that, in 1895, U.S. production was 19 percent greater than Britain's. By 1900 American production was almost four times greater than Britain's; and this supremacy continued throughout the first seventy years of the twentieth century. In 1945, America's mills were at their peak, making over 62 percent of the world's steel. By 1968, however, the American share of the world's market had declined to only 22.5 percent; and in 1971—for the first time since 1890—America's output was surpassed by that of the U.S.S.R.

The last quarter of the nineteenth century, however, had been a heady time—the glory years of phenomenal growth and expansion. In 1875, 1.75 million tons of finished iron and steel products were manufactured. Of this, 81 percent was iron production and 19 percent was steel. Most of the steel (81 percent) was rolled into rails. By 1886, total production had increased nearly 250 percent to 4,331,000 tons. Of this amount, only 47 percent was in iron products, and most of the steel (nearly 70 percent) was being rolled into rails. Ten years later, total production was in excess of 5.5 million tons, three-quarters of it being steel. At the end of the century, production stood at two and one-half times greater than production five years earlier, and over seven times greater than in 1875. Nearly all of it was now steel (84 percent), but only about 28 percent of the steel was being rolled into rails: most was now being put to more diversified uses. In the overall evolution of the industry, open hearth steel was replacing Bessemer as the major form of steel production.

The principal consumers of iron and steel products during the latter part of the nineteenth century were the railroads, which purchased an average of 1.5 million tons of steel rails per year. In the 1890s, however, as railroad expansion slackened somewhat and city development became more pronounced, steel for the construction industry—especially I-beams—became more predominant. These two major uses of steel were followed, in order, by: shipbuilding, the machinery industry, agriculture, pipe for oil and gas producers, and tinplate for the metal container industry.

In the characteristic functioning of the industry in 1875, iron ore was shipped to the blast furnace area from Michigan or Minnesota, or from local ore supplies, and was then converted to pig iron. The pig iron was then shipped to finishing mills, to be puddled. In most cases the puddling and rolling mills did not produce their own pig iron. Puddling was a process by which the pig iron was converted to wrought iron before it was rolled into finished iron products. Most of the iron produced was rolled into rails—nearly one million tons. The rest was used for sheets, wire, plates, bars and structural shapes. In general, the industry was characterized by a large number of small-to-medium sized firms, with the average blast furnace producing less than fifty tons per day (15,000 to 20,000 tons per year). The finished iron producers were similarly small: even the rail mills generally produced on a small scale.

In the next few years, however, the industry was to dramatically transform itself by the adoption of the Bessemer process. As Peter Temin has noted: The Bessemer process . . . represented an unorthodox leap in the . . . production of iron, the jump forms a point of discontinuity in the otherwise more gradual development of sophistication in production techniques.[3] The minimum economic size of the Bessemer plant became far larger than anything known before—a development which led to a different industrial structure in steel making than had prevailed in iron making. Also, the advantages of integrating all stages of production were more pronounced for Bessemer steel than for iron, and this would lead directly to the large integrated firms of the 1890s.

Although the Bessemer process was established on a commercial basis in the United States in 1867, it was not until the 1880s that it became dominant in the making of rails and, in so doing, took precedence in the entire industry. The great advantage of Bessemer steel was that it could produce a product superior in strength and durability to puddled iron products, and at only slightly higher cost. The problem was that establishing a Bessemer steel plant required a great deal more capital than the older puddling plants, with a first class Bessemer plant costing about $200,000 to build.

By 1886 Bessemer steel surpassed iron as the predominant product in the industry; and this was to remain true to the end of the century. During the 1890s, however, a new form of steel making—the open hearth process—emerged to challenge the status of Bessemer steel. Although only one-third of all steel produced in 1900 was of the open hearth variety, the proportion would rise increasingly as the twentieth century progressed.

Unlike Bessemer steel, the open hearth process was a logical development of the puddling process. Thus it was more attractive to many of the old iron makers who had resisted the conversion to Bessemer steel. Also, the replacement of the demand for rails by the need for other products made of higher quality steel furthered the transition away from the Bessemer process. This was to complete the final transition of the industry from iron to steel during the late nineteenth century. Several smaller firms which did not adopt the open hearth method opted for the crucible steel process, which enabled them to produce smaller quantities of very high quality tool steel for a small, highly specialized and profitable market.

The conversion of an older iron industry to steel production, particularly to Bessemer steel, was to profoundly alter the corporate structure of the industry. An industry dominated by small firms owned by single individuals or simple partnerships gave way, by the end of the century, to larger integrated firms; nearly all of these were corporations, some controlled by investment bankers.

Part of the story of the evolution of the iron and steel industry can be told from a relatively simple chart showing the growth in the average size of blast furnaces and rolling mills.

As can be seen in Table 1, the average capitalization of blast furnaces increased nearly fourfold from 1869 to 1899, while the capitalization of steelworks and rolling mills increased over 600 percent. Similarly, the average annual production of the blast furnace saw a thirteenfold increase, while that of rolling mills and steel works was nearly eight times greater by the end of the period. Finally, the average size of the firm—in terms of the numbers of wage earners employed—also increased, although not as dramatically, with a 250 percent increase in blast furnaces and 350 percent increase in steel works and rolling mills. Thus the average iron and steel firm by 1900, whether producing pig iron or finished iron and steel, was significantly more expensive to establish, had a profoundly higher annual productivity, and was a large-scale employer of labor.

TABLE 1
Averages for Iron and Steel Establishments, 1869-1899

	Capital (x 1,000)	Yearly Production (tons x 1,000)	Number of Employees
Blast Furnaces			
1869	$145	5	71
1879	262	10	122
1889	426	29	110
1899	643	65	176
Steel Works and Rolling Mills			
1869	156	3	119
1879	267	7	220
1889	661	14	332
1899	967	23	412

SOURCE: Peter Temin, *Iron and Steel in Nineteenth-century America: An Economic Inquiry* (Cambridge: Harvard University PRess, 1964), p. 166; from U. S. Census of Manufacturers, 1914, *Abstract,* pp. 640-641; Appendix C. Table C.8.

Yet looking at the average size of the iron and steel plants somewhat obscures the fact that, while some plants grew rather slowly over this period, other plants experienced phenomenal growth rates. In 1880 only nine companies had a capacity to produce over 100,000 tons per year—having an average capacity of 205,000 tons, with Carnegie Steel the leader at 450,000 tons. Just twelve years later several companies exceeded a 250,000-ton capacity, while Carnegie Steel and Illinois Steel could produce over 1,000,000 tons per year. Each firm had been capitalized at twenty-five million dollars; but Carnegie Steel grew so rapidly during the following eight years that it was re-capitalized at $320 million in 1900. By this time it was producing nearly four million tons of finished steel products. Several other firms were showing the same growth tendencies, although having lesser capacities: Illinois Steel, American Steel and Wire, Federal Steel, American Bridge, National Tube, National Steel, American Tin Plate, American Sheet Steel, American Steel Hoop, and Jones and Laughlin Steel.

Sheer growth in size, however, was only part of the story of these giants: the other side was the increasing movement toward integration. At first, in the late 1880s and 1890s, the movement was principally toward vertical integration to obtain ownership of ore and coal mines, blast furnaces and transportation facilities. As mentioned above, the inducement for vertical integration grew naturally out of the production demands of Bessemer converters. The motive for horizontal integration in the latter years of the 1890s, however, came primarily from the desire to obtain greater control of the marketplace in order to stabilize the prices of steel products.

These integrative movements of the 1890s produced the industrial giants mentioned above and led to the eventual formation of U.S. Steel in 1901. Capitalized at nearly one and one-half billion dollars, with a productive capacity of over nine million tons, U.S. Steel controlled 37 percent of the nation's iron and steel capacity and 60 percent of the Bessemer steel making capacity.

The formation of U.S. Steel was followed by the creation of other giants in the early twentieth century: Bethlehem Steel, Republic Steel, National Steel, Jones and Laughlin, Inland Steel, Amco Steel, Youngstown Sheet and Tube, and several other large firms—Lukens Steel, Sharon Steel, Pittsburgh Steel, Wheeling Steel, Crucible Steel, Alan Wood Steel, Phoenix Steel and others. The small,independent iron and steel entrepreneur had, for all practical purposes, vanished. He had been replaced in the iron and steel industry by the investment banker and the professional manager.

It shall be the major purpose of this book to trace the rise of hundreds of men and families to postitions of wealth and power in the rapidly expanding iron and steel industry of the late nineteenth century. It will then trace the manner in which these same families consolidated and improved their social positions during the twentieth century, even though the original source of their wealth and power—their iron and steel firms—had slipped from their grasps. To a large degree, it is a story of continuity and social homogeneity. Even while the industry itself went through an organizational and technological revolution, the social position of these independent iron and steel entrepreneurs remained virtually unchanged.

NOTES

1. For those wishing an in-depth analysis of the iron and steel industry, the most comprehensive source is William T. Hogan S. J., *Economic History of the Iron and Steel Industry*

of the U.S., 5 volumes (Lexington, Mass: D.C. Heath, 1971). Volume 1 deals with the period to 1900.

In addition, there is an excellent study by Peter Temin, *Iron and Steel in 19th Century America: An Economic Inquiry* (Cambridge: Harvard Univ. Press, 1964), which deals with the industry from 1830 to 1900.

Finally, there is a study by a geographer, Kenneth Warren, *The American Steel Industry, 1850–1970: A Geographical Interpretation* (Oxford, Eng.: Clarendon Press, 1973). All three books have extensive bibliographies for the curious reader.

2. Quoted in Warren, *American Steel Industry,* p. 11.

3. Temin, *Iron and Steel,* p. 4.

John N. Ingham

THE IRON BARONS

Introduction

Over a quarter of a century ago, Thomas C. Cochran issued a call for a new approach to the study of American businessmen. Rather than focusing upon the unique, the episodic and the pathological, he stressed that "the entrepreneurial historian is interested in the cultural patterns and social structures which have produced these assumed types [of businessmen]."[1] Rather than analyzing individual businessmen, or simply dealing with entrepreneurial decision making, Cochran implored historians to uncover the social and cultural institutions—both inside and outside the business firm—which had created particular types of business leaders. In response to this challenge, there have been some excellent studies of the economic and business world itself; but relatively little has been written concerning the social lives of American businessmen.[2]

Perhaps the most significant works in this latter area have been done by a team of historians at Harvard's Entrepreneurial Research Center, and by a sociologist. William Miller, Irene Neu and Frances Gregory at the Entrepreneurial Research Center have each undertaken quantitative investigation of particular aspects of the business community. The pathbreaking studies of these scholars deal mainly with the social origins of businessmen of the 1870s and the early twentieth century. They are instructive in demonstrating that the widely accepted belief that these businessmen were recruited from the ranks of the new, lower-class immigrants was misleading. By showing that these businessmen, in fact, came from generally upper-middle-class, White-Anglo-Saxon Protestant households, the authors provide intriguing glimpses into the possible operation of the social structure *vis-à-vis* business entrepreneurship. Unfortunately, these insights remain more speculative than definitive. The authors provide no clear picture of what the social structure was like at that time, how it was changing, what the precise interrelationship was between it and the newly emergent business community, or how the latter differed from the business elite of earlier days.[3]

The sociologist, E. Digby Baltzell, has perhaps provided the best approximation of a full-scale structural treatment of the businessman in his social, economic and political setting.[4] His analysis of the development of the Philadelphia upper classes provides an excellent context within which to place the rise of some of the newer industrial giants of the late nineteenth century. His study is quite informative about the power of the traditions of the older upper classes in shaping the life-styles and aspirations of the newer elites in Philadelphia.

Yet, significant questions concerning the social roles of American businessmen remain unanswered in Baltzell's book. First of all, since he studied only Philadelphia, we are left with no concrete sense of the typicality of the environment he covered.[5] Philadelphia was an old seacoast city, with extremely well-entrenched upper classes. This calls into question its typicality for the balance of the American urban, business environment. Secondly, as a sociologist, Professor Baltzell was more concerned with the implications of the past for the present, rather than with the past for its own sake. Because of this disciplinary bias, he provided a clear conception of the manner in which social traditions in Philadelphia have shaped its contemporary situation at the upper-class levels; but we are left much less clear as to what the implications were for the nineteenth and early twentieth centuries.

The limitations of previous work on businessmen, then (with the partial exception of Baltzell), has been the narrow framework within which businessmen have been viewed. Generally, most studies have simply analyzed the businessman within the entrepreneurial decision-making framework. It is imperative that this perspective be broadened to view the businessman within an institutional context which had a profound and intricate impact upon his entire life. The present study proposes to fill that important gap.

Although the institutional context within which the businessmen functioned included a great variety of elements, only three major influences will be analyzed in this study: family; social institutions; and city or community. These phenomena are not isolated, but completely interrelated and involving constant interaction.

To abstract businessmen from this institutional context, as most historians have done, is simply to ignore reality. In the family and social institutions we have two of the most powerful primary groups in the life of any individual or society. With their intimate, ongoing contact, they constitute what Charles Horton Cooley has called "the Nursery of Human Nature."[6] Together, they form much of what is seen as the basic human nature of the individual and the culture of a society. The locale in which he resided (the traditions, culture and general self-image of the area), although including many influences of a more secondary nature, also had a profound effect on the individual and society. Thus, ignoring this institutional context neglects the most important realities in the life of a businessman.

By referring to an institutional context, then, we are referring to something akin to a "social system," only in more restricted terms. As Talcott Parsons has noted:

> A social system consists in a plurality of individual actors interacting with each other in a situation which has at least physical or environmental aspects, actors who are motivated in terms of a tendency to the "optimization of gratification" and whose relation to their situation, including each other, is defined and mediated in terms of a system of culturally structured and shared symbols.[7]

Although it is not possible to reconstruct the entire social system of the nineteenth century, even at the upper-class level, it is possible to isolate and analyze three of the most important institutions. Even these cannot be reconstructed in their entirety; but enough will be done to give a sense of their interaction and influence. An extensive survey of the general importance of these institutions shall be given in Chapter 3.

One element of the institutional context which demands more explanation is that of the city or community itself. Although on one level there was a great deal of similarity among the six cities under investigation (Pittsburgh, Philadelphia, Bethlehem, Cleveland, Youngstown and Wheeling)—all had select neighborhoods, club systems, and complex kinship groupings—the variety of differences among them was as important as their similarities. For example, the traditions and the tenor of life in the older seacoast cities differed in a myriad of ways from those in the newer, less developed cities of the western areas. In addition, the prevailing ethno-cultural or religious group in a community did much to set the tone of that area, to stamp it with a certain particularity. These aspects are at times difficult to classify and even less amenable to quantification, very often involving symbolic relationships existing in men's minds. This difficulty in no way reduces their importance for a complete examination of the institutional context.

To illustrate both the difficulty and the importance of this analysis of the role of the community in the institutional complex, an example from one of the cities under investigation will be given. If one takes the case of the city of Pittsburgh, and considers its cultural and psychological role toward the older seacoast cities such as Philadelphia, an interesting and complex comparison results. Although Pittsburgh's iron and steel entrepreneurs differed little from those in Philadelphia, or from American businessmen generally, there had long been a stereotype about these Pittsburgh steelmen. This view saw the city as the seedbed of "shirtsleeve millionaries," of barefoot boys from poor families who amassed great wealth and power by dint of their own work and intelligence. Yet, as this study will show, Pittsburgh iron and steel men were largely the sons of businessmen, from upper-middle-class and upper-class backgrounds. Was there no substance to the stereotype? Was it simply a myth, a fantasy concocted in the mind of some imaginative journalist? Although this may have been partially true, it does seem that there was also some reality behind it.

What we seem to witness in late nineteenth-century Pittsburgh is not so much the rise to wealth of a group of poor boys but the rise of one of the cultural minorities of the eighteenth century to positions of relative social acceptance by the older upper class in the seacoast cities. The group on the rise was the Scotch-Irish; and "Pittsburgh is the very center of the Scotch-Irish population in America. At one time, seven-eighths of the businessmen of the city were Scotch-Irish, and even now, it is said, three-fourths of the entire population are of that blood."[8] Thus, what happened in Pittsburgh in the late nineteenth century was less the rise of a group of individuals from poverty origins to wealth, than it was the rise of men and families—already wealthy and part of the upper-class social system in that city, —to positions of relative parity with seacoast elites in cities such as Philadelphia. Yet, as ever in situations of social change and mobility, the stereotypes and images of the city and its people as poor and crude, from backgrounds considered inferior by the seacoast elites, died hard.

The idea that the Scotch-Irish might be considered a minority group in the later nineteenth century may be a little difficult for the reader to digest. After all, in a study of social distance in the 1920s, people of Scottish origin ranked next to the English in the degree of acceptance by native Americans.[9] Yet, this had not always been the case. In the early eighteenth century, after the first major waves of Scotch-Irish immigration, attitudes soured among native Americans (primarily of English ancestry). The stereotype developed for the Scotch-Irish was very much like that given to the Catholic Irish in the nineteenth century and to blacks in the twentieth century: "Scotch-Irish . . . were regarded as quick tempered, impetuous, inclined to work by fits and starts, reckless, too much given to drinking. No contemporary observer praised them as model farmers."[10] Their experience as a colonizing group in Ireland, amid a hostile and violent native population, outfitted them with traits and a temperament ideal for frontiersmen and Indian fighters; but hardly made them congenial neighbors. This resulted in a divided view concerning them. On the one hand, they were used to combat the Indians, particularly needed by the pacifist Quakers; on the other hand, they were greatly feared and hated by these same seacoast groups.[11] But what of the nineteenth century? Had the situation changed? If so, how much had it changed?

To be sure, great alterations in the social position of the Scotch-Irish, and in their relationship to the dominant, largely English society, had taken place. This was due to several factors: the maturing of the Scotch-Irish settlements; the increased wealth and stability of the group; and, most importantly, the coming of the Catholic Irish. When faced with the challenge of this large and seemingly more dangerous new group of outcasts, ethnocentrism drew the English and the (once socially subordinant) Scotch-Irish together as allies against the common enemy. The Scotch-Irish then became defenders of the establishment, and vigorous defenders at that.

This development brought the Scotch-Irish into the mainstream of respectability in American society; but it is doubtful that they had yet won acceptance at its uppermost levels. This remaining social distance was evidenced by the establishment, in 1889, of the Scotch-Irish Society of America. The goals of the society seemed to have been twofold. On the one hand, they wished to demonstrate that they were as American and as patriotic as any group in society. In fact, as has been the case with many a newly emergent group, they continually alluded to the idea that they were the most uniquely American of all.[12] They felt that their role as the true American had been ignored by Puritan historians; and it was one of the functions of the society to correct this imbalance.[13] The other function, seemingly somewhat at variance with the first, was to provide members with a sense of their own unique Scotch-Irish heritage, a set of traditions to be passed down to their descendants.[14] This seeming contradiction, however, is again quite characteristic of minority groups passing through a marginal situation.[15]

Thus, when Pittsburgh emerged as the center of the iron and steel industry, its entrepreneurs—largely Scotch-Irish—seemed to be men on the move; and, indeed they were. But it was not poverty they were forsaking; it was a negative cultural stereotype. As such it was a very important form of mobility, but sharply divergent from the standard myth.

Inter-urban comparisons, then, are an important dimension in the institutional nevertheless of great importance for a total understanding of the role and position of businessmen in the late nineteenth century. There are certainly other institutions which affect the lives of businessmen; but the three under analysis in this study seem to cover the major elements of the situation. Within the three areas chosen, however, a certain selection process was involved. These areas of selection will be examined in some detail in order to demonstrate what is to be studied and what aspects have been omitted.

In choosing the cities for study, the selection process was limited, first of all, by the fact that a relatively small number of areas in the United States had iron and steel establishments. Among those which had these establishments, a number of small towns and isolated areas with a single small firm were eliminated. These places were judged to be too heterogeneous and inconsequential to figure importantly. Beyond these, there were two major centers of steel production in the United States which are not included.

The city of Boston had a rather extensive iron and steel industry in the earlier nineteenth century, but by the 1870s it was dying out. It did not, therefore, fit very well into the more dynamic concepts of growth to be used for analysis in this study. In addition, as the iron and steel industry declined in Boston, many of that city's entrepreneurs established firms in the cities considered in this study—a notable example being the National Tube Company in Pittsburgh.

The other city omitted from the study was Chicago. It is true that Chicago, as a middle-western city, would have provided additional insights for this study; but it was concluded that sufficient insight into the Chicago situation had already been gained, since several steel manufacturers from Cleveland, Youngstown and Pittsburgh established some of the more important steel firms in Chicago. Also, consolidation came earlier to Chicago than to the other cities. A very large number of firms were absorbed first into Illinois Steel and then Federal Steel, both of which were controlled by investment banking groups. Thus the independent iron and steel entrepreneur, upon which this study is based, had been virtually eliminated from the Chicago scene by the late 1880s.

In order to illustrate the range of social environments represented by each of the cities chosen for this study, a brief analysis of each will be given. Pittsburgh was a natural selection since it was the center of the iron and steel industry. It had a large number of the older, medium-sized iron rolling mills, many of which dated from before the Civil War. Alongside these were several of the huge new steel enterprises which emerged after the 1870s. It was in the latter firms that a significant number of the so-called robber barons rose to prominence. Socially, Pittsburgh had a fairly strong antebellum upper-class system, which was sufficient to provide a powerful backdrop against which to place the rise of these newer elites. In addition, the upper-class system provided a glimpse of the rise to national acceptance of one of the early cultural minorities—the Scotch-Irish.

Philadelphia offers some interesting comparisons to Pittsburgh. Most of the city's iron and steel industry was dominated by older, relatively small-scale firms. There were, however, some very large, new steel firms controlled by Philadelphians; but these were almost all located in cities outside Philadelphia—in Bethlehem, Harrisburg and Johnstown. Thus very few of the Robber Baron type rose within the Philadelphia economic environment, although several wealthy Philadelphians did attain that status as absentee owners in other areas. Also, Philadelphia was one of the older coastal cities, with a well-established upper-class system of great prestige and fairly recognizable social gradations.[16]

Bethlehem provides yet another unique dimension to the study. Although it had its own (largely German-American) social structure dating back to the eighteenth century, during the years under study the steel industry in the city was almost completely controlled at the upper levels by Philadelphians. Several native Bethlehemites of German or English extraction occupied managerial positions; but ownership and the highest executive positions rested largely with absentee Philadelphians. Thus Bethlehem, rather early in the nineteenth century, displayed some of the characteristics of present day industrial cities with their separation of ownership and day-to-day management. Its social structure also had the look of modernity, with the truncated social system similar to that described by W. Lloyd Warner in *Yankee City*.[17]

Cleveland, in many ways, occupied a middle position between Pittsburgh and Philadelphia, exhibiting some characteristics of each along with its own unique features. It had some very large firms which emerged during the late nineteenth century, and a large number of smaller-scale firms like those in Philadelphia. Cleveland men, similarly, controlled some large steel firms in other areas of Ohio. The city also had a social structure which was rather unique. It was a young city, on the order of Pittsburgh. But, because of the exodus of old-line New Englanders of impressive pedigree to Ohio, its social structure at the upper levels had many features of coastal cities such as Boston or Philadelphia. Yet its social system never quite coalesced, always maintaining an aura of transiency or uncertainty that only seemed to increase over time. Thus, in the end, it failed to achieve a relative social stability like that at the upper levels of Pittsburgh.

Youngstown's iron and steel industry in the late nineteenth century was controlled by three or four families—who were able to dominate the industry well into the twentieth century. Socially, Youngstown was like Cleveland in several ways. It was a young city; and, like Cleveland, it was part of the Western Reserve, attracting many old New England families. But Youngstown appeared, in many ways, to exhibit the traits of a small town in the nineteenth century; and none of the other cities studied displayed quite the same degree of homogeneity and cohesiveness as did this small city.

Wheeling had several very large firms and few smaller ones. It drew its iron and steel executives from more heterogeneous backgrounds than was the case in the other cities. Wheeling steel manufacturers displayed no marked ethnic, religious or geographical backgrounds in their origins. What was distinctive in their social origins, though, was the large number who rose from authentically working-class origins to positions of wealth and influence. No other city approached them in this category. With a less rapid growth rate than the other cities in the twentieth century, however, Wheeling experienced a dwindling elite and failed to develop a strong upper-class structure. Increasingly, Wheeling found itself drawn into the social orbit of the Pittsburgh upper classes in the twentieth century.

It is apparent, then, that a broad range of economic and social environments are represented in the six selected cities. Although they do not include every possible social and economic phenomenon of the time, they seem to be fairly representative of the entire industry and of American urban life in the late nineteenth and early twentieth centuries.

To obtain the sample of nineteenth century iron and steel manufacturers in this study, all volumes of the *Directory of Iron and Steel Manufacturing Plants in the United States and Canada*[18] from 1874 to 1901 were consulted. From these volumes every listed officer from every iron and steel plant, regardless of size, in the six selected cities was extracted. Since a few firms in each city chose not to list their officers in these volumes, these names were found in various city and local directories. This produced a total of 907 iron and steel manufacturers in 164 different companies. These men were then traced through county and city histories, biographical compendiums, and individual family histories, with the result that a total of 77 percent were located. The breakdown of this, by city, is shown in Table 2.

TABLE 2
Iron and Steel Manufacturers, by City

	Number Listed*	Number Located	Percentage Located
Pittsburgh	469	360	77%
Philadelphia/Bethlehem	144	118	82
Cleveland	123	86	70
Youngstown	97	70	72
Wheeling	74	62	84
TOTALS	907	696	77%

*Listings in *Directory of Iron and Steel Manufacturing Plants in the United States and Canada,* 1874-1901, plus occasional listings in local city directories.

The descendants of all the nineteenth-century steel manufacturers, down to the present day, were identified in order to trace the degree, nature, and importance of intermarriage patterns in assimilating the various groups into a unified, coherent upper-class group. This brings the total number of individuals under study to about 12,600. The group is far too large to analyze effectively: thus, the main analysis will deal with the 696 nineteenth-century steel manufacturers. Only in the analysis of the institutional complex of the urban upper class—especially in the marriage patterns and club memberships—is the far larger number of heirs brought under consideration.

The procedure of this study shall be first to examine the social backgrounds of the nineteenth-century iron and steel manufacturers. This will allow us to see, in some depth, the various kinds of backgrounds represented by these men—in terms of ethno-cultural traits, religion, arrival of the family in America, father's occupation, education, and other variables. This will allow the first categorization of them into different family groupings within their city. Then, an in-depth analysis of the role of the various social institutions of the cities in creating a coherent upper class will be studied, paying particular attention to the fate of the heirs of the nineteenth-century iron and steel men.

Two terms used extensively throughout this study are of such importance that they call for special definition. Since both have several popular and technical meanings, it is imperative that the reader understand precisely what is meant when the terms "elite" and "upper class" are used in the course of this analysis.

The term "elite" is not used in quite the same sense as traditionally employed in social theory. Pareto, Mosca, and Mills use the term in a political sense; that is, as a quite cohesive *class* of high ranking individuals who control the economic, social and political life of their environments.[19] It shall be used here in a more restricted sense—as a group of individuals who have attained the principal economic decision-making positions in the iron and steel industry. Nothing is inferred about their power or lack of it in other spheres of life.

Here, the term "upper class" describes a social class rather than describing a purely economic category; it stresses non-economic, social relationships.

> A "Social Class" is the largest group of people whose members have intimate access to one another. A class is composed of families and social cliques. The interrelationships between these families and cliques in such informal activities as dancing, visiting, receptions, teas and larger informal affairs constitute the function of social class.[20]

Such a concept is not without political implication. For, as Max Weber asserts, the social upper class, or status group, is closely interrelated with some degree of economic and political power.[21] Although not strictly a "Ruling Class," they constitute a very powerful and influential group within their community, a group in which membership is not only socially desirable, but necessary to maintain long-term social, economic and political power.

These elite and upper-class groups, then, within the institutional context of the late nineteenth and early twentieth centuries, are to be the subject of investigation in this study.

NOTES

1. Thomas C. Cochran, "The Legend of the Robber Barons," *Pennsylvania Magazine of History and Biography* 74 (July, 1950): 307-321.

2. The most important of the works dealing with economic and business structures are by Alfred D. Chandler, Jr. See especially his *Strategy and Structure: Chapters in American Business Enterprise* (Cambridge, Mass.: Harvard Univ. Press, 1962). See also: "Beginnings of Big Business in American Industry," *Business History Review* 33 (Spring, 1959): 1-31; and "The Railroads: Pioneers in Modern Corporate Management," *Business History Review* 39 (Spring, 1965): 16-40.

3. Frances W. Gregory and Irene D. Neu, "The American Industrial Elite in the 1870s: Their Social Origins," and William Miller, "The Business Elite," all reprinted in William Miller, ed. *Men in Business,* revised edition (New York: Harper & Row, 1962).

4. E. Digby Baltzell, *Philadelphia Gentlemen* (New York: Free Press, 1958). See also his more impressionistic work, *Protestant Establishment: Aristocracy and Caste in America* (New York: Random House, 1964).

5. See Herbert Gutman, "The Reality of the Rags-to-Riches 'Myth': The Case of the Paterson, New Jersey, Locomotive, Iron and Machinery Manufacturers, 1830-1880," in *Nineteenth Century Cities: Essays in the New Urban History,* edited by Stephan Thernstrom and Richard Sennett (New Haven: Yale University Press, 1969), pp. 98-124.

6. Charles Horton Cooley, *Social Organization* (New York: Scribners, 1907), Chapter 3.

7. Talcott Parsons, *The Social System* (Glencoe, Ind.: Free Press, 1951), pp. 5-6.

8. Scotch-Irish Society of America, *Proceedings,* Second Congress, 1890, p. 6.

9. Emory Bogardus, *Immigration and Race Attitudes* (Boston: D.C. Heath, 1928).

10. James G. Leyburn, *The Scotch-Irish: A Social History* (Chapel Hill: Univ. of North Carolina, 1962, pp. 190-191.

11. See, particularly, speech by Alexander K. McClure at the First Convention of the Scotch-Irish Society of America, *Proceedings,* I (Pittsburgh, 1889), pp. 184-185.

12. See the several speeches at the First Convention of the Scotch-Irish Historical Society, *Proceedings,* I, 1889.

13. Ibid., p. 26.

14. Ibid., p. 16.

15. See Judith Kramer, ***The American Minority Community*** (New York; T.Y. Crowell, 1970) for a discussion of this point on a variety of ethnic and racial minorities in America.

16. Baltzell, ***Philadelphia Gentlemen;*** Nathaniel Burt, ***The Perennial Philadelphians*** (Boston: Little, Brown, 1963); and Struthers Burt, ***Philadelphia: The Holy Experiment*** (New York: Doubleday, 1945).

17. W. Lloyd Warner, ed. ***Yankee City,*** abridged edition (New Haven: Yale Univ. Press, 1963).

18. Published in Philadelphia for the years 1874 to 1901.

19. Vilfredo Pareto, ***The Mind and Society,*** 4 volumes (N.Y.: Harcourt, Brace, 1935); Gaetano Mosca, ***The Ruling Class*** (New York: McGraw-Hill, 1936); C. Wright Mills, ***The Power Elite*** (New York: Oxford Univ. Press, 1956).

20. A Davis, B.B. Gardner and M.R. Gardner, ***Deep South: Social Anthropological Study of Caste and Class*** (Chicago: Univ. of Chicago Press, 1941), p. 59.

21. See Harold M. Hodges, ***Social Stratification in America*** (Cambridge: Harvard Univ. Press, 1964), p. 49, for a succinct statement of Weber's view of "class."

1

Social Analysis of Iron and Steel Entrepreneurs: General Characteristics and a Pittsburgh Model

Placing the nineteenth-century businessman within his proper social environment is a difficult task. The investigation of the social origins of businessmen has usually been rather limited, dealing with highly generalized categories such as religious affiliation, father's occupation, and ancestry. Although this level of analysis is important, any meaningful understanding of the true social context of businessmen must attempt to get beneath these categories. To accomplish this, it will be necessary to examine in more depth the local environments from which these men emerged and rose to prominence. Thus, while Chapters 1 and 2 will compare the broader areas of social characteristics of nineteenth-century iron and steel manufacturers with results of previous studies, succeeding chapters shall investigate this local environment in greater detail.

GENERAL CHARACTERISTICS

Until quite recently, the "rags to riches" view about the social origins of American business leaders in the late nineteenth and early twentieth centuries has prevailed in popular thought.[1]

> The most typical figure of the industrial age was undoubtedly Andrew Carnegie. A poor immigrant boy from Scotland, he followed and helped to perpetuate the American tradition of rising from poverty to riches, and his success he ascribed entirely to the political and economic democracy which obtained in the country. By dint of unflagging industry and unrivaled business acumen and resourcefulness and especially through his extraordinary ability to choose as associates such men as

> Charles Schwab, Henry Frick and Henry Phipps, and to command the devotion of his workmen, Carnegie built up the greatest steel business in the world, and retired in 1901 to chart the genius of "Triumphant Democracy" and to give away his enormous fortune of three-and-a-half hundred million.[2]

In the mid-1950s Frances Gregory, Irene Neu, and William Miller, historians affiliated with the Research Center in Entrepreneurial History at Harvard University, challenged this notion.[3] By accumulating data about the backgrounds of businessmen, they concluded that the typical one tended to be, in fact, of White-Anglo-Saxon-Protestant background from a middle-class or upper-class family, with a father who was also a businessman. Their actual social origins were, in fact, precisely the opposite of the prevailing myth.

What of the 696 iron and steel manufacturers in our study? Do they resemble the mythical figure, or the collective portrait generated by Gregory, Neu and Miller? They conform to the latter.[4] Only 12 percent of the iron and steel manufacturers were born outside the United States. This figure corresponds almost exactly with Gregory and Neu's figure on steel manufacturers, and is only slightly higher than their totals for all manufacturers of the early twentieth century. It also nearly replicates the 1880 American population as a whole, of whom all but 13 percent were native Americans.[5] Table 3 illustrates these comparative figures.

TABLE 3
Comparative Figures on Origins of American Businessmen

	SOURCES				
Origins	Iron Barons *N*=693	Gregory & Neu (All Mfgrs.) *N*=247	Gregory & Neu (Steel Mfgrs.) *N*= 80	Miller *N*=187	Census, 1880
Native	88%	90%	86%	90%	87%
Foreign	12	10	14	10	13
TOTAL	100	100	100	100	100

SOURCES: Information for "Gregory & Neu" taken from Frances W. Gregory and Irene D. Neu, "The American Industrial Elite of the 1870s," in William Willer, ed. *Men in Business* (New York: Harper & Row, 1962), p. 197; "Miller" from William Miller, "American Historians and the Business Elite," in Miller, *Men in Business,* p. 322; "1880 Census" computed from U.S. Department of Commerce, Bureau of the Census, *Historical Statistics of the United States* (Washington, D.C., 1975), tables on pages 8 and 14.

Beyond this, 16 percent of the iron and steel manufacturers were native sons of immigrant fathers; but another 59 percent were members of colonial families which had come to the United States before 1800 (with fully 24 percent arriving before 1700). Thus a minority of men came from relatively recent immigrant families and the majority—as Table 4 illustrates—came from among the "oldest" American families.

TABLE 4
Immigration Years for Families of Nineteenth-Century Steel Manufacturers in U.S., *N*=565

Period of Immigration	Percentage of Steel Manufacturers' Families
After 1850	8%
1800-1849	32
1750-1799	25
1700-1749	10
1600-1699	24
TOTAL	99

*Due to rounding-out of the percentages above.

Figures on national origins for iron and steel manufacturers also approximate the findings of Gregory, Neu and Miller—the main exception being that a larger number of the former came from Scotland and Northern Ireland. While fully one-third of the iron and steel manufacturers were of Scottish and Scotch-Irish origin, Gregory and Neu found only 18 percent, and Miller 20 percent. This reflects the large number of Scotch-Irish iron and steel manufacturers in the Pittsburgh area, whose totals play a disproportionate role (over 50 percent) in the study. There is also a variation in Germanic background: Gregory and Neu found 4 percent Germans among all their manufacturers and 9 percent among steel manufacturers; Miller found 12 percent, and our own study reveals 13 percent. The comparison of national origins is shown in Table 5.

Sixty-five percent of the iron and steel manufacturers were either Episcopalian or Presbyterian—the "elite" religions of the nineteenth century—as compared with figures of only 49 percent for Gregory and Neu and 55 percent for Miller. These differences undoubtedly reflect variations in denominational status in the different cities, the high proportion of Presbyterians in the Pittsburgh group in our study, the high proportion of Unitarians and Congregationalists (32 percent) among Gregory and Neu's Boston capitalists, and a very high percentage of unspecified Protestants in Miller's study. Fully 98 percent of the iron and steel manufacturers were Protestant. This compares favorably to Gregory and Neu's 100 percent figure and Miller's 90 percent. The findings of 2 percent Catholic and approximately 0.5 percent Jewish were above those of Gregory and Neu, who found none of either persuasion, and below those of Miller, who found 7 percent Catholic and 3 percent Jewish. A complete comparative breakdown by denomination appears in Table 6.

Few of these men were from lower-class backgrounds: the vast majority (71 percent) were the sons of relatively well-to-do fathers already among the mercantile, manufacturing or banking elite in their city. Gregory, Neu and Miller found similar backgrounds, although at lower levels (51 percent and 55 percent, respectively) than those for iron and steel manufacturers. Thirteen percent of the iron and steel entrepreneurs were the sons of professional men—doctors, lawyers, ministers, and

TABLE 5

Comparative Figures on Ancestral Origins of American Businessmen

	SOURCES					
Ancestral Origins	Iron Barons N=624	Gregory & Neu (All Mfgrs.) N=175	Gregory & Neu (Steel Mfgrs.) N=58	Miller N=162	American Population 1790	American Population 1920
English & Welsh	53%	71%	69%	53%	60.1%	41.1%
Scottish & Scotch-Irish	30	18	15	21	14.0	
Irish	2	–	–	–	3.6	11.2
German	13	4	9	12	8.6	16.3
Other	2	7	7	14	13.7	31.7
	100	100	100	100	100.0	100.0

SOURCES: "Gregory & Neu" taken from Frances Gregory and Irene Neu, "American Industrial Elite in the 1870s," in Miller, ed. ***Men in Business*** (New York: Harper & Row, 1962), p. 200; "Miller" from "Recruitment of the American Business Elite," in Miller, ed., Business Elite" in Miller, ed., ***Men in Business,*** p. 323. Figures on ancestral origins of "American population" were taken from William Miller , "The Recruitment of the American Business Elite," in William Miller, ed., ***Men in Business,*** pp. 327, 337. He adapted his data from American Council of Learned Societies, "Report on Linguistic and National Stocks in the Population of the United States" in ***Annual Report of the American Historical Association, 1931,*** 3 volumes (Washington, D.C., 1952). Estimates on national origins were made only for the years 1790 and 1920.

TABLE 6
Comparative Figures on Religious Preferences of American Businessmen

Religion	SOURCES				
	Iron Barons *N*=666	Gregory & Neu (All Mfgrs.) *N*=144	Gregory & Neu (Steel Mfgrs.) *N*=51	Miller *N*=174	American Population 1850
Episcopal	23%	25%	29%	25%	4.5%
Presbyterian	42	14	26	21	14.6
Methodist	5	6	8	9	30.5
Baptist	2	4	8	5	22.7
Quaker	4	8	13	0	-
Unitarian & Congreg.	2	32	8	6	1.0
Lutheran	2	0	0	0	-
Other Protestant	19	11	8	24	22.0
Total Protestant	99	100	100	90	95.3
Catholic	2	0	0	7	4.6
Jewish	0	0	0	3	.1
TOTALS	101	100	100	100	100.0

SOURCES: "Gregory & Neu" taken from Frances Gregory and Irene Neu, "American Industrial Elite in the 1870s," in Miller, ed., ***Men in Business*** (New York: Harper & Row, 1962), p. 200; "Miller" from "Recruitment of the American Business Elite," in Miller, ed., ***Men in Business,*** p. 334. Data on religious heritage of the "American population" were taken from Miller, "Recruitment of the American Business Elite," p. 334. He adapted his data from J. D. B. De Bow, ***Statistical View of the United States*** (Washington, D.C.: U.S. Census Office, 1854), pp. 136-137.

public officials, all upper-class or upper-middle-class occupations in the nineteenth century. This corresponds favorably with the 16 percent observed by Gregory and Neu, but is considerably below Miller's 29 percent. Miller's larger finding can be attributed primarily to the increased growth of these professions by the early twentieth century. In all, 83 percent of the iron and steel manufacturers came from backgrounds in the urban upper and upper-middle classes. This compares favorably with the 67 percent observed by Gregory and Neu and the 84 percent by Miller.

The main difference between our figures and those of Gregory and Neu, lies in the latter's rather large percentage of men who were sons of farmers (25 percent). Only 6 percent of the iron and steel manufacturers were sons of farmers, even less than the 14 percent observed by Miller for the early twentieth century. Just 10 percent of these iron and steel men were the sons of blue-collar workers, many of whom were skilled craftsmen in the iron and steel industry. The totals of Gregory and Neu (8 percent for all manufacturers and 11 percent for steel manufacturers) are similar; but Miller found only 2 percent who were the sons of workers. These occupational origins are illustrated in a comparative fashion in Table 7.

The "typical" iron and steel manufacturer, then, does not conform very closely to the Andrew Carnegie type. Rather, he was most likely born in the United States, as was his father, and his family had probably been established in the country in the seventeenth or eighteenth centuries. With ancestors from Northern Ireland, England, Scotland or Wales, he was either Presbyterian or Episcopalian. His father was already a member of an economic elite, being a merchant, banker or iron manufacturer.

The typical iron and steel manufacturer differed markedly from the average or "typical" American of the time. Although, as noted above, the ratio of immigrants to native Americans is approximately the same, in most other characteristics they diverge widely. The high percentage of iron and steel manufacturers with family origins in the British Isles (83 percent) is similar to a figure of 78 percent for the population of 1790, but far higher than the 53 percent for 1920. Although data is lacking for 1880, the extensive immigration to America from Germany and Catholic Ireland by that time must have significantly decreased the proportion of the population from the Protestant countries of the British Isles. Thus, the high percentage of iron and steel manufacturers in this category must have differed significantly from the percentage in the total population.

Similarly, the high proportion of Episcopalians and Presbyterians among the iron and steel elite (75 percent), was far above the 19 percent estimated for the American population in 1850. The percentage of Catholics and Jews, though very small among the steel manufacturers, closely approximates their percentage of the total population in 1850. It should be noted, however, that between 1850 and 1880 large numbers of Catholics immigrated to the country; so their percentage of the total population was probably higher in that year. The most underrepresented religious denominations, however, were the Methodists and Baptists, who were 30.5 percent and 22.7 percent of the national population, respectively, but only 7 percent and 2 percent of the iron and steel elite.

TABLE 7

Comparative Figures on Occupation of Fathers of American Businessmen

Father's Occupation	SOURCES				
	Iron Baron *N*=568	Gregory & Neu (All Mfgrs.) *N*=194	Gregory & Neu (Steel Mfgrs.) *N*=57	Miller *N*=167	American Population Mid-19th Cent.
Businessman	71%	51%	48%	55%	8.1%
Professional	12	16	16	29	2.3
Skilled Workman	10	—	—	—	—
Unskilled Worker	0	—	—	—	—
All Workers	10	8	11	2	30.9
Farmers	6	25	27	14	58.7
TOTALS	99	100	100	100	100.0

SOURCES: "Gregory & Neu" taken from Frances Gregory and Irene Neu, "American Industrial Elite in the 1870s" in Miller, ed., ***Men in Business*** (New York: Harper & Row, 1962), p. 202; "Miller" from Gregory and Neu, "American Industrial Elite in the 1870s," p. 202. (Miller adjusted his figures in line with criteria used by Gregory and Neu. The adjustments result in slight changes from his original figures.) "American Population" from Miller, "Recruitment of the American Business Elite" in Miller, ed., ***Men in Business,*** p. 336. He adapted his data from C. Wright Mills, ***White Collar: The American Middle Class*** (New York: Oxford University Press, 1951).

The greatest difference from the national population, nonetheless, lay in occupational background. While 71 percent of the fathers of steel manufacturers were businessmen, only 8.1 percent of employed Americans in the mid-nineteenth century were so categorized. Comparable figures for professional fathers were 12 percent for steel men and 2.3 percent for the national population, while 10 percent of the steel manufacturers were the sons of blue-collar workers and 6 percent were sons of farmers. These groups made up 30.9 percent and 58.7 percent of the American occupations, respectively, in 1850. Then iron and steel entrepreneurs, then, derived from an occupationally elite segment of society.

This still leaves major questions about what kind of society this was, and just how these iron and steel entrepreneurs fit into it. To fully understand this phenomenon, it is necessary to investigate them in more detail in their local environments. The need to go beyond general categories and statistical compilations to describe the social context of American businessmen was illustrated by the fruitful work of E. Digby Baltzell. In his book *Philadelphia Gentlemen,* he sensitively provided an excellent social context within which to place the rise of some of the newer business leaders of the late nineteenth century.[6] Advancing from the work of Gregory, Neu and Miller, his study points to the power that the traditions of older upper-class groups had in shaping the lifestyles and aspirations of the newer business elites in Philadelphia. What had been implicit in the Neu, Gregory and Miller studies—the strong orientation of nineteenth-century American businessmen toward the upper social and occupational classes—is given flesh and life in Baltzell's book. We are able to understand far more clearly why it was that so few from outcast cultural groups and lowly economic origins were able to rise to the top: the older upper classes had constructed a web of tradition and manners which did much to keep out the uncouth and to temper the aspirations of the impetuous.

Similarly, we shall investigate the iron and steel manufacturers within their local environments, stressing the nature and role of the upper-class social systems in these cities, and stressing the nature of acceptance and adaptation for steel manufacturers of varying backgrounds attempting to achieve economic and social status. As we shall observe, each city had a different kind of social system at its upper levels: some were newly formed; others had been functioning for generations; some were able to exert a nearly exclusive influence on elite selection in the iron and steel industry; others were barely able to make their existence felt. These differences in upper-class social systems, then, had a profound effect on the type of men who were able to rise to economic power and achieve ultimate social acceptance in each of the cities.

PITTSBURGH'S IRON AND STEEL MANUFACTURERS

Pittsburgh has often been used as the example *par excellence* of the "rags to riches" rise of the American businessman. Herbert Casson wrote in 1904:

> Pittsburgh has about one hundred shirt-sleeve millionaires and a very few silk hat ones. Without a single exception, the steel kings and coal barons of today were the bare-footed boys of yesterday. In this respect no other American city is as genuinely Republican, as thoroughly American as Pittsburgh. Its motto should be "From Rags to Riches."[7]

Yet, the 360 Pittsburgh iron and steel manufacturers studied differ only slightly from steel manufacturers in other cities, or from American businessmen in general in the late nineteenth century.

Just 12 percent of the Pittsburgh steel men were immigrants, and only 19 percent were native sons of immigrants (totaling 31 percent of them with recent immigrant origins). These figures are similar to the entire sample of iron and steel manufacturers. Pittsburgh steel men are also representative in the case of the times of their families' arrivals to the United States—with 90 percent (of those for whom information is available) coming before 1850, 54 percent before 1800, and 10 percent in the seventeenth century.

Only in ancestral origins is there a marked divergence of Pittsburghers from other steel manufacturers or businessmen: 42 percent of Pittsburgh's iron and steel manufacturers came from Scotland and Northern Ireland. Men of Germanic origin were also disproportionate among the Pittsburgh steel elite, at 17 percent—more than one and one-half the times the proportion in any other city studied. This is difficult to explain, since Pittsburgh's German-American settlement was not particularly large. Although 23 percent of the German origin steel makers in Pittsburgh were immigrants who had been involved in some stage of the iron and steel industry in their native land, the majority (57 percent) were second and third generation families who had come to Pittsburgh in its early years. Thus, while a minority obviously had immigrated specifically to Pittsburgh—the acknowledged center of steel production—to take advantage of their skills, most did not have a tradition in the industry. In this respect Pittsburgh does not seem to differ much from Philadelphia, whose German-American community had been in America for several generations, coming over as farmers and tradesmen rather than as manufacturers.

Most germane to this issue, perhaps, was Pittsburgh's role as the expeditor of the rise of several cultural minority groups of the late nineteenth and early twentieth centuries. Both the Scotch-Irish and the Germans still faced a certain amount of prejudice and discrimination in seacoast cities, but found their way unfettered in Pittsburgh. Although most of the men in these groups were far removed from immigrant passage and menial labor, the popular stereotypes of them made it seem as if they were indeed rising "from rags to riches."[8]

In religious heritage and fathers' occupations, there is very little difference between the Pittsburgh steel elite and the manufacturers in the other five cities. Seventy percent of the Pittsburgh steel manufacturers were the sons of businessmen; and of these, 59 percent were the sons of manufacturers, many from the iron and steel industry. Fourteen percent were sons of professional men; 9 percent were sons of workingmen, nearly all skilled workmen in the iron and steel industry; only 6 percent, the precise figure for iron and steel manufacturers as a whole, were sons of farmers. Table 8 gives a complete breakdown on the relevant biographical characteristics of Pittsburgh steel men.

Contrary to legend, then, the Pittsburgh iron and steel entrepreneurs came from White-Anglo-Saxon-Protestant, urban upper-class and upper-middle-class backgrounds. Yet that background was perceived as culturally and ethnically inferior to groups in other cities. This is portrayed graphically in Marcia Davenport's novel of the steel industry in Pittsburgh, *Valley of Decision.* At the wedding of the son of a wealthy, prominent Boston financier, the Bostonian guests are heard to say: "Have you ever heard of these people before, Georgiana? Certainly not, Serena. Nobody has ever heard of anyone in Pittsburgh."[9] What, then, was the nature of Pittsburgh society at the upper levels in the late nineteenth century, and what was the relationship of the Pittsburgh steel men to this society?

Settlers came to Pittsburgh as early as the 1760s, but not until the late 1780s did the city begin to acquire its characteristic Scotch-Irish population. In 1784, Arthur Lee uttered a rather famous appraisal of Pittsburgh's new population, which may reveal as much about Mr. Lee and other Eastern seaboard aristocrats as it does about Pittsburgh: "Pittsburgh is inhabited almost entirely by Scots and Irish who live in paltry log houses and are as dirty as in the North of Ireland, or even Scotland. The place, I believe, will never be considerable."[10]

As the young city's trade and industry grew, the small elite of largely Scotch-Irish businessmen grew along with it. Most of the families belonged to the First Presbyterian Church, intermarried with one another, and lived within a few blocks of one another in what is now the city's central business district.[11] By the time of the Civil W[illegible] Pittsburgh had a locally significant and closely knit core of elite families which had begun to acquire the trappings of a local upper class. Who were the Pittsburgh iron and steel manufacturers and how did they fit into this emerging social system?

Seventy percent of Pittsburgh's iron and steel manufacturers were the sons of businessmen, and another 14 percent were sons of professionals, all from the upper class and upper middle class. Forty-three percent of all Pittsburgh steel makers were the sons of prominent manufacturers, merchants, bankers or other businessmen in Pittsburgh, forming the core of a powerful postwar upper class whose influence was to be felt in the city for some time to come. Added to this were a series of families from elite origins (10 percent) who migrated to Pittsburgh in the late nineteenth century to engage in the iron and steel industry. Thus, the great majority of Pittsburgh iron and steel makers were from families which had been prominent in business or the professions, either in Pittsburgh or elsewhere, prior to the Civil War. Of the remainder, 34 percent were from middle-class to upper-middle-class, native or immigrant backgrounds, while only 2 percent were from clearly lower-class or poor backgrounds. We shall discuss each of these categories of Pittsburgh steel masters in more detail below.

TABLE 8

Social Characteristics of Pittsburgh Steel Manufacturers

Birth/Parentage *N*=357	%	Immigration of Family *N*=304	%	Religious Heritage *N*=331	%	Ancestral Origins *N*=325	%	Father's Occupation *N*=339	%
Native/ Native	68	After 1850	10	Episcop.	17	English & Welsh	37	Manuf.	59
		1800-1849	37	Presbyt.	54	Scottish & Scotch-Irish	42	Merchant	9
		1750-1799	36	Methodist	4			Banker	2
Native/ Foreign	19	1700-1749	7	Baptist	1	Irish	2	Total Business	70
		1600-1700	10	Quaker	1	German	17	Doctor	2
Foreign	12			Unitarian & Congreg.	1	Other	2	Lawyer	1
				Lutheran	3			Minister	3
				Other Protestant	15			Teacher	1
				Total Protestant	97			Public Off.	8
				Catholic	3			Total Professional	14
				Jewish	1			Skilled Worker	8
								Unskilled Worker	1
								Total Worker	9
								Farmer	6
TOTALS	99		101		101		100		99

Pittsburgh Iron and Steel Manufacturers from Elite Origins

PRE-CIVIL WAR PITTSBURGH IRON MANUFACTURING FAMILIES Despite the extensive technological changes in the iron and steel industry after the Civil War, changes which included the introduction of the Bessemer and open hearth systems of steelmaking, 31 percent of Pittsburgh's postwar iron and steel manufacturers were members of families which had been engaged in iron and steel production before the war.

These 112 individuals were members of thirty-five separate families, indicating the strongly familial nature of the iron and steel business of that period. With an average of 3.2 iron and steel company executives per family, the degree to which many of Pittsburgh's post-Civil War iron and steel firms remained essentially family enterprises is readily apparent.

Viewed in individual terms, steel makers from pre-Civil War iron and steel backgrounds were not much different from the other Pittsburgh steel men. There was a larger proportion from Scotch-Irish backgrounds (35 percent), compared to only 25 percent Scotch-Irish among the other 248 Pittsburgh iron and steel men. This was somewhat balanced by the higher percentage from Scotland among the other iron and steel men. The percentage of men from English origins was nearly identical. The percentage of Germans was also similar, with 18 percent of Germanic background among the former groups, and 15 percent among the latter. In general, then, the variation of ancestral origins was rather slight and inconsequential.

In religious background the differences were more striking. In particular, the percentage of Presbyterians among members of pre-Civil War iron families (63 percent), was significantly higher than the 44 percent recorded among other Pittsburgh steel men. The number of Lutherans was also higher, 8 percent compared to less than 1 percent. In addition, nearly all the Baptist and Quaker Pittsburgh steel men were from pre-Civil War iron families. The percentage of Episcopalians and Methodists was nearly identical. Some of these differences, however, were caused by the larger number of unspecified Protestants and others for whom no information was available concerning Pittsburgh steel men as a whole. Although it is significant that 95 percent of the other Pittsburgh steel makers on whom information could be found were Protestant, the fact that there were no Catholics or Jews among the pre-Civil War iron masters is of even greater importance. However limited the opportunities for Catholics and Jews in the post-Civil War iron and steel industry, it was even more restricted before the war.

Figures on the date of family arrivals in America also reveal some important differences. Although the number with families coming to America in the seventeenth century was virtually identical, the members of pre-Civil War iron families had more than twice as many arriving during the eighteenth century (63 percent to 25 percent). This was counterbalanced by the larger number of men among the other Pittsburgh steel families which came to America during the nineteenth century (46 percent to 24 percent). If Pittsburgh iron and steel manufacturers as a whole do not conform to the recent immigrant stereotype, it is even less characteristic of the men from pre-Civil War iron families.

Similarly, this "old family" pattern among men descended from pre-Civil War iron origins was reflected in the fact that only 3 percent were immigrants and 16 percent native sons of immigrant fathers—compared to 16 percent and 12 percent respectively for the rest of the Pittsburgh steel men. Thus, 81 percent of the men descended from pre-Civil War iron backgrounds were native sons of native parents—well above the 63 percent for other Pittsburgh steel masters.

The "typical" Pittsburgh steel manufacturer from pre-Civil War iron-making origins, then, was either Scotch-Irish or English, and was Presbyterian; his family had come to America during the eighteenth century, making him at least third or fourth generation American by the end of the nineteenth century.

The iron and steel men analyzed above represent not only a generalized business background, but a specialized one in pre-Civil War iron making. Although it is not surprising that those involved in the iron industry in an earlier period would continue their influence—even dominance—in the iron and steel industry after the Civil War, there is one rather surprising element. As noted above, the iron and steel industry went through a veritable revolution in the last decades of the nineteenth century—a revolution placing extensive new demands in terms of technological expertise and capital formulation. The fact that such a large number of these pre-Civil War iron families were able to adapt themselves successfully to this change indicates a remarkable resiliency on their part.

DESCENDANTS OF PITTSBURGH'S PRE-CIVIL WAR BUSINESS AND PROFESSIONAL ELITE In addition to the men from pre-Civil War iron families, another 22 percent of Pittsburgh's iron and steel elite came from families which had been engaged in other aspects of the city's business and professional elite in the antebellum period. These eighty-five men from forty-eight different families emanated from a variety of mercantile, manufacturing, banking and professional activities before the war and into the burgeoning iron and steel industry in the postwar period. This was accomplished in spite of the increasing complexity of the technological and organizational system of the industry in the late nineteenth century. Almost identical in background to the descendants of prewar iron families, these men had comparable differences with the 275 other Pittsburgh steel men. In particular, a greater percentage were Scotch-Irish or Scottish than among the balance of Pittsburgh steel men, while the proportion of Germans and English was nearly identical.

There was a similar pattern in religious background. As with the pre-Civil War iron families, a far greater percentage of the men from antebellum business and professional families (65 percent) were Presbyterian than were Pittsburgh steel men generally (45 percent). As with the pre-Civil War iron men, there were no Catholics or Jews among this group, and in other religious aspects they conformed to the total group of Pittsburgh steel manufacturers.

The men from business and professional families differed most in terms of the dates that their families immigrated to America: in general the prewar iron families had been in America for a longer period of time. While 72 percent of the latter group came to America during colonial times, only 53 percent of the business and professional families did so. Correspondingly, 40 percent came during the nineteenth century, compared to 24 percent of the iron families. More of those in the business and professional group were relatively recent immigrants to America. As a result of these differences, the men from business and professional families conform more closely to the pattern of the other 275 iron and steel men, in terms of family arrival in America. But few were immigrants themselves: the categories "sons of immigrants" and "no information" showed the greatest percentage increase over the pre-Civil War iron group. As a result, a major difference between the pre-Civil War business and professional families and the other 275 steel manufacturers was in the markedly higher percentage of immigrants in the latter group (15 percent), compared to only 2 percent among the former.

Whereas the families of descendants of pre-Civil War iron manufacturers were, by definition, engaged in iron manufacturing, the economic backgrounds of the present group were more varied. Nevertheless, some 58 percent were involved in some kind of manufacturing activity before the Civil War—particularly glass, coal, textiles, oil refining or brewing. Another 14 percent were engaged in mercantile pursuits, with 22 percent of those in banking or one of the professions. Six percent attained prominence in government and politics.

The typical iron and steel manufacturers who derived from pre-Civil War business and professional classes in Pittsburgh, then, differed in only minor respects from men of pre-Civil War iron families. They were most likely Scotch-Irish, English or Scottish, with a small but significant German minority. They were most likely Presbyterian and native sons of native parents. Unlike the men from antebellum iron families, however, their families arrived in America at a later period—with 71 percent coming after 1750, and 40 percent after 1800. Very few, however, were immigrants themselves.

These two groups of families, then, made up the core of Pittsburgh's antebellum upper class. They were families which had attained prominence in iron manufacture, or in some other economic or professional pursuit in Pittsburgh before the war, and then moved into the burgeoning steel industry in the late nineteenth century. As such, barring any social or personal impediments to their standing, they were natural candidates for membership in a local upper-class status group of talent and birth.

In spite of the fact that most of these men were firmly part of the local upper-class or upper-middle-class prior to the Civil War, they were of cultural origins which were generally disdained by the older, seaboard upper-class groups in the nineteenth century. Part of a social upper class in the making, they were "comparable in kind, if not in degree, with those of the older cities of the east."[12]

ELITE MIGRANTS TO PITTSBURGH Another thirty-four individuals, representing twenty-nine separate families, came to Pittsburgh during the late nineteenth century, bringing with them fairly high economic and social prestige previously gained in other areas—particularly in the older seacoast cities.

Comparing this group, first of all, to the pre-Civil War Pittsburgh elite families, produces some significant and important variations. There were major differences in the area of ancestral origins. Whereas 36 percent of the Pittsburgh prewar elite were of Scotch-Irish ancestry, only 19 percent (of those for whom information was available) of the elite migrants emanated from the North of Ireland. Conversely, fully 63 percent of the latter had English origins, compared to only 31 percent among the Pittsburgh elite. Another area of importance was the absence of any elite migrants of Germanic background, compared to 16 percent in this category among the Pittsburgh elites.

These variations between the Pittsburgh pre-Civil War elite and the elite migrants persisted in the area of religious affiliation, with the latter group having nearly twice the proportion of Episcopalians (32 percent to 17 percent), and only a little more than half as many Presbyterians (35 percent to 64 percent). Nor were several Protestant denominations—Baptist, Methodist, Lutheran, Quaker—found among these migrants, although they did contain the only Unitarian among the Pittsburgh steel makers. An area of similarity in religious identification lay in the fact that both groups were composed entirely of men from Protestant backgrounds. None of the Pittsburgh steel men from pre-Civil War elite backgrounds were Catholics or Jews.

The elite migrants were also from families which had generally been in America longer than was the case for the Pittsburgh's prewar elites. While 68 percent of the Pittsburgh elite were from colonial origins, 92 percent of the elite migrants were so classified. Of greater significance was the fact that 38 percent of the elite migrant families had immigrated during the seventeenth century, compared to 11 percent of the Pittsburgh elite, while 63 percent of the former group had arrived before 1750, compared to 18 percent for the latter. The elite migrants were from families of longer duration in America, with only 8 percent arriving during the nineteenth century, compared to 33 percent among the Pittsburgh elite.

As would be expected, similar patterns were evidenced in the category of "nativity", where 94 percent of the elite migrants were native sons of native parents, compared to 77 percent of the Pittsburgh prewar elite group. In both cases, however, the proportion of immigrants was identical—3 percent. The Pittsburgh group was distinguished by the larger number of native sons of immigrant fathers, with 19 percent in this category.

These differences with the Pittsburgh elite adhere to a general pattern, one which becomes even more pronounced when the elite migrants are compared to the total group of Pittsburgh steel men in the late nineteenth century. Again, in ancestral origins, the Pittsburgh group as a whole is more heavily Scotch-Irish than the elite migrant group is, and has less than one-half as many from English backgrounds.

The absence of a large German minority among the elite migrants remains significant.

The pattern of religious difference was also similar in many respects, with 56 percent Presbyterians among the Pittsburgh group, compared to 35 percent among the migrants. On the other hand, the percentage of Episcopalians among the migrants is nearly twice that among the Pittsburgh steel men generally. The most important area of difference, however, lies in the fact that the total group of Pittsburgh steel makers counted 3 percent Catholics and 1 percent of Jewish origin, none of whom were from the pre-Civil War elite groups, migrant or local.

The patterns of family arrival in America were similar to those discussed above, but weighted even more strongly toward the elite migrants. With only 51 percent of the Pittsburgh steel men being from colonial origins, the 92 percent of the elite migrants in this category is that much more striking. Similarly, although 66 percent of the Pittsburgh group generally were native sons of native parents, the elite migrants had 94 percent with this parentage. Even more striking, 13 percent of the Pittsburgh group were immigrants, compared to only 3 percent oamong the migrants.

The typical Pittsburgh steel man from *elite migrant* origins, then, differs in important respects from the typical steel man from elite origins in Pittsburgh. He tended to be English in ancestral background, and as likely to be Episcopalian as Presbyterian. He was of an old family, one which had most likely come to America before 1750. The great majority of these elite migrants came to Pittsburgh from eastern seacoast cities (83 percent), with the largest proportion emanating from New England (44 percent). The economic status of these families had been established in business enterprises similar to those of the prewar elite in Pittsburgh, with 66 percent having fathers who were manufacturers, merchants or bankers. A significant variation, however, lay in the large minority among the migrants (18 percent) whose fathers were politicians or high governmental officials. Among these were a governor of Maine, a state legislator, a congressman, and a cabinet official.

As a composite, then, these men represented important variations in family backgrounds from the pre-Civil War Pittsburgh elite. Although the differences in economic origins were generally not strongly pronounced, the cultural distinctions were clear. This again reflected upon Pittsburgh's role in the rise of cultural minorities of the nineteenth century.

As a group the transplanted elite seemed to be able to quite easily transfer to Pittsburgh the prestige gained in other areas. This allowed them relatively easy entrance into the higher economic ranks of the city; and, apparently, the doors of the social upper class were opened to them. Since, however, so many of these families—particularly those from Boston and New England—preferred not to remain in the Pittsburgh area or to transfer their principal social connections (especially marriages) there, this last point is difficult to establish. Only a small minority became permanent additions to Pittsburgh social and economic upper classes.

COMPOSITE PORTRAIT OF PITTSBURGH STEEL MEN FROM PRE-CIVIL WAR ELITE BACKGROUNDS We have seen, then, that 63 percent of the Pittsburgh iron and steel entrepreneurs in the late nineteenth century originated in families of upper-class economic and social backgrounds prior to the war. In composite terms, these 231 individuals were either English, Scotch-Irish or Scottish (74 percent), and a significant minority (14 percent) were of Germanic origins. They were all of Protestant religious heritage, with 60 percent Presbyterian and 19 percent Episcopalian. Sixty-four percent were members of colonial families which had arrived in America before 1800, with 21 percent of these coming before 1750. They were, in the main, men who represented the preferred economic and social origins of the middle and late nineteenth century.

This in itself is certainly enough to dispel the "rags to riches" myth about Pittsburgh. As noted above, the characteristic which seemed to earn them the label of "poor boys from dismal backgrounds"—namely, their Scotch-Irish heritage—was also losing its importance in the late nineteenth century. This is evidenced by a variety of factors. First, several families, such as the Dilworths, were able to move into the very highest echelons of society in eastern cities. Second, those transplanted elite families who did transfer their residence and loyalties to Pittsburgh showed little reluctance to embrace the Pittsburgh upper-class social system, including marriage with the city's best families—nearly all of whom were of Scotch-Irish heritage.

Therefore, the overwhelming majority of iron and steel manufacturers in Pittsburgh were clearly of elite origins. But what of the remaining 36 percent? If these men should prove to be of lower-class, poverty backgrounds, then a strong case could still be made for the relatively deprived origins of the Pittsburgh steel elite. In other words, if a significantly large percentage of Pittsburghers were from lower social origins, it would still indicate that the city was a haven for poor boys striving to make good. It is necessary, then, to examine in some detail the social origins of this remaining 36 percent.

Pittsburgh's Iron and Steel Entrepreneurs from Immigrant or "Common" Backgrounds

What sort of backgrounds did these men represent? How many were immigrants or sons of immigrants? How many were from working-class families? Were any, whether of native or immigrant origins, from authentically lower-class backgrounds? In summary, how many were truly in "rags" before they assumed the riches of the late nineteenth century?

The answers to these questions are of great importance. Stephen Thernstrom has perceptively demonstrated the importance of "one step" mobility for lower-class immigrant groups in the late nineteenth century.[13] The popular influence, however, of the myth of the self-made man has been observed by Moses Rischin and Irwin G. Wylie.[14] As Rischin has noted, "The American Gospel of Success continues to be without doubt America's most persistent claim to the fealty of everyman."[15] If it can be shown that over one-third of these iron and steel manufacturers actually did emanate from lower-class social origins, then strong support for the "American Gospel of Success" in actual social practice is indicated. If not, then it must remain a powerful and important bit of mythology in American life and culture.

In order to investigate these iron and steel entrepreneurs who derived from non-elite origins, they will be divided into two broad categories: recent immigrants and native Americans. Each of these groups will be further subdivided according to family economic origins: skilled working class, middle class, and those from authentically poor origins.

A total of 19 percent of the steel manufacturers were first or second generation immigrants who had arrived rather late in the nineteenth century; but of this group only a very small percentage can be seen as truly "poor." Many were skilled workers or sons of skilled workingmen. Several were also from European manufacturing and mercantile families. A significant number, especially those from Northern Ireland, had important familial connections in Pittsburgh to give them easy entrance to high positions. Let us consider in more detail each of these different groups.

IMMIGRANT SKILLED WORKING-CLASS FAMILIES Sixteen individuals, representing fourteen separate families, derived from skilled immigrant working-class origins. They constituted 4 percent of the total number of Pittsburgh steel manufacturers and 23 percent of those of recent immigrant status. The men from these families, although generally without wealth or social prestige upon their arrival in America, possessed vitally important skills in the iron and steel industry—a resource which could be put to highly beneficial use in an America starved for technological expertise. These men were able to convert this scarce commodity into relatively rapid mobility into the higher echelons of the steel industry.

When compared to the Pittsburgh iron and steel men from elite origins, significant differences emerge. Although the largest number of men from skilled working-class families (31 percent) were from England, another 25 percent were from Germany, and those from the North of Ireland and Scotland had a combined total of 32 percent. Although not representing a radical departure from the elite group, they do signify an important variation on the theme already developed. Despite some proportional differences, this group of immigrants from skilled working-class backgrounds did not add any new ethnic stocks to the Pittsburgh scene.

The religious heritage of these skilled immigrants showed a similar pattern. Whereas a majority of the elite families were Presbyterian and 19 percent were Episcopalian, only one-third of the skilled immigrants were Presbyterian and none were Episcopal. Rather, they represented more distinctly working-class denominations within Protestantism: 17 percent were Methodist, 17 percent German Evangelical; and 25 percent unspecified Protestants. Of significance is the fact that, whereas all of the elite families discussed above were Protestant, only 92 percent of the skilled immigrants were so; the other 8 percent were Catholics. This represents a more radical departure from the elite groups than does ancestral origin.

Finally, as recent immigrants, the time of arrival of their families in America differed substantially from the elite families. All of the skilled immigrants came to America during the nineteenth century, with 67 percent arriving after 1850. Although resembling the elite families of the area in many respects, these men had generally left Europe to take advantage of their skills in the New World. The great majority were drawn to Pittsburgh, not for cultural reasons, but due to the economic attraction of the expanding postwar iron and steel industry.

These immigrants from working-class backgrounds, then, possessed resources which allowed them to easily overcome their comparatively "low" origins. For the majority, the possession of a rare skill in new steel-making techniques was sufficient; for others, familial connections helped ease their passage. All, however, entered the steel industry in the late nineteenth century in a fairly advantageous stance. They were not just lowly workmen toiling their way to wealth and power, but men possessed of some rare skill or valuable connection which made their accession to elite levels relatively easy.

RECENT IMMIGRANTS OF MIDDLE-CLASS BACKGROUNDS Another forty-nine individuals, representing thirty-two separate families, seemed to fall most clearly into the category of middle-class immigrant families. They made up 14 percent of the Pittsburgh iron and steel manufacturers and 70 percent of those of recent immigrant background. These iron and steel manufacturers derived from families who had achieved a degree of economic and social success in Europe. This produced a variety of resources for them to exploit in America—business skills, formal education, wealth, and familial connections.

In terms of ancestral backgrounds, they were closer to the pre-Civil War elite families of Pittsburgh than they were to the skilled immigrants. The 72 percent from the British Isles was an almost identical proportion to the 74 percent from these origins among the elite families. Also, the 16 percent from Germany nearly duplicated the percentage in this category among the elite.

The difference in religious heritage was more pronounced. Although the largest number of these middle-class immigrants were again Presbyterian, the proportion was substantially lower—at 43 percent, compared to 60 percent among the elite families. The percentage of Episcopalians was nearly identical. The most important differentiation lay in the fact that only 85 percent of the middle-class immigrants were Protestant. Fully 10 percent were Catholic and another 4 percent were Jewish. In this respect they resembled the skilled working-class immigrants, and represented a more drastic departure from the earlier elite of Pittsburgh.

Similar to the skilled immigrants, all the middle-class immigrants came to America during the nineteenth century. Sixty-seven percent, however, came prior to 1850—compared to only 31 percent of the skilled immigrants. Among immigrant families, these men represented families of middle-class origin in Europe who came to America at an earlier time. They were generally not dependent upon the exploitation of their skills in the new steel industry, but instead used wealth, education, and social position to establish a variety of business ventures in the new environment.

The family economic background of these men in Europe reflects this economic diversity: 57 percent were the sons of businessmen, while another 8 percent had fathers in the professional ranks. Eight percent were the sons of governmental officials, and 16 percent relied primarily upon exceptional educational advantages. Only 6 percent were graced by strong family connections with elite families in America. The immigrants of this group, then, were able to start their careers in America at relatively high positions, since they could transfer with ease the skills, money, education, and family positions which they had acquired on the European scene. They started in an advantageous position and were able to maintain or improve this position with relative ease. Even less so than those from skilled working-class backgrounds, they hardly represent the poor-immigrant-to-riches image of the Andrew Carnegie archetype.

THE "POOR" IMMIGRANTS Despite the popularity of the Andrew Carnegie archetype, only five Pittsburgh steel men were immigrants from poor backgrounds. Since two of these were Andrew Carnegie and his brother Tom, only three men outside the Carnegie family (less than 1 percent of the total) reflected this archetype. Further, all five men were officers in the Carnegie mills: thus, outside of this establishment in Pittsburgh, the poor-immigrant-to-steel-mill-owner syndrome never occurred.

These five men represented a variety of ethnic backgrounds. The Carnegies were Scottish; H. W. Borntrager was German; William R. Jones was Welsh; and Henry Phipps was English. Their religions were similarly working class and mixed, with no Presbyterians or Episcopalians among them. Four of the five, however, came as small boys to America prior to 1850; only Borntrager arrived as a young man after that period. Thus, essentially, the four grew up in America, poor, but highly acculturated to the American norms—more like second generation rather than first generation immigrants.

Since the backgrounds and careers of Andrew and Tom Carnegie, along with that of Henry Phipps, are already fairly well known, our analysis will focus upon Borntrager and Jones, making comparisons and contrasts to the Carnegies and Phipps when appropriate.

William R. Jones was born in Hazelton, Pennsylvania, the son of John G. Jones who had immigrated to America from Wales seven years earlier, in 1832.[16] John Jones was a poor pattern maker and an itinerant Methodist preacher. William Jones received only sporadic education in the schools, and, at age ten, was apprenticed to the molder's trade at Crane Manufacturing Company. By age fourteen, he had become a journeyman machinist. Working for various companies around Pennsylvania, he came to Cambria Iron Company as a machinist in 1859. In 1872, he became assistant superintendent at the concern. In 1873 he joined Carnegie Steel as master mechanic, moving up to general superintendent in 1879. He served in that post until he was killed in a mine accident in 1889.

Although not strictly an immigrant, William Jones shared many of the characteristics of Andrew Carnegie's background. Both of their fathers were skilled workers who had spent much time without work, thus causing each of their families to live in poverty. As a result, neither son received much formal education; each went to work at an early age, where he picked up skills which would be useful later in life. Unlike Carnegie, William Jones had little interest in ownership; he preferred a large salary to the stock offers which Carnegie made him. As a result, his son was a well-educated engineer and surveyor, but did not own a business in Pittsburgh or elsewhere.

Henry W. Borntrager had been born in Germany in 1839, and came to the United States in 1861.[17] He evidently did not acquire much in the way of useful skills in Germany: his first job in America was as a laborer in a Pittsburgh boat yard. He then worked for a time as a stocker at a small engine concern, and then became a laborer in a Carnegie Steel mill at $30 per month. In just a few years, at age twenty-eight, he was named manager of the Kloman mill at Carnegie, and later became a partner in the firm. He remained there until 1892, when he resigned due to ill health.

Thus, in most ways Borntrager conforms to the image of the poor but hard-working and talented immigrant who was able to grab his "main chance" in America and rapidly rise to fame and fortune. Only the fact that he was a distant cousin of Kloman—one of Carnegie's partners—dims this picture somewhat. How much this aided him in his rise at Carnegie Steel is difficult to calculate; but it must at least be given due consideration. Few made it by dint of hard work alone.

These were about the only "poor" men of recent immigrant background who rose to prominence on the Pittsburgh scene. There may have been a few others, so obscure that their biographies are lost forever; but this would be a very small minority of the total group of Pittsburgh steel manufacturers. Although there were a fairly large number of immigrants or sons of immigrants among the Pittsburgh steel entrepreneurs, only a handful, at best, conform to the "rags to riches" myth. The majority had either skills which gave them ready entrance to elite status, or they had family connections, money or education to assist them.

The last group of Pittsburgh steel manufacturers is rather difficult to classify. They were neigher immigrants nor sons of immigrants, and some were even from rather "old" American families. Yet, they were not part of a business or professional elite in Pittsburgh or elsewhere. A total of 16 percent of the Pittsburgh steel men fit into this category. They might be termed men from a "common" background. Neither of recent immigrant origin or from upper-class or upper-middle-class backgrounds, they represent the native lower-middle class and lower class. But exactly what kind of backgrounds did they have? If they were truly a native poor or marginal group who rose to economic and social prominence in the nineteenth century, it could symbolize a significant form of social mobility for a small, but important group of Pittsburgh steel men. There were two subgroups of men from "common" origins: those from the middle class, and those from more humble origins. The difference lay in class background and educational advantages. Middle-class respectability and a college education marked the first, and more important, group; disadvantageous circumstances were characteristic of the second.

"COMMON MEN" FROM NATIVE MIDDLE-CLASS BACKGROUNDS A total of fifty-five iron and steel manufacturers from fifty separate families derived from middle-class native American backgrounds. As such, they represented 15 percent of the total, and 19 percent of all the men from native American, non-immigrant origins.

Comparing them to iron and steel manufacturers from elite backgrounds, their percentage from Scotch-Irish origins was identical. There were somewhat fewer from English backgrounds; but the most striking difference lay in the larger proportion of middle-class native Americans from Germanic origins (29 percent), compared to 14 percent among the elite families.

Religious preference illustrates a similar divergence. Although Presbyterianism ranked as the preferred religion for both groups, the percentage in this denomination among middle classes was less than one-half of the 60 percent found among elite families. The percentage of Episcopalians was also about one-half that of the elite families. A major element of the religious variation between the two groups lay in the fact that 8 percent of the men from middle-class families were of Catholic heritage, while there were none of this persuasion among those of elite origins.

Data on the time of arrival of their families in America exhibited little difference from the elite families—at least for those on whom information was available. In both cases 64 percent were members of colonial families arriving before 1800, while the balance came over between 1800 and 1850. All of those men in the middle-class group were native sons of native fathers, none having recent immigrant origins.

In comparing these men from middle-class origins to those who immigrated more recently, a somewhat altered pattern emerges. Although a similar percentage emanated from England, Scotland or the North of Ireland, a higher proportion of the native middle class were of Germanic background (29 percent), compared to 19 percent among recent immigrants.

In religious preference the two groups were more similar. Presbyterians and Episcopalians dominated both, nearly one-half the total in each. The proportion of Catholics was similar (8 percent and 10 percent respectively); but there were no Jews among the native American group, while there were 2 percent of Jewish origin among the recent immigrants.

Family arrivals, of course, were at different times for each group: all of the recent immigrants arrived in the nineteenth century, and 64 percent of the men from native American families came before that time. Thirty-six percent of the native American group, however, did arrive between 1800 and 1849, compared to 60 percent of the recent immigrant group. In other words, a majority of the recent immigrants and a large minority of the native American group had lived in America for a similar number of years prior to the Civil War.

An intricate and complex question about these native Americans of middle-class status concerns the factors which elevated them to this status. For two-thirds of the group, the factor was the possession of educational advantages and training well beyond the norm for American society at the time. Another 13 percent had strong familial connections with individuals who had previously secured elite status; and 7 percent were the sons of men who ran small businesses; another 13 percent had fathers in the lower white-collar ranks of business or government.

These men from middle-class native American backgrounds possessed the types of advantages accruing to this group. Having familial connections with enough wealth to acquire sufficient education, they found the road to elite status less arduous than would be the case for men from truly deprived backgrounds. With comfortable and respectable families, they were able to achieve their goals more easily than those from authentically poor circumstances.

NATIVE AMERICANS FROM LOWER-CLASS BACKGROUNDS Only four men came from authentically lower-class, native American backgrounds, lacking in wealth, educational advantages, and, seemingly, family connections of any sort. Comprising only 1 percent of the total, these men were forced to climb the ladder of success without aid. Combined with the poor men of poor immigrant origins, however, the total percentage from truly disadvantaged beginnings was only about 3 percent. In three of the four native American cases, the men were sons of poor farmers who could not afford to give their sons even meager educational opportunities. The fourth man was the son of a poor tailor who was similarly handicapped.

A brief biography of a few of these men should indicate the kinds of backgrounds represented and the degree of difference between themselves, the native Americans of middle-class backgrounds, and the poor immigrants.

Alexander M. Byers was representative of the sons of poor farmers in this group.[18] Born in 1827 in Mercer County, Pennsylvania, he was forced to leave school at an early age. While still very young he began working for the Henry Clay Furnace Company and at age sixteen became superintendent. In 1854 he went to Cleveland to assume management of the Spang Iron Company. Three years later he came to Pittsburgh, where he organized his own iron company, one which remained in the family until well into the twentieth century. Thus, although the Byers family had little or no money, and although Alexander Byers was able to secure only a meager education, he was able—through luck, skill, or possibly family connections —to rise very quickly within the steel industry.

Alvah C. Dinkey had a background similar to that of Alexander Byers.[19] He was born in 1866 on his father's farm in Carbon County, Pennsylvania. He attended school only until age thirteen, then became a water carrier at Carnegie Steel. He then advanced up the ranks at that firm, becoming in succession: telegrapher in

1882; machinist's apprentice; and secretary to the superintendent of the light and power division in 1899. In 1901 he was made superintendent of all plants for the firm. He then served as president of the Carnegie Steel division of U.S. Steel, until 1915 when he became president of Midvale Steel.

Of German origin, the Dinkey family had been in Pennsylvania since 1743; and some members of the family had acquired minor prestige as local officials and businessmen. But Alvah Dinkey's father was a rather poor farmer, and it is not clear to what degree family connections might have helped Alvah Dinkey in his rapid climb up the occupational ladder.

The other men of poor, native stock shared backgrounds quite similar in most respects to the two men outlined. The major question which exists for all but one of the men (E. R. Crawford) is the degree to which family connections may have aided them in their rise to wealth and success. Although no overt aid was found in any case, each man (with the one exception) was from a family of some prestige and relevance in its area. This makes their rapid ascent somewhat suspect at least, giving them perhaps some of the advantages shared by the men from native middle-class origins.

SUMMARY

Pittsburgh steel men, then, appear to conform closely to the patterns developed for business entrepreneurs in other areas of the country. They do not resemble the Andrew Carnegie archetype. Twenty-nine percent of the 360 iron and steel entrepreneurs were of English origin, and another 28 percent were from the North or Ireland. Altogether, 73 percent emanated from the British Isles, and 16 percent had Germanic origins.

They were overwhelmingly Protestant (97 percent), only 3 percent Catholic and less than 1 percent Jewish. Of the Protestants, 56 percent were Presbyterian and 17 percent were Episcopalian. Other Protestant denominations received scattered percentages of the balance.

A majority (54 percent) of the late-nineteenth-century Pittsburgh steel manufacturers were members of families which had immigrated to America prior to 1800. The greatest number, however, came over during the period between 1750 and 1850 (74 percent). This orientation was reflected in the fact that 68 percent were native sons of native fathers; 19 percent were native sons of immigrants, and only 12 percent were themselves immigrants.

In addition, 63 percent of these men came from families which were part of a pre-Civil War economic elite, either in Pittsburgh or elsewhere. Another 34 percent came from middle-class or skilled working-class backgrounds in Europe or America. This left only 3 percent who appeared to conform more closely to the Andrew Carnegie archetype. Of this group, half were from older, native American families, leaving only about 1.5 percent from poor immigrant stock.

Beyond these aspects, however, certain other trends about the nature of the Pittsburgh iron and steel manufacturers begin to be evident. The first is the disproportionate number of men from the native and immigrant lower-middle-class and lower-class backgrounds who rose within the Carnegie firms. Just as Andrew Carnegie himself was unique in his social origins, it becomes increasingly clear that nearly all those who shared his origins among the Pittsburgh steel elite got their start in his steel firm. Subtract the Carnegie Steel executives from the ranks of Pittsburgh steelmakers, and one would be hard-pressed to find a single example who fits the Andrew Carnegie archetype.

Similarly, the importance of the steel firm itself is seen when one observes another group of outsiders—the transplanted elites. Most of these men came to prominence within only a few firms—most notably at National Tube Works and McKeesport Rolling Mill, and to a much lesser degree at Carnegie Steel. Although these men were unlike most of the Carnegie executives in their social origins (being of elite or upper-class backgrounds), they were "outsiders" as far as the Pittsburgh scene was concerned. They found little receptivity among the "old family" steel firms of Pittsburgh, and they started their own, more nationally oriented firms (as even the name National Tube would attest).

Although the transplanted elite and the common men at Carnegie derived from markedly different social backgrounds, neither experienced great success in gaining acceptance into the older upper-class structure of Pittsburgh. Probably the transplanted elite could have assimilated if they had wished to root themselves to the Pittsburgh scene; but few of them chose to do so. Thus, they remained external to much of the old family economic and social structure of the city. The Carnegie men were generally more interested in gaining social success in Pittsburgh; but since few of them were able to do so, they were forced to transfer their attentions elsewhere. Like Charles Grey in J. P. Marquand's *Point of No Return,* these Carnegie men found themselves blocked by the more rigid status system in their home community, and were forced to move to New York to find social success.

What we observe in Pittsburgh, then, is a group of old family elites faced with challenges by new groups on the business and social scene. Although this development threatened the hegemony of the older upper classes, it did not supplant them. In fact, the upper-class elites displayed a remarkable resilience in retaining their positions as social arbiters and economic magnates, assimilating certain members of these new groups, allowing others to move on to broader pastures where they could not upset the local balance.

NOTES

1. An excellent discussion of this view is contained in William Miller, "American Historians and the Business Elite," in William Miller, ed. *Men in Business,* revised edition (New York: Harper & Row, 1962), pp. 309-328. See also, John N. Ingham, "Robber Barons and the Old Elite: A Case Study in Social Stratification," *Mid-America* 42, 3 (July, 1970): 190-204, for a more extended discussion of popular literature on this subject.

2. Samuel Eliot Morison and Henry Steele Commanger, ***The Growth of the American Republic,*** II, (N.Y.: Oxford Univ. Press, 1950), p. 135; quoted in Miller, ***Men in Business,*** p. 320.

3. See Francis W. Gregory and Irene D. Neu, "The American Industrial Elite of the 1870s: Their Social Origins"; and William Miller, "American Historians and the Business Elite," and "The Business Elite in Business Bureaucracies: Careers of Top Executives in the Early Twentieth Century," and "The Recruitment of the American Business Elite." All essays are contained in Miller, ***Men in Business.***

4. Gregory and Neu surveyed 100 Bessemer open hearth and crucible steel manufacturers in the 1870s; Miller surveyed sixteen steel manufacturers in the early twentieth century.

5. Figures adapted from the Bureau of the Census, ***Historical Statistics of the United States: Colonial Times to 1770*** (Washington, D.C.: Dept. of Commerce, Bureau of the Census, 1975).

6. E. Digby Baltzell ***Philadelphia Gentlemen,*** (Glencoe, Illinois: Free Press, 1958).

7. Herbert Casson, ***The Romance of Steel*** (New York: A. S. Barnes, 1907), p. 207. See also Stewart Holbrook, ***Iron Brew*** (New York: Macmillan, 1939), p. 275, for a similar appraisal.

8. There is little in the way of systematic investigation of ethnic stereotypes of these early groups. A survey of colonial literature, especially on Pennsylvania, however, illustrates the degree to which both the German and Scotch-Irish were cultural underdogs. See Glenn Weaver, "Benjamin Franklin and the Pennsylvania Germans," ***William and Mary Quarterly,*** third series, 14 (1957): 536-559, for his work on the Germans in colonial Pennsylvania. For the Scotch-Irish, the best work is James G. Leyburn, ***The Scotch-Irish*** (Chapel Hill: Univ. of North Carolina Press, 1962). See also Irwin G. Wylie, ***The Self-Made Man in America: The Myth of Rags to Riches*** (New Brunswick, N.J.: Rutgers Univ. Press, 1954) for an analysis of the general literature on the "rags to riches" myth.

9. Marcia Davenport, ***Valley of Decision*** (New York: Scribners, 1942), p. 29. This best-selling novel, although not great literature, is a remarkably accurate and incisive view of the nature of Pittsburgh's steel industry and society. Mrs. Davenport was married to the son of a prominent steel manufacturer in Philadelphia, Russell W. Davenport.

10. Quoted in William G. Johnston, ***Life and Reminiscences from Birth to Manhood*** (Pittsburgh: Privately Printed, 1901), p. 22.

11. The First Presbyterian Church between 1847 and 1851 counted among its pew members: Alexander Laughlin, Thomas Scott, the Irwin family, Neville B. Craig, William F. Willock, Robert and James Dalzell, Alexander Brackenridge, the Denney Family, Francis G. Bailey, General William Robinson, William Hays, R. T. Beech, William McCandless, Samuel Bailey, the Blair family, Hugh McClelland, Dr. J. R. Speer, William Dilworth, the Willkins family, John Thaw, Samuel Johnston, "judge" Porter and "judge" Riddle, Samuel Rea, Henry Sproul, William M. Darlington, George Cochran, and George R. Smith, among others (Johnston, ***Life and Reminiscences,*** from a chart of pew holders, facing p. 176). The extraordinary degree of intermarriage among these families can be graphically reconstructed from Frank W. Powelson's, ***Founding Families of Allegheny County,*** 4 volumes (Pittsburgh: Privately Printed, 1963); and ***More Founding Families of Allegheny County*** (Pittsburgh: Privately Printed, 1965).

12. Richard C. Wade, ***The Urban Frontier: The Rise of the Western Cities, 1790-1830*** (Cambridge: Harvard Univ. Press, 1956), p. 229.

13. Stephen Thernstrom, ***Poverty and Progress*** (Cambridge: Harvard Univ. Press, 1964).

14. Moses Rischin, ***The American Gospel of Success*** (Chicago: Quadrangle, 1965); Irwin G. Wylie, ***The Self Made Man in America: The Myth of Rags to Riches*** (New Brunswick, N.J.: Rutgers Univ. Press, 1954).

15. Rischin, ***Gospel of Success,*** p. 3.

16. John W. Jordan, ed., ***Encyclopedia of Pennsylvania Biography,*** 31 volumes, (New York: Lewis Publishing, 1914-1963), II, p. 128; ***National Cyclopedia of American Biography,*** 58 volumes (New York: J. T. White, 1893-1964), vol. 15, p. 45; Herbert Casson, ***Romance of Steel,*** pp. 20-23; ***Iron Age,*** July 28, 1898; American Society of Mechanical Engineers, ***Transactions,*** 10 (1889): 838-842; ***The Royal Blue Book*** (Pittsburgh: Privately Printed, 1913) pp. 85-90.

17. ***Iron Age,*** May 6, 1897; Casson, ***Romance of Steel,*** pp. 152-153; John K. Winkler, ***Incredible Carnegie*** (Garden City, N.Y.: Garden City Publishing, 1931), p. 129.

18. Frederick A. Virkus, ed., ***The Abridged Compendium of American Genealogy,*** 7 volumes (Chicago: Marquis Co., 1925-), vol. I, p. 267; ***Iron Age,*** December 21, 1899, September 27, 1900; September 2, 1909; April 7, 1922.

Jordan, ***Encyclopedia of Pennsylvania Biography,*** vol. 3, p. 779; ***National Cyclopedia of American Biography,*** vol. 9, p. 409; John W. Gordan, ed., ***Genealogical and Personal History of Western Pennsylvania,*** 3 volumes (New York: Lewis Publishing, 1915), vol. 1, pp. 117-120; ***Century Cyclopedia of History and Biography of Pennsylvania,*** 2 volumes (Chicago: Century Publishing, 1904), vol. 2, pp. 89-90.

19. ***National Cyclopedia of American Biography,*** vol. 22, p. 97; Gertrude Dinkey, ***Genealogy of the Flory-Dinkey Family*** (Pittsburgh: Privately Printed, 1946); ***Iron Age,*** August 6, 1903, p. 30; October 7, 1915, p. 827; August 13, 1931, p. 674.

Prominent and Progressive Pennsylvanians of the Nineteenth Century, 3 volumes (Philadelphia, 1898), vol. 1, p. 109; William Brown Dickson, ***History of the Carnegie Veterans Association*** (Montclair, N.J.: Mountain Press, 1938), pp. 68-69; Jordan, ***Encyclopedia of Pennsylvania Biography,*** vol. 5, pp. 1476-1478; Pennsylvania Society, New York, ***Yearbook,*** 35 volumes (New York: The Pennsylvania Society, 1901-1934), 1932 volume, pp. 88-89; Frank C. Harper, ***Pittsburgh of Today,*** 5 volumes (New York: American Historical Society, 1931), vol. 5, pp. 904-905; Western Pennsylvania Biographical Association, ***Western Pennsylvanians*** (Pittsburgh: Western Pennsylvania Biographical Association, 1923), pp. 164, 364.

2

The Iron and Steel Elite of Five Cities: A Comparative View

The foregoing chapter has delineated the social origins of the entire group of 696 steel manufacturers, and has analyzed in some detail the role of the 360 Pittsburgh entrepreneurs in relation to the larger number. In this chapter, we shall be looking at the other 336 iron and steel manufacturers in Philadelphia, Bethlehem, Cleveland, Youngstown and Wheeling, comparing them to the total number of manufacturers and to the Pittsburgh model. The final section of this chapter will then present a comprehensive summary of the elite in all six cities.

THE PHILADELPHIA IRON AND STEEL MANUFACTURERS

E. Digby Baltzell has called Philadelphia's business community an "American Business Aristocracy." Analysis of the social origins of that city's iron and steel manufacturers substantiates his view, and indicates the important differences between a seacoast city like Philadelphia and a newer, western city like Pittsburgh.

Just 6 percent of the 118 Philadelphia steel men were immigrants, and only 9 percent were native sons of immigrant fathers. Of all the cities included in this study, the Philadelphia iron and steel elite received the least influence from recent immigrants—a total of only 15 percent in this category. This sense of old family aristocracy was further enhanced by the dates of arrival in the United States of the first members of these families. Fully 61 percent—more than in any of the other five cities—came to America in the seventeenth century, and another 20 percent arrived in the eighteenth century, giving a total of 81 percent with colonial origins.

Seventy-four percent of the Philadelphians were of English or Welsh ancestry; and only 4 percent were of Scottish or Scotch-Irish origin. The only significant non-British-origin group in Philadelphia was the German-Americans, who made up

10 percent of the total. Given the long-standing presence of a relatively large German group in the community, this figure contrasts sharply with Pittsburgh Germans who comprised 16 percent of the iron and steel leaders yet had a less significant community of German-Americans among the general population.

Sixteen percent of the Philadelphia iron and steel elite were Quaker in religion —a distinctive characteristic of that city, reflecting the long and continual influence of the Quakers on the Philadelphia upper-class, generally. The largest number of Philadelphia steel men were Episcopalian (43 percent), and only 15 percent were Presbyterian. The remaining one-quarter were fairly evenly divided among other Protestant groups. There were no Catholics or Jews among the iron and steel elite of Philadelphia.

The fathers of 78 percent of the steel entrepreneurs in Philadelphia—the highest proportion for any of the cities under study—were businessmen. Eleven percent were the sons of professionals; 9 percent were sons of skilled workers (about average for all cities); and only 2 percent were the sons of farmers (less than the low average for all cities). These figures confirm the strong urban upper-class character of Philadelphia's iron and steel elite. A more complete breakdown of these characteristics is shown in Table 9.

Since Baltzell and Nathaniel Burt have told the story of Philadelphia's upper class, it is not necessary to summarize it here.[1] We will describe, however, the nature of Philadelphia steel men from various backgrounds in order to illustrate their continuity with the city's older upper class, and to establish more precisely the social origins and social advancement patterns of those who deviate from this upper-class norm. To understand more clearly the roles these and other families played in the city's iron and steel industry after the Civil War, an analysis similar to that used in Pittsburgh will be undertaken here. The Philadelphia iron and steel men will be divided into four main categories: men from pre-Civil War Philadelphia iron families; men from other families prominent in Philadelphia's antebellum business and professional scene; elite migrants from other areas; and men from middle-class families. Since none were from authentically poor families and few were from recent immigrant or working-class families, most of these will be subsumed under the general middle-class headings.

PHILADELPHIA IRON MANUFACTURERS FROM ELITE ORIGINS

Descendants of Pre-Civil War Philadelphia Iron Families

As was the case in Pittsburgh, a large proportion of the late-nineteenth-century iron and steel manufacturers in Philadelphia derived from families who had been involved in the antebellum iron industry of the city. A total of forty-five individuals were so categorized, representing 38 percent of the entire number—compared to 31 percent in Pittsburgh. Although the economic origins of these men in the two cities were similar, their cultural backgrounds were strikingly different.

TABLE 9
Social Origins of Philadelphia Iron and Steel Entrepreneurs, *N*=118

Birth/Parentage	%	Ancestry	%	Immigration of Family	%	Religious Heritage	%	Father's Occupation	%
Native/Native	85	English & Welsh	75	1600-1699	51	Episcop.	43	Manuf.	60
		Scottish &		1700-1749	13	Presbyt.	15	Merchant	13
Native/Foreign	9	Scotch-Irish	4	1750-1799	4	Methodist	2	Banker	5
		Irish	3	1800-1849	14	Baptist	1	Total Bus.	78
Foreign	6	German	10	After 1850	1	Quaker	16	Doctor	2
		Other	3	No Info.	17	Unitarian &		Lawyer	2
		Unknown	7			Congreg.	3	Minister	2
						Lutheran &		Teacher	0
						Germ. Ref.	5	Public Off.	7
						Other Protestant	15	Total Prof.	11
						Catholic	0	Worker	9
						Jewish	0	Farmer	2
TOTALS	100		102		100		100		100

Both groups derived their members in large numbers from the British Isles, with 79 percent of the Pittsburgh pre-Civil War iron men and 93 percent of the Philadelphia group having these origins. But this similarity is somewhat deceiving. Whereas the largest percentage of the Pittsburgh group (35 percent) was from the North of Ireland, with another 31 percent from England, fully 73 percent of the Philadelphia pre-Civil War iron men came from England, with another 18 percent from Wales. Only 2 percent derived from the North of Ireland. Also, where Pittsburgh had a large minority (18 percent) of pre-Civil War, German iron masters, only 4 percent from this group were in Philadelphia.

Religious heritage revealed a similar divergence. Whereas 63 percent of the Pittsburgh men from pre-Civil War iron families were Presbyterian, and 17 percent were Episcopalian, these proportions were reversed in Philadelphia, at 11 percent Presbyterian and 64 percent Episcopalian. Another 22 percent of the Philadelphia group were Quakers; and there were no Lutherans, Methodists, or Baptists among them. Both groups, however, were 100 percent Protestant in origin.

This cultural distinctiveness of the two cities' steel men is further enhanced when one observes data on the dates of their families' arrivals in America. While only 9 percent of the Pittsburgh group came to this country in the seventeenth century, 76 percent of the Philadelphia group did so. The majority (63 percent) of the Pittsburgh iron families arrived during the eighteenth century, most after 1750 (54 percent). Only 15 percent of the Philadelphia group came to America during the eighteenth century, most (13 percent) before 1750. Nor did many of the Philadelphia prewar iron families come over during the nineteenth century (7 percent), compared to the significant minority (24 percent) who did so in Pittsburgh.

This difference was further reflected in the origins of the groups. Although both were made up overwhelmingly of native sons of native fathers, and although neither city had many immigrants among this group, Pittsburgh had a far higher proportion who were native sons of immigrant fathers (16 percent), compared to only 4 percent in Philadelphia.

The two cities' typical steel manufacturers, then, although both descended from pre-Civil War iron families, represented contrasting cultural models. Whereas the Pittsburgh iron men were either Scotch-Irish or English, with a significant minority being German, the Philadelphians were overwhelmingly English in origins. While the typical Pittsburgh iron manufacturer was Presbyterian, his counterpart in Philadelphia was Episcopalian. Further, whereas the typical Pittsburgh iron family had come to America in the eighteenth century, the Philadelphians had arrived a century earlier. Both groups of men were characteristically native; but a significant minority of the Pittsburgh group had fathers who were born abroad. Thus, although the men in the pre-Civil War iron family groups in the two cities shared similar economic origins, they were dramatically divergent in cultural terms. This further reinforces the image of Pittsburgh as representing the rise of the cultural underdog in eastern coastal views.

Nor were the men from the pre-Civil War Philadelphia iron families at variance with the rest of the late nineteenth century steel men in that city. Both groups were overwhelmingly English in origin. The major distinction was in the fact that 18 percent of the pre-Civil War iron men in Philadelphia were of Welsh origin, and only 4 percent Germanic, while the balance of the Philadelphia group had 5 percent and 16 percent, respectively, in these categories.

In religious heritage, there was a greater disimilarity. While 64 percent of the men from Philadelphia pre-Civil War iron families were Episcopalian, only 30 percent of the balance of Philadelphia steel men were of this persuasion. The number of Quakers (22 percent in the former group) was also less, showing only 12 percent among the other Philadelphia steel men. The difference was made up primarily in the larger percentage of Presbyterians (18 percent) and those in other Protestant religions or of unspecified Protestant background. All men in both groups, however, were Protestant.

The figures on immigration to America also indicate some differences between the Philadelphia iron families and the other steel families. Whereas three-quarters of the former arrived during the seventeenth century, only 48 percent of the latter came that early. This difference was partially compensated for by the larger number coming over during the eighteenth century; but the greatest differential appeared in the number who arrived during the nineteenth century—28 percent for the rest of the Philadelphia group, compared to only 7 percent for the pre-Civil War iron families.

Although the great majority of both groups were native sons of native fathers, the larger group of Philadelphia steel men contained more immigrants and sons of immigrants than did the men from the city's prewar iron-making origins. Whereas only 4 percent were native sons of immigrant fathers among the antebellum iron families, 12 percent among the rest of the Philadelphians were in this category. The former group had only 2 percent immigrants, while the latter had 8 percent.

Thus, although the men descended from pre-Civil War iron families were more similar to the rest of the Philadelphia steel men then they were to the men descended from pre-Civil War iron families in Pittsburgh, there were areas of significant variation. While all Philadelphia steel men were from similar ancestral origins, religious diversity, different times of their families' arrivals in America, and contrasting nativity patterns set them apart. Philadelphians from pre-Civil War iron families were an older, more homogeneous group.

Descendants of the Pre-Civil War Business and Professional Elite

Another thirty-five men, representing 30 percent of the total number of Philadelphia iron and steel men in the late nineteenth century, were members of families which had been prominent in phases of the city's business and professional life outside of the steel industry. This total was somewhat higher than the 24 percent in this category for Pittsburgh. There were also other, more distinctive cultural differences between the Pittsburgh and Philadelphia groups derived from pre-Civil War business and professional elites.

There were important differences in ancestral origin. Although 87 percent of the Philadelphia group and 82 percent of the Pittsburgh group came from the British Isles, closer investigation reveals variation. The great majority of the Philadelphians (69 percent) were of English origin, with 9 percent from Southern Ireland and only 3 percent each from Northern Ireland, Scotland and Wales. The Pittsburgh group included 37 percent from Northern Ireland, 29 percent from England and 15 percent from Scotland—a broader sampling from among the countries comprising the British Isles. A point of some similarity between the two groups was the 14 percent and 19 percent Germanic background among the Pittsburgh and Philadelphia groups, respectively.

A comparable pattern is observable in religious heritage. Whereas 65 percent of the Pittsburgh group was Presbyterian, with 18 percent Episcopal and the balance rather evenly divided among several Protestant denominations, the Philadelphians were evenly divided between Presbyterians and Episcopalians, with 34 percent in each group. A large minority, 17 percent were Quaker; and the balance were in other Protestant denominations. As in Pittsburgh, there were no Catholics or Jews among them.

The figures on family immigration were similarly divergent. Although both contained a majority arriving in America before 1800, a larger proportion of the Philadelphia group came over during the seventeenth century (34 percent, compared to 12 percent). Both contained substantial minorities who came over during the nineteenth century; but the Pittsburgh group, at 40 percent, was well above the 29 percent found in Philadelphia.

Despite this difference, figures on nativity for both groups were quite similar. Seventy-two percent of the Pittsburgh group and 74 percent of the Philadelphians were native sons of native fathers. Of the remainder, the Philadelphia pre-Civil War business elite had more immigrants (11 percent, compared to 2 percent), while the Pittsburgh group had a larger percentage of native sons of immigrant fathers, (22 percent, compared to 14 percent).

The economic backgrounds of these two groups of families in Pittsburgh and Philadelphia, despite their cultural differences, were remarkably similar. Ninety-five percent of the Philadelphia prewar elite came from families involved in business activity; the others were sons of government officials and professional men. In Pittsburgh, 78 percent were from business families, and 23 percent from professional or governmental backgrounds. The Pittsburgh group, however, was somewhat more heavily oriented toward manufacturing prior to the Civil War—with 58 percent in this category, compared to 46 percent in Philadelphia. The major element creating this difference in the latter group was the 26 percent who were railway executives, primarily with the Pennsylvania Railroad.

The differences between the Philadelphia men from business and professional families, and those from iron families in the same city, are considerably less striking.

Both groups were overwhelmingly English in ancestry, although there were more Welsh among the iron families and more Germans among the business and professional families. Religious differences were more pronounced, with the former group containing 64 percent Episcopalian and 11 percent Presbyterian, while the latter group had 34 percent in each category. The percentages of Quakers was about the same in each case, and neither contained any Jews or Catholics.

The dates of family arrival also produced some important differences between the two groups. Although a majority of both came to America prior to 1800, a far higher percentage of the iron families came during the seventeenth century (76 percent, compared to 40 percent). Nearly one-third of the business and professional families came during the nineteenth century, compared to only 7 percent of the iron families.

There were also some significant differences in nativity, with 93 percent of the men from pre-Civil War iron families being native sons of native fathers—compared to 74 percent in this category among the business and professional families. Thus the latter group had more immigrants and native sons of immigrant fathers.

The typical Philadelphia steel manufacturers in the late nineteenth century from a pre-Civil War business and professional background, then, differed both from their counterparts in Pittsburgh and from the Philadelphia men from antebellum iron families. Although predominantly English, they were more evenly divided in their Protestant religious preferences. Although more of the families had colonial origins than did their Pittsburgh counterparts, only one-half as many arrived during the seventeenth century, compared to Philadelphia men from prewar iron-making origins. There were more immigrants among them than with the two comparative groups; but the great majority were native sons of native fathers. The iron and steel families who derived from business and professional roots, then, were more varied in their cultural and economic backgrounds than were the men of pre-Civil War iron families. Although nearly all were from relatively old and prestigious Philadelphia families, they had generally arrived in America at a later date, and represented a greater variety of ancestral and religious backgrounds.

Elite Migrants from Other Areas

Philadelphia, like Pittsburgh, had its share of elite families who had migrated from elsewhere to take advantage of the growth of the steel industry in the area. Fourteen individuals, 12 percent of the total (compared to 9 percent in Pittsburgh) moved to Philadelphia in the late nineteenth century. These new arrivals in Philadelphia were virtual replicas of the preexisting elite in the city, particularly resembling the descendants of pre-Civil War iron families. They were also similar in many ways to the elite migrants to the Pittsburgh steel industry, although there were some significant differences.

Like the descendants of Philadelphia's pre-Civil War iron families, the migrating elites were overwhelmingly (100 percent, in fact) English in ancestral origins. Similarly, a great majority (64 percent) were Episcopalian—the same as among Philadelphia's iron families. An important minority were Unitarian, while only 7 percent were Quakers, compared to 22 percent Quaker among the men from pre-Civil War iron-making origins. The vast majority (86 percent) came to America during the seventeenth century, reflecting a similar old family orientation. Finally, all were native sons of native parents, similar to the 93 percent in this category among descendants of pre-Civil War iron families. All of these families had achieved elite status prior to the Civil War. Fifty-seven percent of the men were the sons of businessmen and 36 percent were sons of prominent governmental officials and politicians. The remaining 7 percent had fathers in the professional ranks.

Although these elite migrants to Philadelphia were similar in many respects to their counterparts in Pittsburgh, there were some important variations. First of all, whereas all of the Philadelphia migrants had come from New England, only 44 percent of the Pittsburgh group had come from this area. This factor, generally, was the root cause for other differences between the two.

Although a majority of the Pittsburgh migrants were of English origin, significant minorities were Scotch-Irish (19 percent) and Scottish (11 percent). The religious heritage of the Pittsburgh group was also more varied, with only 32 percent Episcopalian and 35 percent Presbyterian. Six percent were Unitarian, and the rest were distributed among several denominations. All men in both groups were Protestant. In terms of family arrival in America, the Pittsburgh group was not as old as the Philadelphia migrants, with only 38 percent in Pittsburgh coming during the seventeenth century. The majority (54 percent), unlike the Philadelphia elite migrants, had come to America during the eighteenth century. In terms of nativity, however, the groups were similar, with 94 percent of the Pittsburgh migrants being native sons of native fathers.

Despite these cultural variations, the two migrant elite groups represented similar pre-Civil War economic backgrounds. Sixty-six percent of the Pittsburgh migrants were the sons of businessmen, and 18 percent were sons of governmental officials and politicians—a slight variation from the 57 percent and 36 percent, respectively, among the Philadelphia migrants. Reflecting the general coloration of the areas to which they were migrating, these two elite groups displayed the same cultural dichotomy as between other complementary groups in the two cities. This would seem to suggest that elite migrants selected their areas of destination with an eye to cultural homogeneity as well as to economic opportunity.

Summary of Philadelphia Iron and Steel Men from Elite Origins

Some 80 percent of the individuals involved in the iron and steel industry in Philadelphia derived from the oldest and most prestigious families on the eastern seaboard, the great majority of them from Philadelphia itself. Although this situation was similar to that in Pittsburgh, the ability of such large numbers of the older upper class to attain prominent positions in Philadelphia's iron and steel industry is even more surprising. Since few of these men had been involved in a large-scale antebellum iron industry (and more were identified with banking and mercantile ventures), their ability to adapt themselves to the rapidly evolving steel industry stands as strong testimony to the resilience of these upper classes.

A majority of the late nineteenth-century iron and steel manufacturers in both Pittsburgh and Philadelphia traced their backgrounds to the pre-Civil War economic elite. In Philadelphia, however, they comprised 80 percent of the total, whereas they made up 64 percent in Pittsburgh. This figure reflects the degree to which the steel industry in Philadelphia was even more strongly dominated by preexisting economic elites, offering significantly reduced opportunities to men from divergent social and economic origins.

The data would indicate that Philadelphia was also less receptive than Pittsburgh to men from other than English, old family origins. Seventy-six percent of the men from elite origins in Philadelphia were English in ancestry, with those from Welsh backgrounds comprising the only significant minority (10 percent). In Pittsburgh, the elite families were more culturally diverse, with members of cultural minorities of the time gaining increased opportunities. In Pittsburgh only one-third were English, while 32 percent were Scotch-Irish, 14 percent German and 9 percent Scottish.

Religious heritage of the elite groups of the two cities also reflected a strong divergence. While the Philadelphia elite counted 53 percent Episcopalian and 18 percent each for Presbyterians and Quakers, the Pittsburgh elite was 60 percent Presbyterian and 19 percent Episcopalian. An important similarity, of course, is that both were comprised entirely of men from Protestant backgrounds.

Although the elite groups of both cities derived substantially from colonial origins (83 percent in Philadelphia and 71 percent in Pittsburgh), a far higher proportion in Philadelphia were from families which had come to America during the seventeenth century (two-thirds, compared to only 14 percent in Pittsburgh). Twice as many of the Pittsburgh elite were relatively recent migrants to America during the early nineteenth century (48 percent, compared to only 3 percent in Philadelphia). Thus, in general, Philadelphia elite families had been in America about a century longer than the Pittsburgh families.

Despite these cultural distinctions, the two groups from pre-Civil War elite origins were similar in nativity. Eighty percent of the Pittsburgh elite and 87 percent of their Philadelphia counterparts were native sons of native parents. Neither group included many immigrants, but Pittsburgh had more than twice as many men who were native sons of immigrant fathers (16 percent, compared to 7 percent).

In summary, then, the typical steel manufacturer from pre-Civil War elite origins in Philadelphia differed in important cultural respects from his counterpart in Pittsburgh. He was far more likely to be of English ancestry, Episcopalian in religion, and from a family which had arrived in America a full century before the representative member of the Pittsburgh antebellum elite. The extent to which Pittsburgh symbolized the rise to status of the cultural underdog is made more graphic by this contrast.

PHILADELPHIA IRON AND STEEL MEN FROM MIDDLE-CLASS ORIGINS

The extent of social and cultural differentiation between Philadelphia and Pittsburgh iron and steel manufacturers is further exemplified by the fact that none in the Philadelphia group emanated from either immigrant or native American poverty backgrounds. Although there were only 3 percent in this category in Pittsburgh, the fact that not even this small a percentage could find room at the top of the economic pyramid in Philadelphia is of some importance.

Whereas men from middle-class and skilled iron-and-steel worker origins comprised one-third of the postwar steel elite in Pittsburgh, they represented only 20 percent of the total in Philadelphia. In some respects the two groups reflected a similarity in cultural backgrounds; but in several important aspects they differed from one another, tending to further substantiate the cultural dichotomy between the two cities.

In ancestral origins, men derived from the middle class in Philadelphia deviated widely from the English prototype of the pre-Civil War elite in that city, and they more closely resembled their middle-class counterparts in Pittsburgh. Yet there was an important variation in these non-English origins between the two middle-class groups. Although generally the same ancestral countries were represented in the two groups, the proportions were quite different. While Germans comprised 41 percent of the total in Philadelphia and 23 percent in Pittsburgh, 38 percent in the latter city were Scottish or Scotch-Irish, compared to 6 percent in the former. A larger number in Philadelphia were Welsh or French in ancestral origin.

There were also important religious distinctions between the two groups. The Philadelphia men from middle-class origins were widely dispersed among a variety of Protestant denominations, not one of which attracted more than 13 percent of the total. In Pittsburgh, Presbyterians were predominant. Of fundamental importance, however, was the fact that although 88 percent of the Pittsburgh group was Protestant, 9 percent were Catholic and 2 percent Jewish. There were no Catholics or Jews among Philadelphia steel men from middle-class origins.

Of greater significance were the dates of family immigration in America. Fully 59 percent of the Philadelphia group were members of colonial families, compared to only 16 percent among their counterparts in Pittsburgh. While a majority of those coming to Pittsburgh in the nineteenth century arrived prior to 1850 (53 percent), a large minority (31 percent) came after that time. There were only 8 percent in this latter category in the Philadelphia group.

This generally old family standing among men from middle-class origins in Philadelphia was further attested by the fact that 75 percent were the native sons of native fathers; 17 percent were native sons of foreign-born fathers; and only 8 percent were immigrants. In Pittsburgh, while 48 percent were native sons of native parentage, another 24 percent were the sons of immigrants and fully 28 percent were themselves immigrants.

The foregoing analysis reveals some important characteristic differences between the men from middle-class origins in each city. Whereas in Pittsburgh certain ancestral origins (Scotch-Irish, English and German), along with the correct religious background (Presbyterian or Episcopalian), appeared to be requisite for acceptance into the post-Civil War economic elite, in Philadelphia these factors seemed to have been less important than the length of time one's family had resided in America. To gain entrance to the economic elite in Philadelphia, the aspirant in the iron and steel industry had to be a native son of native parentage, from a family with antecedents in colonial America. These factors were of less importance in nineteenth-century Pittsburgh.

Thus, within this context, the apparently radical differences in some areas between Philadelphia iron and steel men from prewar elite origins and those from middle-class origins in that city appear more muted. Despite the fact that less than half as many of the men from middle-class backgrounds were of English heritage (33 percent compared to 76 percent), and a far larger proportion were of Germanic origins (41 percent, compared to 5 percent), this is offset by important similarities. In the same manner, the absence of a majority of Episcopalians, Presbyterians and Quakers among the middle-class men is less crucial. The striking fact is that a majority of men in both the elite and the middle-class groups were derived from families which had been in America prior to 1800. Although the number in this category for the pre-Civil War elite was much higher (78 percent compared to 59 percent), and although a larger proportion came during the seventeenth century in that group (62 percent compared to 17 percent), the most important aspect is that the length of residence of their families in America was the point of continuity and relative homogeneity between these two groups. To achieve economic success in late nineteenth century Philadelphia, the number of generations one's family had resided in America superseded other criteria.

Summary

The Philadelphia iron and steel elite, then, were from relatively higher social, economic and cultural origins. when compared to Pittsburgh. The iron and steel elite in the two cities did not differ, however, so much in substance as they did in degree. Both cities drew a majority of their iron and steel manufacturers from the pre-Civil War business and professional elite. Although Philadelphia had a substantially higher proportion from these elite categories (80 percent, compared to 64 percent in Pittsburgh), the major distinction between the two appears in the type of men who came from non-elite origins. In Pittsburgh it was possible for a small percentage of men to derive from poverty and deprived circumstances, or to be of Catholic or Jewish heritage. This was not the case in Philadelphia. Further, Philadelphia entrants into the economic elite in the late nineteenth century were from families which had been in America for a longer period of time, with fewer immigrants and sons of immigrants among them.

Although one does not find a "rags to riches" pattern in either city, it is apparent that the Pittsburgh steel elite represents a group of men from more divergent cultural origins. Typical of the migrants to America in the late eighteenth and early nineteenth centuries, the steel elite in Pittsburgh marked the arrival to status of a series of cultural minority groups, particularly the Scotch-Irish.

Philadelphia, an older seacoast city, had a more restrictive social and economic system. It was relatively more difficult for a recent immigrant to achieve economic success in the iron and steel industry there than in Pittsburgh. This did much to eliminate from consideration several of the cultural minority groups which had found success in Pittsburgh. With the exception of a minority of men from Germanic backgrounds, few from non-English origins were to find success in Philadelphia. This matrix of old family Protestantism with English antecedents worked against the rise of any steel makers of Catholic or Jewish background in Philadelphia.

THE BETHLEHEM SUBGROUP: SOCIAL ORIGINS

Within the group of Philadelphia iron and steel manufacturers, there was an important subgroup of manufacturers in Bethlehem, Pennsylvania. This rather confusing overlap results from the fact that the Bethlehem Iron Company, the principal iron and steel firm in the city, was owned and controlled at its highest executive levels by upper-class Philadelphians. At the middle-management level, however, many natives of Bethlehem, of English and German extraction, had a strong and continuing influence on the firm. They were all local men, reared in the area; and, to a large degree, they remained socially separate from the Philadelphia group. Thus they form an interesting counterpoint to the Philadelphia manufacturers, in spite of the fact that they did not differ substantially in terms of broad social origins. The differences were primarily of a more subtle social and ethnic nature, and these will be examined in more detail in Chapter 5.

Bethlehem was distinct and separate from the Philadelphia families who owned and controlled the Bethlehem Iron Company. Although it is impossible to determine whether the failure to maintain extensive social contacts between the two groups was by mutual consent or imposed unilaterally by one side, it is clear that English-origin families from Bethlehem could gain some marginal acceptance in Philadelphia's upper-class circles, while those of Germanic background did not. Whether the latter desired this acceptance or not is impossible to determine. Whatever the case, it is clear that Bethlehem, with its separation of ownership and control and its truncated social system in the mid-nineteenth century, resembled "Yankee City" in the 1930s. The Philadelphia families at the top of the economic pyramid maintained a separate and distinct set of social relationships from native Bethlehemites in high-management positions of the iron company.

Separation of the Bethlehem subgroup from the main group of Philadelphia iron and steel manufacturers also reveals that the great majority of those men of German extraction among the city's iron and steel manufacturers (11 percent of the total) were actually residents of Bethlehem, and were distinctly separate in nearly every social detail from the main group of Philadelphians. This only serves to reinforce Baltzell's description of the Philadelphia business elite as an "aristocracy." Not only were they predominantly from the uppper classes and upper middle classes of the eastern seacoast, but they were quite uniformily English, Welsh and Scotch-Irish in their backgrounds. Separating the Bethlehem subgroup from the Philadelphia whole serves to accentuate the upper-class homogeneity of the Philadelphia group.

CLEVELAND IRON AND STEEL ENTREPRENEURS

Cleveland was a "young" city: it was not settled in any numbers until the mid-nineteenth century. By 1840 it still had only 6,071 inhabitants. Ten years later it numbered 17, 034. After the 1850s, however, growth accelerated, reaching 43,000 in 1860, 93,000 in 1870, 160,000 in 1880, 261,000 in 1890, and 382,000 in 1900. During the three decades of exceptionally rapid growth—1870 to 1900, when the population increased by over 400 percent, the iron and steel industry grew to maturity in Cleveland.

Who were to become the iron masters in Cleveland? From what segments of the population did they emanate? Cleveland was a city of two cultures. As a part of the Western Reserve owned originally by Connecticut, many New England families were given lands there, and some of these, in turn, became the earliest settlers. The original society, institutions, and leaders of the Western Reserve were a transplanted Yankee culture. A large percentage of the post-1870 arrivals to Cleveland, however, were immigrants from Europe. By 1870, only 58 percent of the city's inhabitants were native Americans. Further, four-fifths of the native population had been born in Ohio, indicating the relative stability and parochialism of that segment of the population. Of the 42 percent who had been born abroad, 51 percent of these came from Germany, 41 percent from the British Isles, and only 8 percent from other countries. By 1900, although 67 percent of the population was native, only 34 percent were natives with native parentage. Of the one-third of the population who had emigrated from foreign countries, half came from Germany and Austria, 29 percent from the British Isles, 8 percent from Hungary, 6 percent from Russia, 2 percent from Italy, and 4 percent from other countries.[2] Of the large new population of Cleveland in this thirty-year period, then, a majority had emmigrated from Germany, and another 30 percent or so had come from the British Isles. Added to this was a growing minority from southern and eastern Europe, who were to form an important segment of the population in the twentieth century.

The iron and steel elite did not reflect this population proportionately, but was drawn overwhelmingly from the small minority of early New England settlers. Of the eighty-six Cleveland iron and steel manufacturers in the late nineteenth century, 78 percent were natives and 22 percent were immigrants. Although this figure is lower than the percentage of immigrants in Cleveland generally, it is the highest of any of the cities presently under study. Native iron and steel men who were the sons of immigrants comprised 13 percent of the total in Cleveland. Table 10 gives a comparative breakdown of these figures.

The bimodal nature of Cleveland's iron and steel elite appears clearly in the times of family immigration to the United States: 17 percent were from families who came to America after 1850—a far higher percentage than for the other cities studied. Another 30 percent were from families which had come to America between 1800 and 1849. A total of 47 percent came to America after 1800 (all relatively "new" families)— a figure for which Cleveland ranked only behind Pittsburgh.

Conversely, 30 percent of the Cleveland iron and steel elite came to America during the seventeenth century, and 23 percent arrived during the eighteenth century. With 39 percent coming before 1750 and 47 percent after 1800, Cleveland's steel entrepreneurs were comprised nearly equally of families of more recent immigrant origins and older colonial families. Table 11 demonstrates, in comparative fashion, this bimodal aspect of Cleveland's iron and steel elite.

TABLE 10
Origins of Cleveland Population and Its Iron and Steel Manufacturers

Origins	Cleveland 1870 *N*=93,000	Cleveland 1900 *N*=382,000	Cleveland Iron and Steel Men *N*=80
Native, total	58%	67%	78%
Native, with native parents	N.A.	34	65
Foreign	42	33	22

SOURCE: Bureau of the Census, Department of Commerce, *Historical Statistics of the United States* (Washington, D.C. 1975).

TABLE 11
Families of Steel Manufacturers in Three Cities: Periods of Immigration

Period	Percentage of Manufacturers' Families		
	Cleveland *N*=80	Pittsburgh *N*=304	Philadelphia *N*=98
After 1850	17	10	1
1800-1849	30	37	17
1750-1799	14	37	5
1700-1749	9	7	15
1600-1699	30	10	61
TOTALS	99	101	100

Ancestral origins, however, indicate considerable cultural homogeneity in the Cleveland group. Seventy-six percent were either English or Welsh, second only to Philadelphia's 80 percent in this category. Another 17 percent were Scottish or Scotch-Irish, leaving only 6 percent German and another 7 percent coming from other countries. Thus, despite a nearly even division between "old" and "new" families, 93 percent of the steel manufacturers were from the British Isles. This was higher than the 86 percent found in Philadelphia in these categories. The German percentage among the Cleveland steel men was also proportionately low (6 percent), especially since about 50 percent of the immigrants to Cleveland in the late nineteenth century were of Germanic origin and a substantial number of the native inhabitants also derived from this group. Table 12 demonstrates the Cleveland figures on ancestral origin, compared with figures for the population of Cleveland, and compared with iron and steel manufacturers in Pittsburgh and Philadelphia.

In religious heritage, the Cleveland iron and steel elite was more diverse, with only 22 percent Presbyterian, 17 percent Episcopalian, 9 percent Baptist, 5 percent each for Unitarians and Congregationalists, and 11 percent divided between the Methodists and the Disciples Church. A major reason for these lower percentages, however, is the large number of unspecified Protestants (35 percent) among the Cleveland group. All iron and steel entrepreneurs in Cleveland were Protestant.

Occupations of the fathers of the steel elite reinforce this impression of relative homogeneity. Seventy-five percent were sons of businessmen. Another 3 percent were the sons of professionals (all ministers). Thus, a total of 78 percent were from families in the economic upper class and upper middle class. Yet, this figure is somewhat lower than for any other city studied. Of the 21 percent not from these upper-class origins, 12 percent were the sons of skilled workers, and 9 percent of farmers—higher in the case of workers for any other city except Wheeling. Table 13 gives a comparative breakdown of fathers' occupations for iron and steel men for Cleveland, Pittsburgh and Philadelphia.

Although the Cleveland iron and steel elite was composed almost equally of old and new families, it was relatively homogeneous in cultural, religious and economic origins, with a slightly higher minority (than in Pittsburgh or Philadelphia) from working-class and immigrant backgrounds. To better facilitate a comparative analysis of the Cleveland iron and steel manufacturers, they will be divided into categories similar to those created for Pittsburgh and Philadelphia: men descended from the pre-Civil War economic elite in Cleveland; elite migrants from other areas in the late nineteenth century; men from the native American middle class and skilled working class; recent immigrants from middle-class and skilled working-class origins, and poor immigrants from apparently lower-class backgrounds.

DESCENDANTS OF CLEVELAND'S PRE-CIVIL WAR ECONOMIC ELITE

Despite the fact that Cleveland was a young city which did not significantly develop until the 1840s and 1850s, 42 percent of the iron and steel manufacturers

TABLE 12
Comparative Ancestral Origins: Three Cities

Country of Origin	Percentage of Cleveland Immigrant Population* 1870	1900	Percentage of Cleveland Steel Mfrs. *N*=81	Percentage of Pittsburgh Steel Mfrs. *N*=325	Percentage of Philadelphia Steel Mfrs. *N*=110
England & Wales	13	29	76	37	80
Scotland & Ireland	2		17	42	4
Ireland	26		—	2	3
Germany	51	50	6	17	11
Other	8	20	1	2	3
TOTALS	100	99	100	100	101

*Percentages on Cleveland immigrant population in 1870 were recomputed from slightly different breakdowns given in Rose, ***Cleveland: The Making of a City*** (Cleveland: World Publishing Co., 1950).

TABLE 13
Occupations of Fathers of Steel Manufacturers in Three Cities

Father's Occupation	Percentage of Steel Mfrs. Cleveland *N*=86	Pittsburgh *N*=360	Philadelphia *N*=110
Manufacturer	52	59	60
Merchant	18	9	13
Banker	5	2	5
Total Business	75	70	78
Doctor	—	2	2
Lawyer	—	1	2
Minister	3	3	2
Teacher	—	1	—
Public Official	—	8	4
Total Professional	3	15	10
Workers	12	9	9
Farmers	9	6	2
TOTALS	99	100	99

in the late nineteenth century were members of families which had been prominent in the economic activity of the city prior to the Civil War. Although this figure represents an eminently respectable percentage (given the later development of Cleveland), it was well below the 68 percent in this category in Philadelphia and the 55 percent found in Pittsburgh. Cleveland, to a greater degree than either of these two older cities, tended to draw its late-nineteenth-century iron and steel elite from sources other than its own indigenous prewar economic elites.

The majority (72 percent) of these thirty-six men were of English ancestry. This figure was nearly identical to the indigeneous elite in Philadelphia, and is well above the 31 percent in this category among the prewar elite in Pittsburgh. Another 22 percent of the Cleveland steel men in this group were either Scottish or Scotch-Irish, and the remaining 3 percent were of French origin. This differed substantially from Philadelphia, where men of Welsh and German ancestry comprised the two largest minorities. Cleveland's antebellum elite was also somewhat different from those found in Pittsburgh, where the Scotch-Irish and Scottish were the largest single group, at 45 percent, with Germans comprising 16 percent of the total.

The indigenous, pre-Civil War elite in Cleveland, then, varies in important respects from its counterparts in Philadelphia and Pittsburgh. With a substantial over-representation of men from English origins among the elite, Cleveland appears much like Philadelphia. Yet, since the largest minority group in Cleveland were the Scottish and Scotch-Irish, this aspect lends some of the cultural flavor of Pittsburgh. The absence of any prewar elites of Germanic background (an important minority group among both the Pittsburgh and Philadelphia elite) also gives a certain uniqueness to Cleveland.

Analysis of data on religious heritage for the men from the pre-Civil War economic elite in Cleveland also indicates a striking divergence from the patterns in both Pittsburgh and Philadelphia. Whereas a majority of the indigenous Pittsburgh elite was Presbyterian and the largest minority was Episcopalian, Philadelphia had a reversal of this pattern. In Cleveland, the pre-Civil War elite was nearly evenly divided between these two religious denominations, with 36 percent Presbyterian and 31 percent Episcopalian. The only other religious persuasion of any significance among the Cleveland group were the Baptists, at 14 percent. In both Philadelphia and Pittsburgh, Baptists constituted just 1 percent of the total. Philadelphia, with a large minority of Quakers, differed from both Cleveland and Pittsburgh in this respect. A major point of similarity among the antebellum elite in all three cities was the fact that all were Protestant.

In terms of ancestry and the length of time their families had resided in America, the Cleveland prewar elite group more nearly resembles its counterpart in Philadelphia than that in Pittsburgh. A majority of the Cleveland group (54 percent) had come to America during the seventeenth century, corresponding to the 62 percent of the Philadelphia elite in this category. Only 11 percent of the Pittsburgh group immigrated to America at such an early date. The Cleveland and Philadelphia groups also had about the same percentages arriving during the eighteenth century, with 21 percent and 20 percent, respectively. Unlike Philadelphia, however, a majority of the Cleveland families who arrived during the eighteenth century came after 1750. In this respect, Cleveland somewhat resembled the Pittsburgh prewar elite, where a great majority of the 56 percent who arrived during the eighteenth century also came after 1750. Thus, although the Cleveland steel men descended from pre-Civil War economic elites in that city, most resembled their Philadelphia counterparts in terms of time of arrival in America; a large minority (46 percent) immigrated *after* 1750, in this respect more closely resembling their counterparts in Pittsburgh.

In terms of nativity, men of all three cities were similar, with the pre-Civil War elite in Cleveland resembling Philadelphia more than Pittsburgh. Eighty-six percent of the group in Cleveland were native sons of native parentage; 8 percent were native sons of immigrants; and 6 percent were immigrants. This replicates almost exactly with the 85 percent, 9 percent, and 6 percent corresponding in Philadelphia. Pittsburgh was somewhat more unique. Although 78 percent were native sons of native parentage, fully 19 percent were the native sons of immigrants, and only 3 percent were immigrants.

Analysis of pre-Civil War economic backgrounds reveals a similarity between the Cleveland group and those in Pittsburgh and Philadelphia. In all three cities the families of a vast majority of the men were engaged in business rather than in the professions or politics. Ninety-seven percent of the prewar elite in both Cleveland and Philadelphia were businessmen prior to the war, as were 90 percent in Pittsburgh. A somewhat more detailed analysis of these business activities, however, reveals some important variations between Cleveland and the other two cities. Whereas 87 percent of the men from pre-Civil War elite families in Philadelphia were engaged in manufacturing or railroads, and 81 percent in Pittsburgh, only one-half of the Cleveland elite were manufacturers or railroad executives. A far larger proportion of the steel men from that city's prewar economic elite were merchants or bankers, 25 percent and 22 percent, respectively. In Pittsburgh and Philadelphia only 6 percent in each city derived from mercantile families; only 4 percent in Philadelphia and 3 percent in Pittsburgh had been engaged in banking. This discrepancy undoubtedly reflects the relatively slow economic growth of Cleveland prior to the Civil War, while manufacturing was of less importance than commercial or banking activities.

Cleveland's steel men from the city's pre-Civil War economic elite, then, share some important characteristics with their cohorts in Philadelphia, but also have some features which serve to set them apart. The typical late-nineteenth-century steel manufacturer in Cleveland from antebellum elite origins was English in ancestry, Episcopalian or Presbyterian in religious heritage, and came from a family which had arrived in America during the seventeenth century. A significant minority, however, were Scotch-Irish in ancestry, Baptist in religion, and came from families which had come to America after 1750. In economic background, although a large number were manufacturers prior to the Civil War, an equal number had been engaged in mercantile pursuits and banking. The major distinction of these Cleveland men from indigenous elite origins, then, lay not in their cultural variation from Philadelphia's seacoast elite, but in the nature of their prewar economic activity. This sums up much of what is important about the Cleveland elite: although dominated by an elite whose cultural origins were similar to those in seacoast cities, the newness of the Cleveland area created an alternate set of economic institutions to facilitate the emergence of the iron and steel elite in the late nineteenth century. Most importantly, these men represented the transplantation of both a Yankee culture and Yankee upper class from southern New England to the Western Reserve. From the very founding of the city, they exercised a powerful influence in its affairs. They became intimately involved in the development of the city's iron and steel industry, and represented a major portion of the core of the Cleveland antebellum social upper class. Only a small minority of families represented a variation on this New England old family theme. These positions of leadership and social prominence for the old Yankees were not temporary; for these roles continued well into the twentieth century, and their position in the iron and steel industry represented one expression of a particular cultural segment of the Cleveland upper class that has been highly influential throughout its history.

Elite Migrants to Cleveland

Twelve individuals, 14 percent of the total, were elite migrants to Cleveland in the late nineteenth century. This represents a higher percentage in this category than was the case in either Philadelphia or Pittsburgh (which cities had 12 percent and 9 percent, respectively). These men who migrated to Cleveland after the Civil War, to take advantage of the economic opportunities offered in its steel industry, were remarkably similar to the pre-Civil War elite of the city. They also strongly resembled their counterparts arriving at the same time in Philadelphia, but differed in some significant respects from those migrating to Pittsburgh.

Like Cleveland's steel men from indigenous pre-Civil War elite origins, these migrants to the city were overwhelmingly English in ancestry, but were more varied in religious heritage—since none were Episcopalian. This was offset, however, by the one-third who were Unitarian or Congregational in religion. Twenty-five percent were Presbyterian. The remainder were adherents of the Disciples Church (8 percent) or were unspecified Protestants (33 percent).

The great majority of these elite migrants were also members of families which had arrived in America during the seventeenth century, while another 10 percent had immigrated in the early eighteenth century. A major difference lay in the fact that 20 percent of these men came to America after 1850. However, they were members of a wealthy English steel-making family who purchased a steel mill in late nineteenth century Cleveland. Eighty-three percent of these men were native sons of native parentage. None were the sons of immigrants, but 17 percent were immigrants (the English steel makers).

These elite immigrants to Cleveland, then, not only substantially replicated the city's indigenous elite, but were also similar to the elite group migrating to Philadelphia. All of the migrants to Philadelphia came from New England, as did 75 percent of the Cleveland migrants. The remainder came from England, Kentucky, and New York State. This strongly "Yankee" orientation of both migrating groups was also reflected in a similarity of cultural backgrounds. Both groups were overwhelmingly English in ancestry, with their families coming to America during the seventeenth century. Only in religious heritage was there some variation, with a large number of Episcopalians and Quakers among the Philadelphia migrants, and none of these persuasions among the Cleveland group.

Although a substantial minority of the elite migrants to Pittsburgh were from New England (44 percent), the majority emanated from elsewhere; and this was reflected in the contrasting cultural backgrounds. Although a majority of the transplanted elite families in Pittsburgh were English in ancestry, this proportion was lower than in Cleveland and Philadelphia. Thirty percent of those migrating to Pittsburgh were Scotch-Irish or Scottish, reflecting a divergent cultural orientation. In religion, they were more similar, but the Pittsburgh migrants had far fewer with seventeenth-century family origins. A majority of the Pittsburgh families came to America during the eighteenth century. Thus, in all three cities, the men of prior elite standing who migrated into the area in the late nineteenth century tended to replicate the cultural orientation of the indigenous pre-Civil War elites.

Summary of Cleveland Steel Men from Pre-Civil War Elite Origins

These two groups of Clevelanders from elite origins comprised 56 percent of the total number of steel manufacturers in the city during the late nineteenth century. Although this is an impressive total, it is substantially below the 80 percent from elite origins found in Philadelphia, and lower than the 64 percent in Pittsburgh. Herein lies an important distinction between Cleveland and the two cities previously analyzed: a larger proportion of the men who were able to attain prominent status in the steel industry in Cleveland during the late nineteenth century were from outside the antebellum economic elites. In this sense, the three cities represent a gradient of economic opportunity correlated to the age and maturity of the economic and social system. Philadelphia, the oldest city, was also the least open to men from non-elite origins. Pittsburgh, then a much younger city economically and socially, was substantially more open to non-elite influence. Cleveland, the youngest and least developed of the three, was the most amenable to men from non-elite origins.

What kinds of men constituted the 44 percent from non-elite backgrounds in Cleveland? To what extent did they reflect a cultural, if not economic, unity with the pre-Civil War elites of the city? To what degree did they reflect the arrival of recent immigrants or of men from poor and humble backgrounds? How much similarity was there between these men from non-elite origins and their counterparts in Pittsburgh and Philadelphia? To attempt answers to these questions, the group of Cleveland steel men from non-elite origins will be subdivided into those from native backgrounds, those from immigrant middle-class and skilled working-class origins, and immigrants from poverty and deprived circumstances.

CLEVELAND DESCENDANTS OF THE NATIVE AMERICAN MIDDLE CLASS Fifteen of the iron and steel manufacturers in Cleveland in the late nineteenth century, 17 percent of the total, were from rather solidly established native American middle-class and skilled working-class families. Although their economic origins separated them from Cleveland's elite families, their cultural backgrounds were somewhat similar.

Sixty-nine percent of them were of English ancestry. The largest minority (15 percent) were Germanic (which set them apart from the elite families), but the remainder were Welsh or Scotch-Irish. Their religious heritage was more varied, and the majority were unspecified Protestants. The largest minority (27 percent) were members of the Disciples Church, a significant variation from the Cleveland elite families. They also differed in terms of family arrival in America, with all of them immigrating during the eighteenth century—compared to 59 percent of the elite families having arrived during the seventeenth century. In this middle-class group, there were no immigrants or sons of immigrants.

Whereas the ancestral origins of these Cleveland steel manufacturers from native middle-class backgrounds served to tie them more closely to the elites of that city, it was an important point of distinction between themselves and the middle-class families in Pittsburgh and Philadelphia. In the latter cities the middle-class group was a significant vehicle of upward mobility, whereby men from Germanic origins moved to positions of prominence. In Pittsburgh, 29 percent of the men from middle-class status were of German-American background; 32 percent were Scotch-Irish; and 26 percent were English. In Philadelphia, 41 percent of this group were of Germanic ancestry, and 35 percent were English. This represents a variance with the preponderance of men of English ancestry in Cleveland, and only a small minority of Germans. There was little difference in terms of religion or the dates of their families' arrivals in America.

Similar to the native American middle-class families in Philadelphia and Pittsburgh among the iron and steel elite, those in Cleveland were highly dependent upon better-than-average educational opportunities and upon familial connections to facilitate their rise to elite status. Two-thirds of these men possessed these advantages. Another 20 percent had learned important steel-making skills from their fathers. The remaining 13 percent were the sons of men who operated small businesses, providing them with some business skills.

Although there was certainly diversity in the backgrounds of the men from middle-class families, none had emanated from a lower-class mileau. Although some were from the working class, it was a skilled segment of that class. These skills could be important for entrance into the steel industry; and family connections along with sound educational advantages made the position of these men rather solidly middle-class.

CLEVELAND STEEL MEN OF RECENT IMMIGRANT MIDDLE-CLASS OR WORKING-CLASS ORIGINS

Similar to the native American middle-class group described above, was the group of recent immigrants representing 24 percent of the total in Cleveland. Like the middle-class native Americans, these men combined steel-making skills, family connections, and good educations to move rapidly up the ladder of success in the late nineteenth century.

These recent immigrants also resembled the native Americans of middle-class backgrounds and Cleveland's elite families, in that they were preponderantly of English origin—with a further 10 percent Scottish, and 5 percent each Welsh and Scotch-Irish. Another 14 percent were from Germany. In religious heritage, they were also much like the native American middle-class group, although 19 percent were Episcopalian and 10 percent Presbyterian. The majority, however, were unspecified Protestants, with 14 percent of Methodist heritage.

The area of greatest divergence, of course, between the native middle-class group and the recent immigrants, lay in the times of their families' arrival in America. Whereas a majority of Cleveland's elite families arrived during the seventeenth century, and all of the families of middle-class origins came during the eighteenth century, all of the recent immigrant group came to America during the nineteenth century (57 percent arriving prior to 1850). Thus, in large measure, one observes a quite homogeneous group in Cleveland. The vast majority of the steel makers are of English origin, and all are Protestant. Only the dates of arrival of these immigrant families in America served to set them apart from the other steel manufacturers in Cleveland.

The ancestral origins of Cleveland's recent immigrants of middle-class background distinguishes them from their counterparts in Pittsburgh. Only 13 percent of the Pittsburgh group was English, while 25 percent were German and 32 percent Scottish or Scotch-Irish. There was greater cultural diversity among the immigrants to Pittsburgh who achieved elite status in the steel industry, when compared to Cleveland. Just as the elite migrants to each city seemed to reflect the social and cultural orientation of the city to which they were migrating, so, too, did the recent immigrants. Recency of immigration proved to be less of an issue than was the possession of the "proper" cultural and social background in association with education, usable skills and—occasionally—familial connections.

RECENT IMMIGRANTS FROM POOR BACKGROUNDS

In Cleveland, as in Pittsburgh, there was a small percentage of the steel men (2 percent) who appeared to emanate from truly deprived and lower-class backgrounds. Two brothers, Henry and William Chisholm, would seem to best fit this category in Cleveland. In fact, they resembled the Carnegie brothers of Pittsburgh in a variety of ways. They were Scottish; their father possessed outmoded skills, resulting in family poverty and little in the way of formal education; and (after arrival in America) their occupational rise was rapid. By the 1880s they controlled Cleveland's largest steel company.

Henry Chisholm, along with his brother William, and their sons, William H., Wilson B., Stewart H. and Henry A. Chisholm, were all officers in Cleveland Rolling Mills in the late nineteenth century.[3] Henry Chisholm had been born in Scotland in 1822, and had immigrated to Montreal in 1842. He followed the carpenter trade in that city for seven years before coming to Cleveland, where he worked for the Cleveland and Pittsburgh railroad. By 1857 he had acquired a modest fortune of $25,000, which he used to found the Cleveland Rolling Mill. In later years, he also owned Union Rolling Mill in Chicago.

His brother, William, was born in Scotland in 1825, came to Montreal in 1847, and engaged in the general contracting business. In 1852 he moved to Cleveland, where he entered the lake carrying trade. Then, after spending a few years in Pittsburgh, he returned to Cleveland and joined Cleveland Rolling Mill as a partner. In 1860 he started his own steel plant, Chisholm Steel Shovel, and he built the Union Steel Screw Works in 1871. He later consolidated these concerns with National Screw and Tack Company.

The social origins of the Chisholm family are a little difficult to analyze, since little is known of Henry's father or their life in Scotland. His father had been a skilled worker, however; and the extreme poverty of the family in its early years in Montreal would indicate that he was not able to practice his trade. Yet, how the Chisholm family was able to rise so quickly in the business world in Cleveland, and how Henry Chisholm was able to accumulate $25,000 in so short a period of time, remains a mystery. There may have been family resources not apparent to the investigator. Based upon available information, however, the Chisholm family would appear to be from origins of authentic poverty, much like that of the Carnegie family in Pittsburgh.

CLEVELAND: CONCLUSIONS

In several respects the iron and steel manufacturers in Cleveland differed little from their counterparts in Pittsburgh and Philadelphia. Almost all were from at least middle-class or skilled working-class families, with 78 percent being sons of businessmen or professionals. Only a minority (22 percent) were immigrants, and just 13 percent were native sons of immigrant fathers. As in Pittsburgh and Philadelphia, all of those men of recent immigrant origin resembled the older immigrant stock—English, Welsh, Scottish, or Scotch-Irish, along with a minority from Germanic backgrounds. None belonged to the newer immigrant groups of the late nineteenth century (Jews, Slavs or Italians), despite the numbers from these groups pouring into Cleveland during these years.

As in Philadelphia and Pittsburgh, most of the Cleveland steel men found their ancestral origins in the British Isles (93 percent in Cleveland, compared to 87 percent in Philadelphia and 81 percent in Pittsburgh). Yet, like Philadelphia and unlike Pittsburgh, most of these men emanated from England itself—72 percent in Cleveland and 70 percent in Philadelphia, compared to only 32 percent in Pittsburgh.

This cultural homogeneity among the Cleveland iron and steel elite, and its orientation toward men of English background, was somewhat offset by the fact that a smaller proportion in Cleveland derived from pre-Civil War elite origins. Only 56 percent were in this category, compared to 80 percent in Philadelphia and 64 percent in Pittsburgh. This was further reflected in the dates of immigration for their families. In Cleveland there was a strongly bimodal pattern in family arrival, with 39 percent coming before 1750 and 47 percent after 1800. Fully 30 percent of the Cleveland steel families arrived during the seventeenth century. The Cleveland steel elite was composed in fairly equal measure of very old and relatively new families of similar cultural backgrounds.

In Philadelphia the vast majority (76 percent) came to America prior to 1750, with 61 percent arriving during the seventeenth century. The iron and steel elite of that city was almost totally dominated by "old families." In Pittsburgh, only 17 percent of the families had come to America prior to 1750, and 47 percent arrived after 1800. Another 44 percent came during the eighteenth century. Compared to either Cleveland or Philadelphia, Pittsburgh had fewer truly "old families," though a somewhat smaller proportion came after 1800 than was the case in Cleveland. With 74 percent of the Pittsburgh steel families coming between 1750 and 1850, few in that city were either very old or very new in America. Cleveland had the most significant pattern in this regard.

Cleveland was somewhat more open to men of recent immigration to America than were Philadelphia or Pittsburgh. Whereas 31 percent of the iron and steel elite in Pittsburgh were immigrants or native sons of immigrant fathers (and 15 percent of the Philadelphia elite were in this category), 35 percent of the Cleveland iron and steel men came from recent immigrant origins. Yet, because the balance of the steel men in Cleveland tended to come from very old New England families of English ancestral origins, these "new men" on the Cleveland scene differed little in their cultural backgrounds. They were new in terms of the recency of their arrival in America, but they were not new social or cultural groups. In this manner, Cleveland differs from Philadelphia (which had few men of recent immigrant origins) and from Pittsburgh, whose recent immigrants tended to represent somewhat newer and more diverse cultural backgrounds.

YOUNGSTOWN'S IRON AND STEEL ENTREPRENEURS

Youngstown, like Cleveland, was part of the Western Reserve, and attracted a large number of old, New England families. At the same time, as a new industrial area in the mid-nineteenth century, it had many of the same economic opportunities as Pittsburgh; and it was located near the centers of the Scotch-Irish culture in Western Pennsylvania. The social origins of the Youngstown iron and steel manufacturers reflected these circumstances: they were in many respects strikingly similar to those in Cleveland, but also shared some important characteristics with Pittsburgh.

Of the seventy men engaged in the iron and steel industry in Youngstown from 1874 to 1900, (on those for whom information could be found) 69 percent were native, 19 percent were immigrants, and 13 percent were native sons of foreign-born fathers. Their families' times of arrival in the United States also correspond closely to the Cleveland case, with nearly one-third each arriving in the seventeenth and eighteenth centuries. Thus, a total of 63 percent of the men were from families which had been in America for at least three generations. Of the remainder, 34 percent came to America between 1800 and 1849, and only 3 percent came after 1850.

Sixty-two percent of the Youngstown iron and steel elite were of English or Welsh origin, and 29 percent were Scottish or Scotch-Irish. Seven percent were from Germany, and the remaining 3 percent emanated from Southern Ireland. Although much like Cleveland, the Youngstown leaders included a substantial portion of men of Scotch-Irish origins, reflecting the Pittsburgh pattern and its proximity to that center of Scotch-Irish culture.

The "elite" religions of the nineteenth century dominated Youngstown steel makers: 13 percent were Episcopalian and 60 percent Presbyterian. The remaining 28 percent were Methodists and unspecified Protestants. There were no Baptists, Quakers, Congregationalists, Catholics or Jews. Fully 80 percent were from upper-middle-class and upper-class economic origins: 60 percent were sons of businessmen and 20 percent were sons of professionals. This compares with the 80 percent figure for Cleveland, 84 percent for Pittsburgh and 89 percent for Philadelphia. Seven percent were the sons of skilled iron workers, and 14 percent were sons of farmers. Table 14 gives a complete breakdown of these social characteristics of Youngstown steel makers.

Youngstown was, of course, much smaller in population than the three cities previously studied. In 1850 its population was less than 3,000. Despite rapid growth in the next half century, it reached only 45,000 by 1900. In 1920 its population was 132,000; in 1940, 168,000. A large proportion of the growth came from Italian and Slavic migration, but few from these groups became steel manufacturers.[4]

The men engaged in the iron and steel industry in Youngstown can be divided into groupings similar to those developed for the cities previously studied. Fifty-three percent of the men were members of families which had been influential in the city's business and professional life prior to the Civil War. Another 3 percent were elite migrants from other areas. Fourteen percent emanated from the native American middle class and skilled working class, while 30 percent were recent immigrants. None in the Youngstown group derived from truly poor or deprived backgrounds.

TABLE 14

Social Characteristics of Youngstown Steel Manufacturers, N=70%

	%		%		%
Birth/Parentage		*Ancestral Origins*		*Father's Occupation*	
Native/Native	69	English	46	Manufacturer	46
Native/Foreign	13	Scotch-Irish	16	Merchant	13
Foreign	14	Irish	3	Banker	0
		German	10	Total Business	59
Immigration of Family		Welsh	9		
		Scottish	10	Doctor	4
After 1850	3	No Information	11	Lawyer	0
1800-1849	29			Minister	0
1750-1799	10	*Religious Heritage*		Teacher	0
1700-1749	17	Episcopal	13	Public Official	16
1600-1699	26	Presbyterian	60	Total Professional	20
No Information	16	Methodist	16		
		Baptist	0	Skilled Worker	7
		Quaker	0		
		Unitarian & Congreg.	0	Farmer	14
		Lutheran	0		
		Other Protestant	11		
		Total Protestant	100		
		Catholic	0		
		Jewish	0		

DESCENDANTS OF YOUNGSTOWN'S PRE-CIVIL WAR ECONOMIC ELITE

Despite the fact that Youngstown was little more than a large town on the eve of the Civil War, thirty-seven of its iron and steel manufacturers in the late nineteenth century were descended from families which had been prominent in its economic structure prior to the war. Of these 51 percent had been involved in some aspect of the iron and steel industry, while the remainder were in banking (14 percent), mercantile activities (5 percent), or other manufacturing pursuits (30 percent).

In this orientation of Youngstown's postwar iron and steel elites toward prewar iron manufacture, the city had more similarities with Pittsburgh and Philadelphia than with its sister city in the Western Reserve, Cleveland. Fifty-seven percent of the men from Pittsburgh's pre-Civil War elite, and 56 percent of that group in Philadelphia, were engaged in iron manufacture prior to the war. Only 31 percent of Cleveland's descendants of prewar elites had been iron manufacturers.

Youngstown bore more resemblance to Cleveland in the ancestral origins of the men from its pre-Civil War elite, with 57 percent being of English ancestry. A large minority (30 percent) were either Scottish or Scotch-Irish—a total exceeded only in Pittsburgh. Twelve percent were German—a higher total among the pre-Civil War elite than in the other cities studied, except Pittsburgh. The remaining 3 percent in Youngstown were Irish.

In religious heritage, the men from pre-Civil War elite backgrounds in Youngstown resembled those in Pittsburgh. Seventy percent of these men in Youngstown were Presbyterian, compared to 64 percent in the latter city. Neither Philadelphia nor Cleveland had as high a percentage. Only 14 percent of the men from the pre-Civil War elite in Youngstown were Episcopalian—the lowest proportion of the four cities studied. The 11 percent Methodist in Youngstown was also far higher than in the cities previously analyzed.

But in dates of their families' immigrations, the Youngstown group was more like its counterparts in Cleveland and Philadelphia than in Pittsburgh. Fully 47 percent of the families came to America during the seventeenth century. This compares quite favorably with the 62 percent in this category among the prewar elite in Philadelphia, and with the 54 percent in Cleveland. Only 11 percent of the Pittsburgh prewar elite group came to America during this time. Another 31 percent of the Youngstown group came between 1700 and 1749, and 19 percent came between 1750 and 1799—giving a total of 97 percent who arrived in America prior to 1800. No other city in the study had such a large percentage of colonial families among the pre-Civil War elite: even Philadelphia had only 72 percent, Pittsburgh had 67 percent, and Cleveland had 75 percent.

This same "old family" orientation was reflected in the figures on nativity. Ninety-seven percent of the men from Youngstown's pre-Civil War economic elite were native sons of native parentage. The other 3 percent were immigrants. None of the other three cities studied thus far contained such a high percentage of native men of native parents among the prewar elites.

The men descended from Youngstown's pre-Civil War economic elite, then, shared some characteristics with both Cleveland and Pittsburgh, and even some with Philadelphia. Yet, although most men from Youngstown's pre-Civil War elite were English in ancestry, nearly as many were Scottish, Scotch-Irish or German. They were most likely to be Presbyterian, although small minorities were Episcopal or Methodist. Of greatest importance, however, was the fact that they were of "old" family: 78 percent of the families had come to America prior to 1750, ensuring that virtually all the steel makers were native sons of native parentage. No other city in the study had fewer men from recent immigrant origins among its pre-Civil War elite.

ELITE MIGRANTS IN THE LATE NINETEENTH CENTURY

Youngstown in the late nineteenth century—unlike Pittsburgh, Philadelphia, and Cleveland—was little affected by elite migrants from other areas. Only two men (representing 3 percent of the total) belonged in this category. Since it would make little sense to attempt to present tabulations on these two men, a brief biography of each will be given, along with comparisons with the indigenous elite.

Edward L. Ford was born in Albany, New York in 1856, of a family whose ancestors had been in that area for several generations.[5] He graduated from Yale University, and then entered the steel industry at Albany and Rensselaer Iron and Steel Company. He was then affiliated with Cambria Iron and Springfield Iron before becoming superintendent at Youngstown Steel in 1882. In 1907 he was elected president of the firm, organizing Brier Hill Steel in 1912. He married the daughter of Joseph G. Butler Jr., a prominent pre-Civil War iron manufacturer in the city.

Mason Evans was born in Philadelphia in 1847.[6] Educated in private schools in the city, he was graduated from the University of Pennsylvania in 1869, and was then admitted to the bar. Shortly thereafter he came to Youngstown as a partner to General Thomas W. Sanderson—one of the most successful attorneys in the city. In 1883 he became affiliated with Commercial National Bank in Youngstown, and became president of that concern. In 1894 he was elected treasurer of Youngstown Iron and Steel Roofing.

Both men, then, shared many characteristics with the city's pre-Civil War elite. They were of old family; both were Presbyterians; one was of English ancestry and the other was Welsh. As such, each was eminently eligible for easy acceptance by the older families of the city. The process of elite migration had little impact upon Youngstown, and the men who did come as a result of the expanding steel industry differed little from those already there. Elite migration did nothing to disturb the status quo of the existing elite.

MEN FROM NATIVE AMERICAN MIDDLE-CLASS FAMILIES

Ten men, 14 percent of the total, emanated from native American middle-class backgrounds. Like the elite migrants to the city, these men differed only slightly from the pre-Civil War elites in Youngstown. Similar to the elite families, the men from middle-class origins were predominantly English and 20 percent each Scotch-Irish and Welsh.

Although one-half were unspecified Protestants, the majority of those for whom denominational information was available (60 percent) were Presbyterian. They were also of old family: like the pre-Civil War elites, all came to America prior to 1800, and fully 80 percent arrived before 1750. All were native sons of native fathers. There were no immigrants or sons of immigrants among them.

The middle-class status of most of the men was achieved due to the relatively substantial amount of education they had received, their family connections, and (in one-third of the cases) the white-collar occupations of their fathers. All of these men were educated at least through high school, and all were able to use this to their advantage in seeking future upward mobility.

Although their economic origins were less substantial than those of elite background in Youngstown, they nevertheless derived from comfortable circumstances.

Further, they shared with that elite group the same general cultural characteristics. This did much to increase the stability of the prewar social system at its upper levels, and eased the entrance of these men into the elite.

MEN OF RECENT IMMIGRANT ORIGIN

Youngstown, like Cleveland, had a disproportionate percentage of men from recent immigrant origins to complement the old family origins of its elite and middle-class families. Thirty percent of the late nineteenth-century iron and steel men in the city were of recent immigrant derivation—higher than the 26 percent found in Cleveland in this category, or the 15 percent in Pittsburgh. Philadelphia had only about 5 percent who would be similarly categorized.

Thus Youngstown, like Cleveland, had a bimodal structure to its iron and steel elite. Whereas a majority of the steel men were from old colonial families of English ancestry—most of whom had originated in New England—a large minority were from among the more recent migrants to America. This structure appeared to be unique to the two Ohio Cities in this study.

Despite their recent immigration to America, these men shared nearly identical cultural origins with the older elite and middle-class families in Youngstown. The greatest number (43 percent) were English, and 24 percent were Scotch-Irish. This compared favorably with the 55 percent English, 15 percent Scotch-Irish and 13 percent Scottish among the older families. Only the 10 percent of Germanic background among the latter group was substantially at variance.

A similar pattern existed with religious heritage. Fifty-two percent of the recent immigrants were Presbyterian, compared to 63 percent of the men from native American families. Another 10 percent were Episcopalian, compared to 14 percent among the older families. The most significant variation was the 33 percent being of the Methodist persuasion among the recent immigrants, compared to only 8 percent in this category among men from native backgrounds.

The only truly major area of differentiation between the native families and those of recent immigrant origin lay in their nativity and the dates of arrival of their families in America. All of the latter group came to America during the nineteenth century, 91 percent prior to 1850. Only 3 percent of the native families arrived during the nineteenth century. In nativity, 43 percent were native sons of immigrants while 57 percent were immigrants themselves.

The recent immigrants among Youngstown's iron and steel elite were, then, not unlike their counterparts in Cleveland and Pittsburgh. Like those in her sister city in the Western Reserve, the largest number in Youngstown were English, although the 61 percent in this category in Cleveland was well above the 43 percent found in Youngstown. As in both Cleveland and Pittsburgh, a large percentage were either Scottish or Scotch-Irish (34 percent), compared to 38 percent in Pittsburgh and 21 percent in Cleveland. Both of the latter cities, however, had significant percentages of Germans among their recent immigrants (Cleveland with 13 percent and Pittsburgh with 15 percent), while Youngstown had none.

Similar to Pittsburgh's recent immigrants, the majority of Youngstown's immigrant families were Presbyterian. Only the one-third proportion of Methodists in Youngstown's group set it apart from those in the other two cities, neither of which had significant numbers among its immigrants. Youngstown, then, like Cleveland and Pittsburgh, drew its fairly large number of recent immigrants from a cultural stock which was not at variance with its older elite and middle-class populations.

SUMMARY

The iron and steel entrepreneurs of Youngstown were much like those in the cities previously analyzed. Almost all were at least of middle-class background, and the others emanated from the skilled working class. Like Cleveland, a smaller percentage (56 percent), were from pre-Civil War elite families. There was somewhat more opportunity in both Cleveland and Youngstown for a man whose family had not achieved significant economic status before the Civil War to be able to do so after that time. This apparent openness in both cities, however, was circumscribed by the cultural backgrounds which were deemed acceptable for admittance into the elite classes.

In Cleveland an acceptable cultural background was one with English origins. In Youngstown, there was more room for a cultural minority group such as the Scotch-Irish to achieve success. In this manner, Youngstown also resembled Pittsburgh, sharing partially that city's status as a cradle of Scotch-Irish culture.

ORIGINS OF THE WHEELING IRON AND STEEL ELITES

Wheeling, West Virginia, had a distinctive iron and steel elite. Although we have noted differences among groups of that elite in Pittsburgh, Philadelphia, Cleveland and Youngstown, all of them had more homogeneous backgrounds and origins when compared with Wheeling. In national and religious characteristics, Wheeling did not differ greatly; but it differed in class origins. It drew from more heterogeneous cultural areas than did the other cities; but more importantly, it drew from lower economic and social backgrounds. Wheeling had a more open, fluid social order in which its iron and steel leaders came from a much wider base than did those in other cities.

Like Cleveland and Youngstown, as well as Pittsburgh, Wheeling was a "new" city in the mid-nineteenth century. Unlike them, however, it was not part of the Western Reserve or of the Western Pennsylvania Scotch-Irish culture; and it did not naturally attract the families from old New England or from Northern Ireland who had flocked to the other cities. Similar to Cleveland and Youngstown, Wheeling had less than 3,000 inhabitants in 1830. During the following decade it experienced its first major growth, to 8,000 persons, making it larger than either of the two Ohio cities. By 1850 it had grown to 11,400—still larger than Youngstown, but smaller than Cleveland. Located at the head of deep water navigation on the Ohio River, and somewhat isolated before the 1820s, Wheeling developed a strategic transportation position in 1825 when the National Road was opened to the city and a canal from Cleveland to Portsmouth, Ohio was built. These gave rise to its initial growth.

Some of the people who had helped develop the iron and steel industry in Pittsburgh came down the Ohio River to take up similar ventures in Wheeling. Among the first were Dr. Peter Shoenberger and David Agnew, who had developed the first iron rolling mill in Pittsburgh. They arrived in 1832; and, finding abundant coal and limestone, Shoenberger and Agnew built the city's first iron puddling mill—"Top Mill"—that same year.

Iron production attracted a heterogeneous group of people to Wheeling in the mid-nineteenth century. Since it was not part of the Western Reserve, was close to Pittsburgh, was a part of Virginia and quasi-southern town, Wheeling drew entrepreneurs from a much broader spectrum than did the other cities studied. It was new, frontier-like, culturally mixed and complex, contrasting sharply with the other iron and steel centers. Just 8 percent of the city's iron and steel men were immigrants; only Philadelphia, an old seacoast city, had a lower proportion. But 15 percent were the sons of immigrants—comparable to Pittsburgh, Cleveland, and Youngstown, and nearly twice as high as for Philadelphia.

Only 8 percent of the Wheeling iron manufacturers' families came to America after 1850. This was well below the totals in this category for Cleveland (17 percent), and about equal to Pittsburgh (10 percent). It was, however, well above that for Philadelphia (1 percent) and Youngstown (3 percent). Two-thirds arrived between 1750 and 1850, with a total of 45 percent coming after 1800. Eleven percent came during the early eighteenth century, and 16 percent had arrived during the seventeenth century. Thus, in terms of family arrival in America, the Wheeling iron men most resembled those in Pittsburgh—they were neither substantially old family nor recent immigrant in origin.

In ancestral backgrounds and religious heritage, the Wheeling group was representative of the entire five-city group. Fifty-two percent came from England or Wales, 35 percent from Scotland and Northern Ireland, and 11 percent were German. In religious heritage, 40 percent were Presbyterian, 29 percent were Episcopalian, and 5 percent each were Methodist and Quaker. Another 14 percent were unspecified Protestants. This gave a total of 93 percent of the steel men being from Protestant origins. The remaining 7 percent were Catholics—the highest total for any of the cities in this study. Wheeling had no Jewish steel makers.

The most striking distinction between the Wheeling men and those in the other cities lay in their fathers' occupations. Although 63 percent were the sons of businessmen, and 15 percent had fathers in the professional ranks, fully 20 percent were the sons of working-class fathers. Even this figure somewhat understates the case, however, since several men were the sons of fathers who had begun as iron workers but had risen to the status of iron manufacturers by the time of the Civil War. Thus, fully 27 percent of the Wheeling iron and steel manufacturers in the late nineteenth century were the sons of men who had been in the working class (primarily as skilled iron workers) at least part of their working lives. Only 2 percent were the sons of farmers.

Wheeling clearly had a more open social order. It never developed a fixed, local aristocracy and its upper social strata remained fluid in the nineteenth and early twentieth centuries. Most of the men coming to economic power were relatively "new men," and the rise from workman to capitalist was greater than in any of the cities studied. All of this is reflected in the fact that Wheeling's iron and steel elite do not fit as neatly into the categories "pre-Civil War business elite," or "native middle class and working class." Many had recently been iron workers, and were from rather modest social origins, despite membership in a prewar economic

TABLE 15
Social Characteristics of Wheeling Steelmakers, N=62

Birth/Parentage		*Religious Heritage*	
Native/Native	77%	Episcopal	29%
Native/Foreign	15	Presbyterian	40
Foreign	8	Methodist	5
Total	100	Baptist	0
		Quaker	5
Immigration of Family		Unitarian-Congreg.	0
1600-1699	10%	Lutheran	0
1700-1749	7	Protestant Unspec.	14
1750-1799	18	Total Protestant	93
1800-1849	23	Catholic	7
1850-	5	Jewish	0
No Information	37	Total	100
Total	100		
Ancestral Origins		*Father's Occupation*	
English & Welsh	39%	Manufacturer	51%
Scotch & Scotch-Irish	26	Merchant	12
Irish	0	Banker	0
German	8	Total Business	63
French	2	Doctor	10
No Information	26	Lqwyer	0
Total	101	Minister	0
		Teacher	0
		Public Official	5
		Total Professional	15
		Worker	20
		Farmer	2
		Total	100

elite. In order to provide an effective comparison with other cities, however, the categories mentioned will be applied here (with some reservations). Of the sixty-two iron and steel manufacturers in Wheeling, 61 percent may be classified as pre-Civil War economic elite in Wheeling; 10 percent as elite migrants in the late nineteenth century; 11 percent from the native American middle class and working class; 15 percent recent immigrants of working-class or middle-class origins; and 3 percent from poor and deprived backgrounds.

DESCENDANTS OF WHEELING'S PRE-CIVIL WAR ECONOMIC ELITE

A significant number of the thirty-eight men from Wheeling's pre-Civil War economic elite emanated from working-class origins in the early nineteenth century. Twenty-six percent had fathers who had begun as iron workers and had acquired ownership interest in iron mills in Wheeling during the 1850s. They represented the workingman-to-capitalist phenomenon that was an important part of Wheeling's steel industry, and thereby served to make the Wheeling elite different from those in other cities. Many of these pre-Civil War elite families in Wheeling were only a few years removed from "horny-handed" toil in the early years of the 1870s. Far fewer of these indigeneous elite families of Wheeling had the background or social position characteristic of the dominant groups in Pittsburgh, Philadelphia, Cleveland or Youngstown.

In ancestral origins the descendants of Wheeling's pre-Civil War elite were most similar to their counterparts in Pittsburgh. Of those for whom information was available, 61 percent were of English background; but 39 percent were Scotch-Irish, the highest percentage of any city outside of Pittsburgh. In religious heritage, however, they differed somewhat from their Pennsylvania neighbors. While 32 percent were Presbyterians, 42 percent were Episcopalian and 8 percent each were Quaker and Methodist. There were no Catholics or Jews among Wheeling's pre-Civil War elite. Although Wheeling prior to the Civil War was more open to men from lower economic origins, they showed a resistance to men from divergent religious backgrounds, a resistance characteristic of the other cities analyzed.

The dates of arrival of their families in America also reveal a pattern similar to those in Pittsburgh. Sixty-five percent of the men on whom information was available arrived between 1750 and 1849. Another 20 percent came during the early eighteenth century, and 15 percent had come in the seventeenth century. In nativity, only Youngstown's pre-Civil War elites had a larger proportion who were native sons of native parents. In Wheeling, 90 percent were in this category and 11 percent were the sons of immigrant fathers. None of the city's pre-Civil War elite were immigrants themselves.

The elite status of these men prior to the Civil War was achieved primarily through iron manufacturing, with 61 percent having economic origins in that industry. Thirteen percent were involved in other manufacturing pursuits—saw mills, paper manufacturing, glass manufacturing, and others. Another 8 percent each were engaged in mercantile activities and banking, giving a total of 90 percent associated with business activities prior to the war. Of the remainder, 5 percent each were professionals or government officials.

In cultural terms, and in a broad analysis of their economic origins, these men from Wheeling's pre-Civil War elite appear similar to those in other cities, especially Pittsburgh. These figures, however, mask some important differences. To explicate these more clearly, the biographies of couple of these families shall be presented.

The Oglebay family was Wheeling's "first family" in terms of social prestige and national repute.[7] Earl W. Oglebay was involved in several iron mills in the city during the late nineteenth century. His family had settled in Wheeling in 1800. He was the son of Crispin Oglebay, a wholesale grocer in the young city, who had also been involved in the Benwood Iron Works. Earl W. Oglebay was born in Bridgeport, Ohio, in 1849, and was educated in private schools in Wheeling and New Brighton, Pennsylvania. After graduating from Bethany College in 1871, he entered his father's grocery establishment. Later, he became a clerk in the National Bank of West Virginia—of which his father was president. In 1877 he succeeded his father as president of the bank, then served in that capacity until his death in 1926. During these same years, he started the iron ore interests in the Lake Superior region. In addition, he was a director of Benwood Iron Works and Bellaire Nail Works in Wheeling, and was vice-president of Cleveland Steel Company.

The Oglebay family most resembled pre-Civil War elite counterparts in Pittsburgh, Cleveland and Youngstown. Of elite status for several generations, the family not only dominated the social and economic scene in Wheeling, but was also recognized for its prestige in other cities. With this more cosmopolitan acceptance, the Oglebay family did not remain long in Wheeling. In the late nineteenth century they moved their business and social interests to Cleveland, and ceased to be part of Wheeling's social structure.

Alexander Glass was secretary of Laughlin and Junction Steel Company in the 1880s and 1890s.[8] His grandfather, Alexander Glass, Sr., had come to America from Ireland in 1812. His father, Andrew Glass, was a nail worker who married Harriet Harris—daughter of Thomas Harris, a skilled iron worker from England (who had started an iron-rolling mill in Wheeling which went bankrupt in the 1850s). Andrew Glass, along with several of his fellow nail workers, organized the Belmont Iron Works in 1849 and the LaBelle Iron Works in 1851. In 1859, he also became part owner of the Jefferson Iron Works in Steubenville, Ohio.

Alexander Glass was born in Wheeling in 1859, and was educated in local schools until he was fourteen. At that time he entered his father's iron mill and learned the nail-making trade. In 1880 he set out on his own. He worked for a time as a clerk at the Wheeling Post Office, then set up an unsuccessful paper mill in Nashville, Tennessee. Returning to Wheeling in 1882, he worked as a clerk for LaBelle Iron and as a bookkeeper for Junction Iron. In the early 1880s he was named secretary of Laughlin and Junction Steel Company. He served there until 1887, was appointed general manager of the East Chicago Steel Works, and then managed the Terre Haute Iron and Nail Company. Returning to Wheeling in 1890, he joined Wheeling Corrugating—which was merged with Whitaker Iron and Laughlin Nail to form the Whitaker-Glessner Company. He remained there until 1902, then served as president of Portsmouth Steel until it was absorbed by Whitaker-Glessner. In 1920, that firm was merged with LaBelle Iron and Wheeling Iron and Steel to form the Wheeling Steel Corporation: Glass was chosen as chairman of the board, serving until his death in 1941.

The Glass family represents cultural and economic origins different from those of the Oglebay family. Of Irish and English background, the Glass family did not come to America until the early nineteenth century. Most importantly, elite status did not come until several years later: both sides of the family were serving as skilled iron workers for several years. Although Alexander Glass's father was an iron manufacturer for several years prior to the war, only a short time before that he was a wage worker.

Stimson H. Woodward, along with his son, Joseph H. Woodward, were officers in LaBelle Nail Works throughout most of the late nineteenth century.[9] Stimson H. Woodward was born in Taunton, Mass., in 1812. Receiving little formal education, he went to work at an early age; and by age eleven, he was an accomplished nail feeder. After spending a few years working in the textile mills of Massachusetts, he moved to Troy, New York, and then to Pittsburgh, where he worked as a nailer for the Shoenberger Iron Works. In 1847 he moved to Wheeling, and became a partner in Belmont Nail Works in 1849. In 1852 he organized the LaBelle Iron Works; and in 1859 he purchased the Jefferson Iron Works. After the Civil War he hearded southward on the Ohio River in search of nail contracts for his firm. While in Alabama, he discovered the vast iron, coal and limestone reserves in the area; and in 1868 he purchased 500 acres of the Red Mountain ore land. In the next few years he purchased several thousand acres of the ore land, but did not develop it immediately. It was not until 1880 that he built the first blast furnace in the area, a year before his death.

Joseph H. Woodward was born in Pittsburgh in 1843, and was educated in Wheeling private schools. After serving in the Civil War he became a traveling salesman for his father's firm, while also serving as secretary of the company. Upon the death of his father in 1881, he moved to Birmingham, Alabama, and formed the Woodward Iron Company there. Becoming president of the firm in 1886, he undertook a program of rapid expansion. In 1911, when the company absorbed the Birmingham Coal and Iron Company, it became the larg est iron and steel firm in the South. He died in 1917.

His brother, William H. Woodward, was born in Pittsburgh in 1840, and was educated in Wheeling. Becoming the first president of Woodward Iron, he served from 1881 to 1886. He then retired to pursue other enterprises in the Birmingham area, and died in 1910. Joseph's son, Alan H. Woodward, who had been born in Wheeling in 1876, became chairman of the board of Woodward Iron and vice-chairman of Wheeling Steel. Joseph's daughter married Oscar W. Underwood, U.S. Senator from Alabama.

The Woodward family amply illustrates the paradoxical nature of Wheeling social origins. They were a "founding family", and an old New England family at that; but they came from working-class origins. They represented the workingman-to-capitalist phenomenon that was an important part of Wheeling's steel industry. This is what makes the Wheeling elite so different: few families fit the pattern of the other cities—the early aristocracy of the city was often only three or four years removed from manual labor.

ELITE MIGRANTS TO WHEELING

Only six men were members of pre-Civil War economic elites who migrated to Wheeling in the late nineteenth century to engage in iron production. Although these men shared cultural origins which were similar to those of the indigeneous Wheeling elite, none in their families had recent experience with manual labor. This merely serves to accentuate the degree to which Wheeling's pattern of mobility into influential levels differed from that of other cities (or conversely, the degree to which the pattern of the other cities was prevalent and characteristic).

In ancestral origins, about half of the elite migrants to Wheeling were English, one-third were Scotch-Irish and 17 percent were German. All were Presbyterian in religious heritage. Half of the men were from families which had come to America during the seventeenth century, while the other families had come during the late eighteenth century. All were native sons of native parents. Although none of the men had been involved in iron manufacture in former cities, two-thirds were from other manufacturing origins—especially tobacco production. The other one-third was engaged in mercantile activities.

The characteristic which most distinguished the elite migrants to Wheeling was the number of them originating in the South. These southern families were in many respects identical to the elite migrants of Pittsburgh, Cleveland and Philadelphia (being English in ancestry and Episcopal in religion, and with seventeenth-century roots in America), but their southern heritage set them apart. And this was another aspect of the Wheeling elite which helped make it unique among the cities studied. Not only were its pre-Civil War elite more influenced by the workingman-to-capitalist phenomenon, but many also had families with roots in the South.

NATIVE AMERICANS FROM WORKING-CLASS AND MIDDLE-CLASS ORIGINS

It was characteristic of the Wheeling social order that the men from pre-Civil War middle-class and working-class origins differed little from the pre-Civil War elite. Their principle distinction is confined almost entirely to the timing of their achievement of elite status in Wheeling. Whereas a large percentage of the pre-Civil War elite in Wheeling rose from workingman to capitalist in the decade just prior to the war, the men in the present group did so in the first few years after the war. Only a very short span of time with elite status separated the two groups.

Since information could not be obtained on the ancestral origins of a great majority of these men, no conclusions may be made in this category. In religious heritage, only one of the seven men was Presbyterian and two were Episcopalians, while the rest were unspecified Protestants. Information was also largely unavailable on times of their families' immigrations to America. For the two on whom information was found, the families had come in the late eighteenth century.All, however, were native Americans of native parentage. Short biographies of a few of these men should indicate the similarity of economic and social origins between themselves and Wheeling's pre-Civil War economic elite.

Joseph D. DuBois was vice-president and treasurer of Belmont Nail in the late nineteenth century.[10] His grandfather, John J. DuBois was born in Philadelphia, and came to Steubenville, Ohio, in the 1820s as a clerk in a drug store. He then worked as a farmer in the area until 1857, when he moved to Iowa. He died there in 1867.

Joseph D. DuBois was born in Jefferson County, Ohio, in 1827 and was educated in country schools. He studied law and was admitted to the bar in Steubenville in 1848. He left his practice after a short time, becoming first a steamboat clerk on the Ohio River, then a steamboat captain. In 1864 he came to Wheeling, where he became secretary and manager of Belmont Nail. He organized the Wheeling and Elm Grove Railroad, retired in 1899, and died in 1909.

Adam W. Kelley was president of Belmont Nail in the late nineteenth century.[11] His father, John Kelley, was a native of Wheeling, and had been a farmer and deputy sheriff. Adam W. Kelley was born in Wheeling in 1815, and was reared on a farm which he helped to run until 1847. In 1853, he began the manufacture of nails; but the company failed in 1855, so he returned to the farm. In 1858, he started another mill, which he ran until 1864, sold out, and moved to Wheeling. In 1879, he purchased Belmont Nail and was its president. He was also a director of Exchange Bank and Belmont Bridge.

Henry M. Priest was president of LaBelle Nail Works in the 1880s and 1890s.[12] He was the son of Valentine Priest, a blacksmith and postmaster in Winterville, Ohio, where Henry was born in 1847. He was educated in village schools; and after attending Hopedale Normal School for a time, he entered Jefferson Iron Works in 1871 as a clerk. In 1874, he was appointed superintendent of the firm; and from 1881 to 1883 he served as secretary. He was then appointed president of LaBelle Iron, where he stayed until 1887, and then became president of Junction Iron. He died in 1899.

William H. Travis was superintendent of LaBelle Nail in the late nineteenth century.[13] He was the son of James Travis, a glass blower from Massachusetts, who came to Wheeling in 1830. William Travis was born in Wheeling in 1840, and was educated in public schools until age eleven. He began working in glass factories, where he remained for four years until he entered LaBelle Nail. He was named superintendent of the company in 1885, and served in that position for several years. He was also prominent in Republican politics, serving two terms on the city council. His son, Henry Travis, born in 1866, became a machinist and engineer at LaBelle Nail.

These families, then, differed little from the founding families, except for the fact that they arrived at elite status in Wheeling somewhat later than did the founders. If a difference were to be insisted upon, these later arrivals can be seen to have come from slightly more middle-class origins than the founding families. This difference is not substantial enough, however, to be truly distinctive.

MEN FROM RECENT IMMIGRANT WORKING-CLASS AND MIDDLE-CLASS ORIGINS

Nine men, 15 percent of the total in Wheeling, derived from recent immigrant working-class and middle-class backgrounds. Again, their role in Wheeling society differs very little in most respects from the early arrivals (or from the later migrants to the city from other parts of the United States). Although possessing some important cultural and religious distinctions from these native groups, the recent immigrants were remarkably similar to them in economic background, and were able to take their place, with relative ease, alongside the other groups as part of the Wheeling iron and steel elite.

Ancestrally, 44 percent of the recent immigrants were English and 20 percent were Scotch-Irish; but one-third were German in the group—the most important source of this nationality in Wheeling. In religious heritage two-thirds of the recent immigrants were Presbyterian; but the other one-third were Roman Catholic. Thus, recent immigration did introduce important minority factions into the Wheeling elite structure. One-third of the nine men in this group represented an important cultural minority: they were Roman Catholics from Germany. The other six adhered to the older cultural patterns of Wheeling.

The six Protestant families differed very little from the pre-Civil War elite families in Wheeling. Generally, only ten to fifteen years difference in the timing of arrival to elite status (along with the fact that they had more recently immigrated to America) gave them a distinctive appearance. The only important cultural difference was the introduction of an important German Catholic minority into Wheeling's postwar elite. They appeared to experience relatively little difficulty in adaptation, however, and took their place alongside English Protestant families of native or immigrant origins in the Wheeling social structure.

WHEELING IRON MANUFACTURERS FROM POOR FAMILIES

Only two of Wheeling's iron manufacturers in the late nineteenth century derived from truly poor, lower-class origins. One of these men was of recent immigrant background, the other from an older, native American family. They shared, however, a similarly deprived existence as youngsters. Since they were essentially similar, a biography of only one of them will be presented to indicate the degree to which they differed from families previously considered.

Nicodemus Reister was superintendent of Belmont Nail in the late nineteenth century.[14] Born in Germany in 1831, he was brought to Wheeling by his parents in 1838. His father, John Reister, had been a hand-loom weaver in Germany, but was unable to find work in his trade in Wheeling. He joined the army and was killed during the Mexican War. Nicodemus was forced to go to work at the age of eight. He began in a glass factory and later became a nail feeder at the Wheeling Iron Company. In 1852 he went to work as a nailer at Belmont Nail, where he was named superintendent in 1863. He was also interested in politics, serving two terms in the city council as a Democrat. His eldest son, Nicodemus C. Reister, was born in Wheeling in 1857 and educated in Catholic parochial schools of the city. After attending St. Vincent's College in Pittsburgh, he joined Wheeling Iron and Steel. In the late 1880s he was named superintendent of Belmont Nail, succeeding his father. Another son, Frank C. Reister, who was born in Wheeling in 1866, became superintendent of Wheeling Iron and Steel in 1899.

Although there were many men with backgrounds in the skilled iron-working trades in Wheeling, Reister was one of the very few who came from true poverty backgrounds. As in the case of Andrew Carnegie, his father was a hand-loom weaver, and was unable to find work in his trade in either Europe or America. In both cases, this forced the families into poverty, and the sons had to go to work while still young boys.

WHEELING: SUMMARY

The most obvious distinctive characteristic of Wheeling iron and steel leaders is the degree to which they came from working-class origins. Whether they came early or late, whether from "old American" origins or more recent immigrant background, a considerable number (and a disproportionately high number compared with other cities) had been "aristocrats of labor"—skilled iron workers drawing weekly paychecks. It should be borne in mind that this segment of the working class was its upper level (a relatively small and advantaged segment), and that those of semiskilled and unskilled labor origins remained almost completely absent from the Wheeling iron and steel elite. We must not create an image, therefore, of a completely fluid society from top to bottom. Rather, Wheeling was a society where the origins of the successful iron and steel leaders reached down beyond the upper class into the skilled levels of the working class; but it represents fluidity only within what was probably the top third of the American occupational and social order.

The key to this phenomenon in Wheeling was the development of two companies, the LaBelle Iron Company and (to a lesser degree) the Belmont Nail Company. Both were formed by several iron workers who pooled their resources to venture into manufacturing; and most of the men stayed in management positions in their firms throughout the century. They represented a successful, and perhaps rare, example of those cases of joint workingmen's action to enter large-scale manufacturing in the nineteenth century. Many of the Wheeling men who were sons of manufacturers were actually the sons of those skilled iron workers who had started these firms in the 1840s and 1850s. Horatio Alger would have been proud of Wheeling.

A FIVE-CITY COMPARATIVE ANALYSIS OF SOCIAL ORIGINS

Our final, collective portrait of 696 iron and steel manufacturers in the five cities analyzed reveals a pattern from which each individual city differed only slightly. Ancestrally, 53 percent of the 624 manufacturers on whom information was available were English or Welsh, and nearly one-third were Scottish or Scotch-Irish. Thirteen percent were German and 2 percent each were Irish or French.

In religious heritage, 43 percent were Presbyterian and 23 percent Episcopalian. In all, 98 percent were Protestant (with the balance of the Protestants fairly evenly divided among Methodists, Baptists, Quakers, Lutherans, and Unitarians). Two percent of the iron and steel manufacturers were Catholic, and less than 1 percent were Jewish.

Twenty-four percent of the men came from families who had arrived in America during the seventeenth century, and 35 percent of their families came during the eighteenth century. Another 32 percent arrived between 1800 and 1849, with the remaining 8 percent immigrating after 1850. Relatively few of these men were of recent immigrant origin: 72 percent were native sons of native parents. Sixteen percent were native sons of immigrant fathers, and only 12 percent were immigrants.

To consolidate the mode of analysis used in each individual city, 66 percent of the iron and steel men derived from families which had attained elite status prior to the Civil War—either in their home city or elsewhere. Another 16 percent were products of the native American middle class and working class, while 17 percent were recent immigrants of similar status. Only 2 percent of the total were from identifiably poor or lower-class families.

These four groups of iron and steel makers, as determined by socioeconomic origins, shared some similarities with one another, but also exhibited some important cultural differences. The majority of the men from pre-Civil War elite status were English or Welsh in origin (56 percent), while one-third were Scottish or Scotch-Irish and 10 percent were German. Among men from the native American middle class, only 45 percent were English or Welsh and just 23 percent were Scottish or Scotch-Irish. Men of Germanic background had a much stronger representation among this group, with 28 percent of the total. Among recent immigrants, 49 percent were English or Welsh, one-third were of Scottish heritage, and 16 percent were German. These recent immigrants, then, tended to be ancestrally more similar to the pre-Civil War elite than were the men from native American middle-class or working-class backgrounds. Of the men from poor or humble origins, the vast majority were either Scottish (46 percent) or German (27 percent).

In religious heritage, a similar pattern prevailed. Forty-eight percent of those from pre-Civil War elite backgrounds were Presbyterian, while 28 percent were Episcopalian. The balance was fairly evenly divided among several other Protestant sects. There were no Catholics or Jews among these prewar elites. The men from native American middle-class backgrounds included 46 percent unspecified Protestants, while 20 percent were Presbyterian and 10 percent Episcopalian; another 20 percent were evenly divided among several Protestant denominations. The recent immigrant group from middle-class and working-class origins had 40 percent Presbyterian, 13 percent Episcopalian, 21 percent unspecified Protestants, and 11 percent Methodist. Of greater significance, however, was the fact that 8 percent were Catholic and 2 percent Jewish. Among those from poor backgrounds, 92 percent were from among a variety of Protestant affiliations, and 8 percent were Catholic. Thus, the three non-elite groups were not only less uniformly Presbyterian and Episcopalian in denomination than the elite groups, but they were also less solidly Protestant. It should be borne in mind, however, that none of these groups was less than 90 percent Protestant. If the newer groups opened doors for Catholics and Jews, the opening was small and highly restricted.

In terms of family arrival in America, the men who were derived from pre-Civil War elite families, naturally, came from markedly older families. One-third came to America during the seventeenth century, and fully 75 percent arrived prior to 1800. Among families of men from native middle-class and working-class backgrounds, only 12 percent came during the seventeenth century, although a nearly equal number had arrived in America by 1800 (74 percent). No families of the men of recent immigrant origin, of course, came before 1800. Of this group, 65 percent arrived between 1800 and 1849, and 35 percent after 1850. The great majority of men from poor backgrounds (70 percent) also came to America between 1800 and 1849.

Figures on nativity showed similar results. Among the pre-Civil War elites, 85 percent were native sons of native parents, while 12 percent were native sons of immigrant fathers. Only 4 percent were immigrants. Men from the native American middle class had an even higher percentage who were born of native parentage (95 percent); only 4 percent were native sons of immigrant fathers. Among recent immigrants of middle-class and working-class backgrounds, 54 percent were immigrants and 44 percent were the sons of immigrants. Men from poor backgrounds were more varied, with 39 percent native sons of native parentage, and 46 percent were immigrants. Only 15 percent were native sons of immigrant fathers.

These broader similarities and differences among the 696 iron and steel manufacturers, however, should not be permitted to obscure the important variations that occurred from city to city. In the first place, the cities reflect contrasting cultural backgrounds. Although each of the areas received an influx of old-line New England families, only two of the cities seemed to have been indelibly stamped by their presence. Whereas Philadelphia and Pittsburgh appeared able to absorb rather large numbers of these New England families into their elite structure without affecting their cultural orientation, Cleveland and Youngstown strongly reflected a transplanted Yankee culture throughout the nineteenth century. This gave the latter cities a basic similarity with each other, and served to set them apart from the other cities in the study. Similarly, despite the influx of large numbers of other groups (and the turning of most of its indigenous upper-class families to Episcopalianism), Philadelphia remained indentifiably Quaker in its cultural orientation. Pittsburgh's cultural distinctiveness derived from its Scotch-Irish origins, as large numbers of its elite were from this group. Wheeling, on the other hand, seems to be identified mostly by its lack of any particular cultural stamp: It was partly southern, partly western, vaguely Scotch-Irish, a river town, and an industrial city.

Also influencing the nature of the elite structure in these cities was the different timing of their social development. Philadelphia, the oldest city in the study, had very few men from newer elite backgrounds. Most of the newcomers were men from other old seacoast cities. Pittsburgh, as a newer city whose traditions were not as well established, provided more opportunities for newer elites in its economic and social life. Both Cleveland and Youngstown, although they were new areas in terms of their actual development, were characterized by the transplanting of old seacoast families who dominated their early development. In Cleveland, this old family dominance weakened somewhat in the waning years of the nineteenth century; but Youngstown's New England families were able to maintain a firm hold on its social and economic system. The most open city was Wheeling—a newly developed city of the nineteenth century, rather than a simple transplantation of a seacoast culture. There were far more opportunities for newer groups to achieve success in Wheeling than there were in any of the other areas.

Another important aspect is the dominant-subordinant relationship among the cities. The most striking and clear-cut example of this occurred between Philadelphia and Bethlehem, with the latter losing its economic independence to the former. This meant that Bethlehem's elite families were restricted to middle-management positions in the city's largest steel company and without ownership rights. They also functioned within the parallel social system, which was subordinate to that of Philadelphia. There were other examples of this kind of relationship. Youngstown was somewhat subordinate, both economically and socially, to Cleveland, although the takeover was never as complete as in the case of Bethlehem and Philadelphia. Wheeling was always in a somewhat subordinate position to Pittsburgh, although Wheeling resisted this throughout most of the nineteenth century. By the end of the period, however, large numbers of its elite had moved to Pittsburgh, drawn into the city's economic and social orbit.

The confluence of these trends determined the context for a clash between old families and new elites. In Philadelphia, the new elites never really got a chance to surface; so no conflict emerged. In Cleveland and Youngstown, although there was some influence from the newer elites, the power of the cultural traditions of the older New England families minimized the conflict there. In Wheeling, the "old families" were essentially new elites anyway; so the conflict was of little relevance. Only in Pittsburgh was there a situation to spark a real struggle between groups. With the old families of the area being predominantly Scotch-Irish, a rising cultural minority of the nineteenth century, they were more susceptible to challenges on both sides. On one side were the Carnegie men, who differed little culturally, but were newer and more impetuous. On the other side were older New England families (represented in the National Tube Company) bringing impeccable social credentials with them to challenge the social standing of the older Scotch-Irish families of Pittsburgh. In the end, these older Pittsburgh families prevailed, repelling both groups; but it is in this city during the nineteenth century that the battle lines were most firmly drawn and the struggle most intense.

The role of the immigrants of the early nineteenth century—the Germans, Welsh, Scottish, Scotch-Irish and Irish— was relatively minor in all cities. However, some distinctiveness emerges from city to city. The immigrant influence in Philadelphia was virtually nonexistent; but in other cities it was more important. Ironically, Wheeling—with the largest number of new men rising to positions of importance—saw few immigrants moving to elite status, although sons of immigrants were in relatively plentiful supply. Even Pittsburgh, a seeming haven for emergent immigrants in popular literature, had relatively few—although the sons of immigrants had a significant impact. The two cities with the largest numbers of immigrants among their iron and steel elite were Cleveland and Youngstown, where they made up about one-quarter of the elite population in each. Why this should be the case is not entirely clear. These were new areas in the nineteenth century: but so were Wheeling and Pittsburgh; and the transplanted old families of Cleveland and Youngstown seem to have maintained a tight hold on the social reins of their cities. Yet, new immigrants viewed these cities as relatively hospitable for elite advancement, since their percentages of immigrants were almost twice that of Pittsburgh and nearly four times that of Wheeling or Philadelphia.

Finally, the uniqueness of Wheeling must be reiterated. Whereas all of the cities in the study retained a basic similarity (differing in degree, but not in kind), Wheeling represents a distinctive case. A far more open, fluid society, without a highly stratified social system or cultural stamp, Wheeling was the vehicle of workingman-to-capitalist mobility. It is only in this city that the dream of the nineteenth century —an industrial democracy open equally to all of equal ability—was most nearly realized.

NOTES

1. E. Digby Baltzell, *Philadelphia Gentlemen* (New York: Free Press, 1958); and Nathaniel Burt, *The Perennial Philadelphians* (Boston: Little, Brown, 1963).

2. Herbert A. Miller, *The School and the Immigrant* (Cleveland: Survey Committee of Cleveland Foundation, 1916), p. 15; William G. Rose, *Cleveland: The Making of a City* (Cleveland: World Publishing Company, 1950), pp. 361, 500-501, 608. (Figures have been rounded for the sake of simplicity.)

3. Elroy McKendree Avery, *A History of Cleveland and Its Environs,* 3 volumes, (Chicago: Lewis Publishing Company, vol. 2, p. 503; vol. 3, pp. 156-157; *Iron Age,* May 14, 1914, p. 1229; August 28, 1919, p. 613; December 14, 1905, p. 1618; October 14, 1920, p. 1019; January 9, 1908, p. 195; January 16, 1908, p. 223; October 12, 1933, p. 46A; March 23, 1899, p. 17.

National Cyclopedia of American Biography, vol. 18, p. 247; vol. 15, pp. 154-155; vol. 27, pp. 451-452; J. Fletcher Brennan, *A Biographical Cyclopedia and Portrait Gallery . . . of the*

State of Ohio, 6 volumes (Cincinnati: J. C. Yarston, 1879), vol. 1, pp. 148-149; vol. 4, p. 1050; Samuel Porter Orth, *A History of Cleveland, Ohio* (Chicago: S. J. Clarke, 1910) vol. 2, pp. 276-277; 958-962, 964-977, 52-55; Casson, *Romance of Steel,* p. 352.

4. Harlan Hatcher, *The Western Reserve: The Story of New Connecticut in Ohio* (Indianapolis: Bobbs-Merrill, 1950), p. 287.

5. *Iron Age,* July 27, 1927; Iron and Steel Institute (Britain), *Journal* 117, (London, 1970-) 463; Joseph G. Butler, *History of Youngstown and Mahoning Valley of Ohio,* 3 volumes (Chicago: American Historical Society, 1921), vol. 3, p. 508.

6. American Iron and Steel Institute, *Biographical Directory* (New York: AISI, 1911), p. 87; *Iron Age,* January 5, 1922, p. 131; Thomas W. Sanderson, *Twentieth Century of Youngstown and Mahoning County* (Chicago, 1907), p. 537 Butler, *History of Youngstown,* 3, p. 750; John Struthers Stewart, *History of Northeastern Ohio,* 3 volumes (Indianapolis:Historical Publishing, 1933), vol. 2, pp. 518-520.

7. *Mining and Metallurgy* 7 (October, 1926): 456; Robert L. Plummer, *Sixty-Five Years of Iron and Steel in Wheeling* (n.p., n.d.); Earl Chapin May, *Principio to Wheeling: 1715-1945* (New York: Harper, 1945), pp. 241, 275-280; Orth, *History of Cleveland,* II, pp. 741-742; *National Cyclopedia of American Biography,* vol. 20, pp. 375-376; Casson, *Romance of Steel,* p. 295; Robert E. Murphy, *Progressive Men of West Virginia* (Wheeling: Wheeling News, 1905), p. 111; *Who's Who in West Virginia* (Wheeling, 1916), p. 179.

8. *National Cyclopedia of American Biography,* vol. 31, p. 78; *Progressive West Virginians, 1923* (Wheeling, 1923), p. 277; *Who's Who in West Virginia,* 1916, p. 209; Gibson L. Cranmer, *History of Wheeling City* (Chicago: Biographical Publishing, 1902), II, p. 825; May, *Principio to Wheeling,* pp. 61-72; *Iron Age,* November 26, 1925, p. 1490.

9. *History of the Upper Ohio Valley,* 3 volumes (Madison, Wisconsin: Brent and Fuller, 1890), vol. 1, pp. 480-482; George W. Atkinson, *Prominent Men of West Virginia* (Wheeling: W. L. Cullin, 1890), pp. 999-1000.

10. Plummer, *Sixty-Five Years of Iron and Steel,* pp. 51-52; May, *Principio to Wheeling,* pp. 228-240; *National Cyclopedia of American Biography,* vol. 21, p. 22; *Iron Age,* December 20, 1917, p. 5105; May 12, 1881, p. 15; December 1, 1910, p. 1260; *National Cyclopedia of American Biography,* vol. 28, p. 219.

11. *History of Upper Ohio Valley,* I, pp. 273-274; May, *Principio to Wheeling,* pp. 135-137; 144-145; *Iron Age,* August 19, 1909, p. 252; *Men of West Virginia,* 2 volumes (Chicago: Biographical Publishing, 1903), vol. 2, pp. 447-449; Cranmer, *History of Wheeling City,* pp. 576-578.

12. *History of the Upper Ohio Valley,* I, p. 347.

13. *Iron Age,* September 21, 1899, p. 17; *History of the Upper Ohio Valley,* II, p. 309.

14. *History of the Upper Ohio Valley,* I, pp. 324-325; Atkinson, *Prominent Men of West Virginia,* p. 989; *Men of West Virginia,* II, pp. 508-510; Cranmer, *History of Wheeling City,* 449-450.

3

Urban Upper-Class Institutions, 1875-1965: The Institutional Context

Each of the cities considered in this study had its pre-Civil War upper-class system which, although of little influence outside the boundaries of the community, functioned as the social arbiter at home. Each of these upper-class systems was also faced with the challenge of assimilating a few of the new and prosperoue elites who emerged in the late nineteenth century. This placed great strains upon the older, less formal institutions of the pre-Civil War upper classes.

Though a larger and more established seacoast city like Philadelphia had already developed many of the more formal trappings and institutions of an upper-class system by the mid-nineteenth century, most of the cities under discussion were able to function in a more informal manner.[1] The pre-Civil War upper class, being small and relatively homogeneous, was able to select its social cohorts without resorting to a series of complex institutions. As E. Digby Baltzell has noted:

> As with so much else in American life, the 1880's mark a turning point in upper-class history; the local, familialistic-communal upper classes were absorbed into a new upper class which was increasingly extra-communal and associationally defined . . . [as] new fortunes of undreamed of proportions were created.[2]

But as these new men—often from exceedingly diverse social origins—moved into positions of wealth and power during the late nineteenth century, the old, informal (if not outmoded) ways were taxed. There arose the need for more formal methods to provide at least the first steps in the process of sorting and selecting. A series of upper-class institutions emerged for this purpose—from neighborhood and religion, which had earlier antecedents, to education and social clubs, which were relatively new to the upper-class scene. These formal institutions were united with an older, informal institution—marriage—to establish a complex yet reasonably logical system whereby the new elites were sorted, tagged and ranked according to status. The system also marked clear steps and stages (a series of hurdles perhaps) that the new elite had to scale before being allowed that most intimate area of social assimilation —marriage into the oldest and "best" families.

Each of these newly evolved institutions depended upon what Ralph H. Turner has called "sponsored mobility" in deciding which families should attain upper-class status.[3] The attainment of sponsored mobility at the social level contrasted markedly with the "contest mobility" system which operated at the economically elite levels of the steel industry.[4] Whereas the latter was relatively more open to men of talent and industry, the former was more strictly circumscribed by ethno-cultural and personal considerations.

At the close of the nineteenth century—partially to aid and abet these procedures in the local community, but also to aid in ranking these families on a more national basis—the *Social Register* was introduced. As more and more families married with families in other cities, some sort of formal, national, social ranking was needed (a social *Dun and Bradstreet)* as the first sort of sifting process to determine whom to invite to one's parties at summer resorts or how to discern the family status of the Harvard boy who was dating one's Vassar daughter.

GENERAL DETERMINANTS OF CLASS POSITION

NEIGHBORHOOD

"[Neighborhood is] a distinct territorial group, distinct by virtue of the specific physical characteristics of the area and the specific social characteristics of the inhabitants."[5] As Kurt Mayer has observed, "outstanding among the highly visible status symbols is residence. Most American towns have a right and wrong side of the tracks—their 'best', 'good', and 'poor' sections."[6] Neighborhood is often the first and most obvious kind of social distinction which the casual observer is able to make in assessing the status configuration of any community. Even knowing relatively little about the social makeup of a particular community, one could quite readily make the three broad distinctions in residential areas, as Professor Mayer has done.

Yet this distinction is crude; and in a study of this nature, the problem of residential and neighborhood analysis is far more subtle and difficult. Since all of the families considered here were possessed of a relatively high degree of wealth—an economic upper class—the ability to afford a palatial residence on the "right" side of the tracks indicates little about class position vis-à-vis other wealthy groups. In order for neighborhoods to serve as a useful analytic tool, further conceptual refinements must be made.

The pioneer sociologist, Charles Horton Cooley, considered the neighborhood, along with the family and playmates, to be a primary group for most individuals.[7]

Yet, most recent investigators of the phenomenon have demonstrated that urban neighborhoods, unlike small towns and villages, do not always manifest this same primary group orientation.[8]

These recent studies have shown that all urban neighborhoods do not display the same degree of cohesion and neighborliness. Two major factors influencing the nature of neighborhoods appear to be the physical structure of the area itself (influencing propinquity), and the degree of social homogeneity of the inhabitants. As Herbert Gans has commented: "Propinquity brings neighbors into contact, but it is because of homogeneity that this contact is maintained on a positive basis."[9] These two attributes, then, propinquity and homogeneity, shall be initially employed as tools for the definition of urban upper-class neighborhoods.[10]

The first—propinquity—shall be ascertained by the relative density of the neighborhood area. Erecting an informal continuum, those at the end of greatest density shall be identified as *urban* neighborhoods, while those showing the lower rates of density shall be identified as *suburban.* In regard to homogeneity, neighborhoods will be ranked as to their relative percentage of iron and steel family members who are listed in the city's Social Register. Those neighborhoods with over 90 percent so listed shall be considered *upper class;* those ranking between 50 and 89 percent shall be considered *elite* in orientation; and those with fewer than 50 percent shall be categorized as *middle class.*[11]

Further, these neighborhoods shall be analyzed in terms of their *retentive, attractive,* and *resistive* qualities.[12] As Professor Baltzell has noted, upper-class neighborhoods "rarely last for more than two or three generations."[13] These properties, then, test the relative staying power of various upper-class neighborhoods within the "filtering" process of housing which takes place in most large cities. The *retentive* category tests the ability of a neighborhood to retain large numbers of upper-class families, as defined by Social Register listings, over a period of time. The *attractive* properties of a neighborhood test its ability to lure upper-class inhabitants, particularly to newly developed areas. And, finally, the *resistive* property attests to a neighborhood's ability to resist the incursion of commercial and other nonresidential uses in this area.

Previous studies of upper-class neighborhoods have revealed certain salient patterns. Walter Firey, in his study of upper-class Boston neighborhoods from 1894 to 1943, discovered a profound shift in upper-class domiciles from urban to suburban areas. In 1894, 79 percent of the Bostonians liste in the Social Register lived within the city of Boston. By 1905, this figure had dropped to 67 percent; and to 60 percent by 1914. In 1929 the Boston upper class was evenly divided between urban and suburban residences. By 1943, however, only 33 percent lived in the city of Boston, with two-thirds now residing in the surrounding suburbs.[14]

E. Digby Baltzell found a similar phenomenon in his study of Philadelphia. During the colonial period and th early nineteenth century, upper-class Philadelphians lived in what later became the downtown business district. After the Civil

War, and until World War I, the upper-class center shifted to Rittenhouse Square; after the war it shifted to suburban areas.[15] This process was shown most clearly in his analysis of directors of the Philadelphia National Bank. In 1890, 83 percent lived within the City of Philadelphia. By 1914, this figure had declined to 53 percent, and by 1940, 83 percent lived in the suburbs (an exact reversal of the proportions in 1890).[16]

Related to this urban-suburban shift in Boston and Philadelphia was the birth, death, and occasionally, rebirth of various upper-class neighborhoods. In Boston, the fortunes of urban upper-class neighborhoods was varied. Beacon Hill, with 15 percent of the upper-class families in 1894, suffered a serious decline in 1905. It was, however, able to partially recover by 1914 and maintain a remarkably stable life as an upper-class domicle to 1943. The Back Bay, however, was not as fortunate: the largest single upper-class area in 1894, with 45 percent of the total, it increased its percentage in 1905. By 1914, a decline had set in, which was rapid and unchecked to 1943, when it contained only 19 percent of the total. At the same time, suburban towns such as Brookline, Newton, and Cambridge were born and grew apace during this period, as they were transformed from isolated, semi-rural villages into elite suburbs.

Similarly in Philadelphia, certain neighborhoods flowered for a time, decayed, and were replaced by new suburban abodes. For much of the nineteenth and early twentieth centuries, the Rittenhouse Square area was Philadelphia's preferred residential domicle for elite families. By the late nineteenth century it had begun to decline as upper-class Philadelphians moved away. North Philadelphia was also an elite neighborhood in the late nineteenth century, but during the twentieth century it became almost completely commercialized, losing its elite residents. As these areas declined, new suburban towns emerged, particularly Chestnut Hill and the various enclaves along Philadelphia's "Main Line."[17]

In our study of five cities, then, we shall be investigating similar phenomena. The neighborhoods in each city will be examined as to their density (urban/suburban) tendencies over time, and their relative social homogeneity. Within that broader framework, they will also be analyzed as to their ability to retain and attract elites and their ability to resist commercial and other incursions. Since this investigation will be comparative in nature, it should be possible to determine the extent to which relative city size, cultural background, physical characteristics and related factors determine neighborhood development at the upper-class levels.

RELIGION AND ETHNO-CULTURAL INSTITUTIONS

> Every American community, from the most rural to the most urban, from Plainville, through Middletown, to Metropolis, has some pronounced pattern of social stratification, and religious institutions and practices are always very closely associated with this pattern.[18]

That American religious denominations have tended toward a general class orientation is familiar to even the most casual observer of American society. An analysis of American religion, published in 1952 by Professor Herbert Schneider, bore witness to this tendency of American religious denominations to reflect class divisions, as shown in Table 1·6.

TABLE 16
Social Class Profile of American Religious Groups

Denomination	Percentage in Upper Class	Percentage in Middle Class	Percentage in Lower Class
Christian Scientist	24.8	36.5	38.7
Episcopal	24.1	33.7	42.2
Congregationalist	23.9	42.6	33.5
Presbyterian	21.9	40.0	38.1
Jewish	21.8	32.0	46.2
Methodist	12.7	35.6	51.7
Lutheran	10.9	36.1	53.0
Roman Catholic	8.7	24.7	66.6
Baptist	8.0	24.0	68.0

SOURCE: Adapted from Herbert Schneider, *Religion in Twentieth Century America* (Cambridge: Harvard University Press 1952), Appendix, 228.

As indicated, several Protestant denominations—Christian Scientist, Episcopalian, Congregationalist and Presbyterian—all tended to contain large minorities of upper-class members, as did the Jews. On the other hand, Methodists and Lutherans tended more toward middle-class status, while Roman Catholics and Baptists contained a majority of lower-class members. A subsequent study by Bernard Lazerwitz, based upon the 1957 religious census, revealed similar patterns. In his analysis, Episcopalians, Jews and Presbyterians were placed at the top of the social structure; Methodists, Lutherans and Roman Catholics in the middle; and Baptists at the bottom.[19]

Yet, a second glance at Table 16 reveals that a majority of Episcopalians, Congregationalists and Presbyterians are *not* in the upper class. Nor were the majority of Methodists and Lutherans middle class. Even among Roman Catholics and Baptists, significant minorities were classified as middle-class, and not inconsequential numbers were ranked as upper-class. Thus, in order to determine the role of religious institutions among the upper class, a more careful and detailed approach must be made.

As Robin Williams Jr. has noted, "the relationships between social class and religious participation are complex."[20] The problem is partially one of viewpoint. Although the majority of members of Episcopalian and Presbyterian denominations are *not* upper class, the majority of the members of the upper class *would* tend to be Episcopalian, Presbyterian or another of the "elite" denominations. Further, these upper-class individuals would tend to belong to certain elite congregations within the denominations, which, because of locational and attitudinal patterns, tended to make them strongly homogeneous.[21]

New elites born into lower-class or middle-class denominations will usually switch to more respectable denominations as they move up the economic ladder. Those who are already of the "proper" denomination will strive to gain acceptance in the most "respectable" congregation in that city—most often coinciding with a move to that upper-class residential area. Therefore, within Protestantism a graded social order exists from denomination to denomination and from congregation to congregation. It functions primarily as a series of steps to be ascended on the path to complete upper-class respectability.

Yet, the foregoing distinctions do not completely clarify the role of religion as an upper-class institution. As Andrew Greeley has commented, "[r]eligion is indeed . . . a meaning-giving cultural system, but the religious denomination is also a belonging-providing ethnic group."[22] In Professor Greeley's view, this ethnic orientation of American churches has been developed largely in reaction to the general societal movement from a *gemeinschaft* to a *gesellschaft* form of social organization, due to intensive industrialization and urbanization:

> In the United States, the churches came to serve an ethnic role; they helped to sort out "who one was" in a bewildering complex society. As a result the various denominations have immeasurably strengthened, as they serve not only a religious need, but a social one as well.[23]

Although this concept of the religious denomination as a quasi-ethnic group has received rather wide acceptance in its application to Jews, Catholics and certain Protestant groups (such as German Lutheran and Dutch Reformed), it is less well recognized as a function of the more upper-class denominations. Yet, as Charles H. Anderson has pointed out, "White Protestants, like other Americans, are as much members of an ethnic group as anyone else, however privileged the majority of them might be."[24]

This identification of the religious denomination as a ethnic group exists most clearly and strongly with Judaism. Although there has been substantial debate upon this issue within the Jewish community, it seems clear that Judaism is more clearly an ethnic identification than a purely religious one. Although American Jews generally have the lowest rate of participation in religious ceremonies or synagogue identification, this does not appear to diminish their self-identification as Jews.[25] In terms of the relationship of Jews to upper-class social institutions, this ethnicity is perhaps seen most clearly. During the colonial period in America, it was evidently possible for a wealthy Jew to embrace Protestantism and be accepted quite easily into the communal life of the Gentile upper classes.[26] Judaism was apparently considered to be a religious affiliation only: upon renunciation of the Hebrew religion and acceptance of a "respectable" Protestant denomination, the aspirant ceased to be Jewish and was rendered acceptable for assimilation.

This situation underwent change during the nineteenth century, to the extent that one should say, "once a Jew, always a Jew." It mattered little by the early twentieth century if a wealthy Jewish individual embraced Episcopalianism or Unitarianism. He was now permanently defined as a Jew, an ethnic designation which could not be altered by a simple change of religion.[27]

A similar, though more complex, process has occurred with respect to Roman Catholics. In the colonial period, persons of Roman Catholic background who had attained wealth seemed to be able to merge into the Protestant upper classes with little difficulty, as the cases of the Drexel and Carroll families, among others, would attest.[28] The coming of masses of poor Irish Catholics in the nineteenth century apparently altered this earlier status to the point that, in the middle and late nineteenth century, ethnic group (Irish) and religion (Catholic) were virtually synonymous.[29] The arrival of later Catholic ethnic groups (Poles, Italians, other Slavic minorities), modified, but did not substantially alter, the situation. A simple change of religion for persons from these Catholic groups would not serve to enhance their respectability among the upper classes.

The notion of Roman Catholicism itself an an ethnic group reappears more clearly in the twentieth century. As Ruby Jo Kennedy Reeves demonstrated in New Haven in 1940, Catholics of every ethnic origin tended to marry with one another.[30] Gerhard Lenski discovered the same phenomenon nearly a quarter-century later in Detroit.[31] Although there are examples of upper-class individuals converting to Catholicism (for one, Marshall Field III), there is little conclusive evidence that wealthy Catholics were able to achieve assimilation into the upper classes by converting to Protestantism. Catholicism, too, had acquired an ethnic stigma which simple denominational change could not overcome.

The notion of Protestantism (and particularly of certain elite Protestant denomination) as embodying ethnic characteristics, however, is a good bit less clear. To begin with, in the early nineteenth century, each Protestant denomination tended to be affiliated with a particular national origin group—Episcopal and Congregational with the English, Presbyterian with the Scottish and Scotch-Irish, and Lutheran with Germans and Scandinavians. The Methodists and Baptists drew from several ethnic groups.[32]

As foregoing chapters of the present study have indicated, as have the results of other studies, a large proportion of the wealthy individuals in nineteenth-century America were English, and a substantial minority were Scottish and Scotch-Irish. The religious denominations of these national groups (Episcopal, Congregational and Presbyterian), then, naturally suggested class and national origins.[33]

An important index of the degree to which any group of persons can be considered to have particular ethnic traits is the degree to which they remain separate from other groups in society in their primary activities. Several community and national studies have shown this to be true of English, Welsh and Scottish groups, and true of high-status religious denominations.

In his study of Burlington, Vermont, in the 1930s, Elin Anderson found that of all ethnic groups in the city the "Old Americans" were the most socially exclusive —with 87 percent declaring that all of their intimate friends were also "Old Americans."[34] Similarly, W. Lloyd Warner discovered that high-status Yankees in Newburyport, Massachusetts, rarely associated with people of other ethnic stocks.[35] In like manner, C. W. King found that Anglo-Americans in a Connecticut town in the 1940s remained socially aloof from other ethnic groups.[36]

This ethnic exclusivity has also been reflected in studies of intermarriage patterns of persons of English and other British backgrounds in several cities. In figures compiled by Charles H. Anderson, it was shown that the endogamous marriage rates of English-Americans in most community studies were about fifty percentage points higher than could have been expected in a random marriage pattern. Only in rural areas in New York State—containing large percentages of persons from English background— was the expected and actual endogamous marriage rate nearly identical.[37]

These marital figures, however, dealt mainly with the first- and second-generation English. In the third generation and after, persons of English stock were increasingly likely to have exogamous marriages. But, their choices continued to be mainly limited to members of Protestant groups.[38] Thus, religion itself became the defining ethnicity among English and cognate groups, particularly among the upper classes.[39]

In his studies of friendship chains, Edwin Laumann found that high-status Episcopalians and Presbyterians had a low index of dissimilarity (.31) toward one another, indicating a high degree of compatibility and interaction, while their indices of dissimilarity toward other Protestant groups ranged from .35 to .79. Their index of dissimilarity regarding Catholics was .40 and .42, respectively, while for Jews it was .67 and .63.[40]

Among the upper classes in America the phenomenon of ethno-cultural and ethno-religious expression was a general movement towards Episcopalianism. Since a majority of the iron and steel elite and the American business elite were of English ancestry, it was this group which tended to lend the ethnic tone and style to the upper classes. For the non-english minority (the Scotch-Irish, Scottish, Welsh, German and French) acceptance on an even par with these predominantly English families presented problems of varying degrees of intensity. The road toward accommodation in the late nineteenth and early twentieth centuries evolved into a subtle shift of ethnic identity away from national origins and towards a religious identification—Episcopalianism. This made it possible for wealthy men from similar backgrounds, particularly British backgrounds, to achieve an ethnic solidarity with old English-origin families by embracing the Episcopal Church.[41]

Thus, in the analysis which follows, we shall be investigating this ethno-cultural and ethno-religious factor among the iron and steel elite in the five cities. We shall examine the degree to which men of non-protestant origins (Catholic and Jewish) were denied entrance to upper-class institutions. We shall investigate the differential acceptance of those from non-English Protestant groups (particularly the Scotch-Irish and Germans) by the older upper classes. Finally, we shall view the emergence of a broader Episcopalian upper class—particularly the denominational changes from Methodist, Presbyterian and Baptist to Episcopalian—along with the growth of other religious institutions, such as Episcopal boarding schools. By this process we shall attempt to analyze, generationally, the means by which elite families finally attained desired upper-class status within the older social upper class—particularly through marriage.

SCHOOLS

> The emergence of the private boarding school in significant numbers at the end of the nineteenth century was only one indication of an increasingly complex society . . . The private prep school was but one manifestation of an America becoming more socially and culturally pluralistic.[42]

Prior to the late nineteenth century, education per se was hardly an important institution of social selection. There were, to be sure, important differences to be observed in the degree and quality of education; but before the advent of the great "common school" movement in the early and mid-nineteenth century, most of the schools and academies catered primarily to the middle and upper classes of the city. This was coupled with the inability of the poor to send their children to school for any extended period. Thus, the principle class and status distinction in education was largely between those who were educated through secondary school, and those who received only a minimal amount of schooling.[43]

With the passage of compulsory public education laws, and the founding of thousands of new public high schools designed to educate the swarms of immigrant children to American ways, the schools became the preserve of the "common" man, with whom the upper classes were increasingly reluctant to have social contact.[44]

The upper classes were alienated from the new public schools for both educational and social reasons. Educationally, they resented the increasing standardization and bureaucratization of these new "comprehensive" high schools. This, they felt, deprived their children of individuality and lessened their chances for admission into prestigious college.[45] On the social side, "the well off and well educated were often distressed by the heterogeneous nature of the student body and its [the high school's] increasingly egalitarian social goals."[46] Barbara Solomon has studied the phenomenon among the upper classes in Boston:

> After the Civil War, fewer and fewer sons and daughters of the proper families attended the common schools, which had become increasingly

> public by 1850 . . . Some parents feared an exposure "to crime or contagion," particularly before the level of high school. Well-bred New England youngsters sensed the real meaning of the separation from foreign-born contemporaries. . . . More and more, America had assumed a limited definition in the minds of adult Brahmins. Their children never doubted in the 1870's that it applied only to those who came from approximately the same class of homes, and knew, in short, "their knives and forks."[47]

For these reasons, a series of private boarding schools were developed from 1880 to 1910 to serve the needs of the social upper class. These private boarding schools can generally be said to have had four social functions. First, they isolated the children of older upper-class families into homogeneous environments where they did not have to mix with those from other social environments. Second, they "served the latent function of acculturating the members of the younger generation, especially those not quite to manor born, into an upper-class style of life."[48] Third, these schools provided a convenient means for upper-class children from one city to meet and form lasting friendships with their upper-class counterparts in other cities. Finally, these schools, isolated in small towns and rural environments, provided an insulation from the increasingly urban and heterogeneous nature of their home communities.[49]

Among these prep schools there was a subtle, but real social gradient, with St. Paul's, St. Mark's Groton, St. George's and Middlesex generally being the most prestigious. At the other extreme were Andover and Exeter, which tended to be the least exclusive, taking in the very wealthy, newly rich and intelligent non-upper-class boys (as scholarship students). The other schools varied between these two extremes.[50] A brief analysis of the most important of these schools for the iron and steel elite will be presented below.

Several of the schools were founded as Episcopal institutions. St. Paul's, established in 1855, "became the most influential model . . . for the scores of private boarding schools found in the decades after the Civil War."[51] In its early years, St. Paul's drew its student body largely from Massachusetts; but, by the 1870s, an important shift began to take place, whereby the middle Atlantic states, especially New York and Pennsylvania, provided the largest number of students.[52]

One of the aims of St. Paul's was "an education which shall fit [boys] either for colleges or business."[53] But until well into the 1870s, most graduates did not go on to college. Nor, despite its Episcopal orientation, were many graduates attracted to the ministry. Less than 2 percent chose the clerical profession.[54] The essential role of St. Paul's was to educate the sons of wealthy families from large cities to assume roles of business leadership.[55]

For these reasons, St. Paul's became the most popular boarding school for the sons of the iron and steel elite in our five cities. It provided an insulated social environment, Christian moral training, and—most importantly for families engaged in America's industrial transformation—it did not divert them to more esoteric scholarly pursuits. As Eton and Harrow in England created generations of army and foreign service officers, St. Paul's created recruits for this country's industrial establishment.

Of the other schools, none of which attained the importance of St. Paul's for the sons of iron and steel elite, a less detailed analysis is necessary. Hotchkiss, founded in 1892, was intended primarily as a "feeder" school for Yale. Of the thirty members of the class of 1896, twenty were preparing for that college.[56] Similarly, Lawrenceville (founded by James McCosh, president of Princeton), was intended as a principal source of students for Princeton.[57] Philips-Exeter was an old academy which was refitted as a college preparatory boarding school. Its studer body was more heterogeneous—rich and poor, white and black, rural and urban— than the other boarding schools.[58] Groton, founded in 1884, was oriented more to older, aristocratic, eastern seaboard families. Although often not as wealthy as those at St. Paul's, they came from families with a tradition of public service—a trait which continued to be reflected in Groton's graduates. No other prep school could boast of such large numbers of graduates among the governmental and foreig service elite in the early twentieth century.[59] However attractive this ideal was to national consciousness of the time, it had little appeal to families enmeshed in the iron and steel industry.

By the time of the outbreak of World War I, then, the development of the upper class prep school was essentially complete. It had assumed a form which was to alter only slightly during the balance of the century. These prep schools can be roughly divided into three groups. First, there were the direct descendants of the eighteenth-century academies—Andover, Exeter, and Deerfield: they were comparatively inexpensive, and drew their students from a relatively broad social spectrum. Second, there were the Episcopal church schools—St. Paul's, St. Mark's, Groton, St. George's and Kent—which drew their students from a restricted clientele of wealthy urban families. Third, there were the nondenominational boarding schools—Lawrenceville, Hill, Choate, Taft, Hotchkiss and Middlesex—which drew their students from much the same groups as the Episcopal schools, but were more strongly oriented towards academic and university life.[60]

By the end of the nineteenth century, as the acquisition of a college education became a necessity both in business and social circles, certain colleges and universities became national centers of higher learning for the American upper class. Several of the cities under observation had local colleges with varying degrees of prestige: Philadelphia had the aristocratic University of Pennsylvania, along with the slightly less prestigious Haverford and Swarthmore, Pittsburgh had the rather middle-class University of Pittsburgh and the Carnegie Institute of Technology; Cleveland had the slightly more prestigious Western Reserve University, with Oberlin College nearby; Youngstown had only the plebian Youngstown University (founded by the Y.M.C.A.), and Wheeling's closest institution of higher learning was the middle-class Bethany College, operated by the Christian Church.

There was increasing interest in sending sons and daughters away to prestigious eastern colleges. The "big three" were Harvard, Yale and Princeton; but Columbia,

Cornell, Dartmouth, Brown, Amherst, Williams, Trinity, Wesleyan and the University of Virginia, along with a few others, were not too far behind. The latter colleges however, were usually the "second choice of those of the upper class who for one reason or another did not choose to go to one of the 'big three.' "[61] Increasingly, in the twentieth century, the sons and daughters of America's iron and steel manufacturers flocked to these citadels of national prestige.

The influx of the sons of the urban rich into these schools—particularly the "big three"—was to profoundly alter the prior status of the schools.

> In the 1880s and 1890s, the future Ivy League colleges were beginning to reflect the social patterns of the "wealthy inhabitants of large cities" whose sons they were more and more attracting. . . . That the sons reproduced the fathers' social patterns when they reached college was hardly surprising.[62]

As denominational schools, Harvard, Yale and Princeton had traditionally catered to a somewhat localized student body selected partially on the basis of religion and family ties. Their emergence to university status at the turn of the century, coinciding with the invasion of wealthy urban elites, altered this former status.[63]

Nowhere, perhaps, were the dynamics of this transformation more profound than at Princeton University. Traditionally a Presbyterian denominational college, even by the early 1880's it began to feel the influx of urban, wealthy, primarily Episcopalian students. The situation seemed critical enough to President James McCosh at the time that he hurriedly built a low-cost dormitory to attract less affluent sons of Presbyterian ministers (to help counter Princeton's growing image as a "rich man's school").[64]

Although the number of Presbyterians at Princeton had dropped to 64 percent in 1885 (down from 73 percent in 1875), with the number of Episcopalians growing from 15 percent to 21 percent, the most dramatic shift came after 1910. Until that time, Presbyterians represented a steadily diminishing majority of the Princeton student body. By 1911, however, they constituted only 41 percent, with Episcopalians standing at 24 percent. By 1933, the two denominations achieved relative parity, with Presbyterians comprising 36 percent and Episcopalians 33 percent.[65] As the American urban upper class increasingly adopted an ethno-religious orientation expressed through Episcopalianism, this was reflected in major upper-class institutions such as Princeton.

The pattern for iron and steel elites was to attend ivy league institutions (particularly Yale) in increasing numbers in the final two decades of the nineteenth century. About the time of World War I, however, there was a pronounced shift toward Princeton as the preferred school. Although less selective than the boarding schools on the basis of social prestige, the ivy league universities nonetheless became important indicators of upper-class status after 1890.[66]

In its analysis of schools, this study will deal only with prep schools and colleges for the elite and upper-class families—primarily because this was the only information readily available. Also, since the day schools were local, it was difficult to rank them very intelligently. With the rather clearly recognized social gradations of prep schools, this was judged to be the most accurate index of social ranking within the school structure. Although the college attended was significant, to a point, it was less so than admission to a really exclusive prep school. Sending a son to Harvard, Yale or Princeton was certainly a step up for a man who had attended a local business college; but it said less about his real social standing than did the prep school his son was able to attend.

SOCIAL CLUBS

> Every American city with a vestige of tradition has one eminently respectable men's club, housed behind brownstone or substantial brick, heavy but impressive in architecture, food and membership. . . . Here is his [the gentleman's] peculiar asylum from the pandemonium of commerce, the acceptance of Democracy and the feminism of our household.[67]

The United States, almost from its origin, has been viewed as a nation of "joiners," as a people with a tendency to form clubs and voluntary associations in numbers far beyond that of European societies. As Alexis de Tocqueville commented: "In no country has the principle of association been more successfully used or applied to a greater multitude of objects than in America."[68] Yet, this tendency toward clubs and associations was not uniform and undifferentiated throughout the population. In the first place, "the most fertile ground for the proliferation of voluntary associations is large metropolitan communities."[69] Even within these metropolitan communities, however, participation was far from uniform. In a study of associational activity in Cincinnati in 1840, Walter S. Glazer discovered that those most active in a wide variety of associations represented only 13.7 percent of the men included in the 1840 Cincinnati *Directory.* More importantly, these men stood out as distinctly wealthier, and more homogeneous culturally, than the community as a whole. They were the social and economic elite of that time.[70] Studies of association membership in present-day society reveals a similar class bias.[71]

The clubs played an important social role within the upper-class subgroup in society. In the late nineteenth century, in each of the five cities under discussion (and in America generally), exclusive "gentlemen's" clubs began to form in the downtown business areas. Graded on the order of exclusivity, they ranged from those which allowed only those with the most impeccable family backgrounds to enter, to those which were really "business" clubs, catering to the business elite regardless of their social background.

It is generally accepted that these gentlemen's clubs "evolved from the London coffee houses of late Stuart and Georgian times."[72] These had emerged during the seventeenth century, becoming permanent private clubs. The oldest continuing club in America is the Philadelphia Club, which began in 1830. It is followed by the Union in New York (1836), the Century in New York (1847), the Somerset in Boston (1851), the Pacific Union in San Francisco (1852), and the Maryland in Baltimore (1857). After the Civil War, exclusive men's clubs were founded in most major cities.

> Today the more distinguished clubs in America include the Somerset and Union in Boston, the Union and Knickerbocker in New York, the Duquesne and Pittsburgh in Pittsburgh, the Pacific Union in San Francisco, the Queen City and Cincinnati in Cincinnati, the Chicago in Chicago, the Maryland in Baltimore, the Buffalo Club in Buffalo, the Detroit Club in Detroit, and the Philadelphia and Rittenhouse in Philadelphia.[73]

Below the level of these aristocratic strongholds in each city are a series of lesser clubs which follow a fairly uniform pattern from city to city.

"The circulation of elites in America and the assimilation of new men of power and influence in the upper class takes place primarily through the medium of urban clubdom. Aristocracy of birth is replaced by aristocracy of ballot."[74] This is, however, a classic example of *sponsored,* rather than *contest* mobility, since the "blackball" process guaranteed that only those acceptable to the older upper-class members would gain entrance.

At about the same time, suburban country clubs emerged. Like the downtown clubs, they were graded on the basis of exclusivity. Unlike the men's clubs, however, they catered to the recreational needs of the whole family. The development of the country club was the result of the convergence of a few factors: (1) the movement of upper-class families into the suburbs, making travel to recreational facilities in the center city more difficult; (2) the increasing unwillingness to use these public facilities anyhow; and (3) the great, and rather sudden, popularity of golf as the recreational pastime—demanding a large area, which almost of necessity must be located outside of the city.

"The country club . . . is a peculiarly American concept."[75] The first, *the* Country Club, was founded at Brookline, Massachusetts, in 1882. In the next few decades, suburban clubs spread like wildfire, proliferating to all major American cities. Unlike the men's clubs in town, however, the country club also spread to smaller cities and towns, so that by the mid-twentieth century there was hardly a town of any substance in America which did not have its "country club set."

These clubs separated the elites from the masses in their leisure or semi-leisure activities, and also provided another convenient means for grading and sorting the upper class and its prospective candidates. Certain club memberships became important badges of attainment, and many a newly rich family in each of the cities worked longer and harder on this social achievement than they had worked to attain business success.

In our analysis of iron and steel elites, we shall be tabulating the incidence of membership in town and suburban clubs. In addition, we shall attempt to establish a social rank ordering of these clubs by comparing the membership lists to the *Social Register* and other social indices. In this manner, the clubs serve as a sensitive and important barometer—when combined with other variables—of relative social position.

MARRIAGE AND KINSHIP SYSTEM

> Intermarriages are one of the key evidences of in-group interaction, and there is certainly a great deal of it within the American upper class.[76]

> In the upper class, status is ascribed to a larger degree according to the extended kinship system rather than on personal achievement alone, and the individual has something to gain in terms by maintaining an attachment to the wider kinship group."[77]

For many years, the prevailing orthodoxy of American sociologists concerning the family and kinship organization of industrial societies followed the ideas of Talcott Parsons and Louis Wirth.[78] They contended that the demands associated with occupational and geographic mobility brought about a family pattern in urban society which consisted of relatively isolated nuclear family units operating without much support from the broader kinship system.

This contention, however, has been challenged recently by a number of students of the American kinship structure.[79] In the more recent view, "family networks and their patterns of mutual aid are organized into a structure identified as a 'modified extended family' adapted to contemporary urban and industrial society."[80] This structure involves nuclear families which interact on the basis of geographic propinquity, affectional ties, mutual aid and other considerations.

Even the most fervent advocates of the isolated nuclear family model for urban industrial society, however, did not claim that it applied to the upper-class family. For instance, Talcott Parsons has commented:

> There are important upper-class elements in this country for which elite status is closely bound up with the status of ancestry, hence, the continuity of kinship solidarity is a —mainly patrilinial— line of descent, in "lineages." Therefore, in these "family elite" elements the symmetry of the multilinear kinship structure is sharply skewed in the direction of a patrilinear system with a tendency to primo-geniture—one in many respects resembling that historically precedent among European aristocracies . . . There is a tendency for this in turn to be bound up with family property, especially an ancestral home, and continuity of status in a particular local community.[81]

Although nearly all commentators on the American family structure agree upon the importance of marriage and kinship systems for the upper class, almost no systematic analysis of this phenomenon has been attempted.[82] This tendency of both historians and sociologists to stress the family and kin structures of middle-class and working-class families is understandable, but unfortunate. As James McLachlan asserts: "In the future, if significant and convincing work on the American 'upper class' . . . is to be done by historians, they would do well to begin with family and kinship systems."[83]

Since it would appear that marriage is the most important, and most intimate, institution of upper-class attainment and ranking, the necessity to study it in detail becomes even more obvious. While it has always been true that marriage stood as the ultimate point of assimilation for families on the rise to the upper classes, the increasing complexity of society, the more national associations, and the larger number of families born of new wealth in the late nineteenth century, brought forth more formal institutions such as prep schools and social clubs which functioned in large measure as a pre-screening process for marital selection.

The marriage, kinship, and family system of the upper class, then, became intimately tied to the rest of the institutional structure of that class in the late nineteenth century. The main problem is that these marriage and kinship patterns are difficult to trace and illustrate in a meaningful manner. The critical conceptual tool to be used in this analysis is that of *endogamy,* as Robert K. Merton has described it in this context.

> Endogamy is a device which serves to maintain social prerogatives and immunities within a social group. It helps prevent the diffusion of power, authority and preferred status to persons who are not affiliated with a dominant group. It serves further to accentuate and symbolize the "reality" of the group by setting it off against other discernible social units. Endogamy serves as an isolation and exclusion device with the function of increasing group solidarity and supporting the social structure by helping to fix social distances which obtain between groups.[84]

The term "endogamy," as defined by George Peter Murdock refers to marriages within the local, kin, or status group to which the individual himself belongs. The complementary term "exogamy" refers to marriages outside these groups.[85]

The iron and steel families, then, were allowed to group themselves by endogamous marriage patterns. As a result, there is a fourfold grouping of families in relation to social class achieved: the *core families* represented the very core of the social upper class of that city, families which intermarried with one another extensively, almost to the exclusion of other families, and had the highest indices of membership in the other prestigious social institutions. The *non-core upper-class families* were those which had at least one marriage into the core families, but tended to have more marriages outside this group, and to have lower percentages of membership in other indices of social prestige. The *marginal upper-class families* usually had a rather high percentage of membership in other social institutions, but no marriages into the core families. For all practical purposes, the marginal upper-class group could be subdivided into the "locals," who were just moving into the fringes of ultimate social prestige and the "cosmopolitans," who were married to prestigious families in other areas—and, for some reason, chose not to participate in the local upper-class structure: the latter were often of higher ultimate prestige than the local group. The final group of families were the *elite families* (non-upper class), those without a significant marriage pattern. Either information was lacking on them, or they were upper-middle-class families who did not move into the upper class—as evidenced by their lack of membership in other prestigious institutions.

After allowing the upper-class families to rank themselves on the basis of their patterns of endogamy, these resulting configurations will be correlated to Social Register listings, club memberships, and school attendance patterns. This should allow for a more complete appraisal of the role of marriage and kinship systems among the upper class, and should also provide a more perceptive and sensitive barometer of relative class standing within the upper-class subgroup.

Marriage, then, will be viewed as the key social variable, correlated with other institutions, but assuming a preeminent role. Although they are much more difficult to work with than the other social rankings, marriages reveal an intimate area of social ranking that is not discernible in any other way. It allows us to view the most intimate social decisions of the respective families.

AN UPPER-CLASS SOCIAL NETWORK

> The saying goes in Llanfinhagel that a neighboring valley is like a dog. If you tread on its tail at one end of the valley, it will bark at the other end.[86]

Implicit in the discussion of marriage and kinship patterns is the idea of the interrelationship of the various elements of the upper-class institutional context. It forms what several anthropologists in recent years have termed a "social network." In the words of Professor J. A. Barnes, "The social network is seen essentially as a network in which all members of a society, or some part of that society, are enmeshed."[87]

Institutional analysis, by its very nature, tends to "minimize the connections *between* institutions . . . An analysis using social networks, on the other hand . . . allows the behaviour in terms of one normative network to be related directly to that in another."[88] The task confronting the present investigator of iron and steel elites, then, is to develop a mechanism whereby this network of affiliations among and between institutions may be articulated.

The task is not a simple one. Network theory, as employed by anthropologists, relies heavily upon participant observer data and dwells principally upon observations of *personal* behavior patterns of one selected individual with his peers within a group. This precise mode of analysis is neither possible nor necessarily desirable in a historical study of this nature, in which no individual receives greater focus than any other.

Yet it would appear that a modified form of network theory could profitably be employed in this analysis. By measuring the *density, content, durability,* and *frequency* of the various relationships of upper-class individuals to one another, a reasonable approximation of the relevant social network may be developed. "Density" refers to the extent to which links which could possibly exist among persons do in fact exist. "Content" concerns the type of relationship—kinship, social club, school, etc. "Durability" implies the relative permanence of relationship—neighborhood as opposed to kinship. "Frequency" simply refers to the relative frequency of contact among persons in a network (business, recreation, family, etc.).[89]

Thus, we should be able to identify "clusters" of persons among the upper class in this social network. A cluster is "a set of persons whose links with one another are comparatively dense . . ."[90] In this manner, it should be possible to establish a morphology of upper-class structure in each city, which will reveal the extent and nature of the relationships and the meaning of this for relative social status and position.

CONCLUSIONS

> In the disorganization, personal and social, that occurs as part of the pilgrimage from the peasant communities to the industrial city, man attempted and still attempts to compensate for the deprivation he endures, and the absence of the social support and the intimacy of the village evolving quasi-*Gemeinschaft* institutions.[91]

Viewed from long range, the phenomenon of the American urban upper class in the late nineteenth and early twentieth centuries is a picture of escape and adaptation. Confronted with an increasingly complex and heterogeneous society, they created a series of institutions which separated them from the mass of their fellow Americans. These institutions provided a sense of community in an urban-industrial world and also stamped their members with a badge of exclusivity and privilege. Thus the kinship ties were stronger and more extended, reflecting the continuing importance of family economic activities, whether in running a family business or managing a family investment trust. Their clubs were either communal islands in the heart of their city's commercial districts, or were pastoral "country clubs," tucked away in rolling hills. Their secondary schools were rural and exclusive, stressing an individualism at variance with a bureaucratic society. They were separated from the rest of America not only by their wealth, but also by their norms and values, which hankered to an earlier and more homogeneous age.[92]

In our analysis of the institutional context and social networks of the urban iron and steel elite, we shall use Pittsburgh as the principal model. An intensive and detailed analysis of the Pittsburgh upper class will be presented in Chapter 4, followed by comparative perspectives based upon analysis of the remaining cities in Chapter 5.

NOTES

1. See E. Digby Baltzell, *Philadelphia Gentlemen* (New York: Free Press, 1958), and Nathaniel Burt, *Perennial Philadelphians* (Boston: Little, Brown, 1963) for extended discussions of Philadelphian's pre-Civil War upper-class system.

2. E. Digby Baltzell, *"Who's Who in America* and the *Social Register:* Elite and Upper Class Indexes in Metropolitan America," in *Class, Status, and Power,* edited by Reinhard Bendix and Seymour M. Lipset, 2nd rev. ed. (New York: Free Press, 1966), p. 268.

3. "Under sponsored mobility elite recruits are chosen by the established elite or their agents, and elite status is *given* on the basis of some criterion of supposed merit and cannot be *taken* by any amount of effort or strategy." Ralph H. Turner, "Sponsored and Contest Mobility and the School System," *American Sociological Review* 25 (December, 1960), also in *Structured Social Inequality: A Reader in Comparative Social Stratification,* edited by Celia S. Heller (New York: Macmillan Company, 1969), p. 353.

4. "Contest mobility is a system in which elite status is the prize in an open contest and is taken by the aspirants own efforts." Turner, "Sponsored and Contest Mobility," p. 353.

5. Ruth Glass, ed. *The Social Background of a Plan* (London: Routledge and Paul, 1948), p. 18.

6. Kurt B. Mayer, *Class and Society,* rev. ed. (New York: Random House, 1964), p. 46.

7. Charles Horton Cooley, *Social Organization* (New York: Scribner, 1909), pp. 22-31.

8. See Suzanne Keller, *The Urban Neighborhood: A Sociological Perspective* (New York: Random House, 1965), for a convenient summary of these views.

9. Herbert Gans, "Planning and Social Life," *Journal of the American Institute of Planners* 27 (May 2, 1961), pp. 134-140.

10. As Baltzell has noted: "[r]esidential propinquity, by limiting social interaction, serve[d] the function of creating and preserving social heritage and life styles of the various . . . units." *Philadelphia Gentlemen,* p. 174.

11. This framework follows, in modified form, that developed by Baltzell in *Philadelphia Gentlemen,* Chapter 9.

12. These concepts were developed by Walter Firey for his analysis of upper-class Boston neighborhoods, "Sentiment and Symbolism as Ecological Variables," *American Sociological Review* 10 (1945): 140-148.

13. Baltzell, *Philadelphia Gentlemen,* p. 178.

14. Walter Firey, "Sentiment and Symbolism." Percentages were adapted from a table presented by Professor Firey.

15. Baltzell, *Philadelphia Gentlemen,* p. 179.

16. *Ibid.,* p. 198.

17. *Ibid.,* Chapter 9.

18. Liston Pope, "Religion and the Class Structure," *The Annals of the American Academy of Political and Social Science* 246 (March, 1948): 89.

19. Bernard Lazerwitz, "Religion and Social Structure in the United States," in *Religion, Culture and Society,* edited by Louis Schneider (New York: Wiley & Sons, 1964), p. 429.

20. Robin M. Williams, Jr., *American Society: A Sociological Interpretation,* 3rd ed. (New York: Knopf, 1970), p. 402.

21. Kenneth Underwood, in his analysis of "Paper City," concluded that upper-class Yankee families clustered in their own exclusive social institutions, which included separate and relatively homogeneous congregations. See *Protestant and Catholic* (Boston: Beacon Press, 1957), pp. 191, 400.

22. Andrew M. Greeley, *The Denominational Society: A Sociological Approach to Religion in America* (Glenview, Illinois: Scott, Foresman, 1972), p. 2.

23. *Ibid.,* p. 125.

24. Charles H. Anderson, *White Protestant Americans: From National Origins to Religious Groups* (Englewood Cliffs, New Jersey: Prentice Hall, 1970), p. xiii.

25. For a discussion of this phenomenon, see Greeley, *The Denominational Society: A Sociological Approach to Religion in America;* Will Herberg, *Protestant-Catholic-Jew: An Essay in American Religious Sociology* (Garden City, New York: Doubleday, 1960); Gerhard Lenski, *The Religious Factor: A Sociological Study of Religion's Impact on Politics, Economics and Family Life* (Garden City, New York: Doubleday, 1963); Marshall Sklare, *America's Jews* (New York: Random House, 1971); Morris Axelrod, Floyd J. Fowler and Arnold Gurin, *A Community for Long Range Planning: A Study of the Jewish Population of Greater Boston* (Boston, 1967); Sidney Goldstein and Calvin Goldschneider, *Jewish Americans: Three Generations in a Jewish Community* (Englewood Cliffs, New Jersey: Prentice-Hall, 1968); among others.

26. E. Digby Baltzell, *Protestant Establishment: Aristocracy and Caste in America* (New York: Random House, 1964).

27. See Baltzell, *Protestant Establishment;* and Stephen Birmingham, *"Our Crowd": The Great Jewish Families of New York* (New York: Harper and Row, 1967) for a more detailed discussion of Judaism and the upper classes.

28. Andrew M. Greeley, *The Catholic Experience in America* (Garden City, New York: Doubleday, 1967), pp. 35-62; see also Baltzell, *Protestant Establishment,* p. 73.

29. See Barbara Miller Solomon, *Ancestors and Immigrants* (Cambridge, Mass.: Harvard University Press, 1956); Also, John Tracy Ellis, *American Catholicism* (Chicago: University of Chicago Press, 1956); Thomas F. O'Dea, "The Catholic Immigrant and the American Scene," *Thought* 31 (Summer, 1956); Thomas T. McAvoy, "The Formation of the Catholic Minority in the United States, 1820-1860," *The Review of Politics* 10 (January, 1948); among others, for a more extended discussion of this point.

30. Ruby Jo Kennedy Reeves, "Single or Triple Melting Pot?: Intermarriage Trends in New Haven, 1870-1940," *American Journal of Sociology* 49 (January, 1944): 331-339. The endogamous marriages of Catholics in New Haven decreased only slightly between 1870 and 1940—from 93.35 percent to 83.71 percent.

31. Gerhard Lenski, *The Religious Factor.* In his study of the Detroit population in 1958, he found that 84 percent of all Catholic respondents were involved in endogamous marriages, while another 14 percent had married non-Catholics who had since converted to Catholicism (pp. 36-37). See also Herberg, *Protestant-Catholic-Jew: An Essay in American Religious Sociology;* and see Greeley, *Denominational Society,* for additional discussion of this point.

32. Charles H. Anderson, *White Protestant Americans,* p. xiv.

33. Suzanne Keller found that 87 percent of the executives of the largest American corporations in 1870 were of British decent. This had declined to only 77 percent by 1900. Similarly, between 15 and 20 percent were of Scottish ancestry, accounting for nearly all of the business elite in the nineteenth century. Keller, "The Social Origins and Career Lines of Three Generations of American Business Leaders "(Ph.D. dissertation, Columbia University, 1953). Mabel Newcomer also found that a substantial majority of business executives in 1900 were of British origin. Newcomer, *The Big Business Executive: The Factors That Made Him,* (New York: Columbia University Press, 1955); see also Gregory and Neu, "The Business Elite of 1870s," and Miller, "Historians and the Business Elite." Pitirim Sorokin, in his analysis of

American millionaires in 1925, found that at least one-half were English, and a great majority were from the British Isles. Sorokin, "American Millionaries and Multi-Millionaries," *Social Forces* 3 (May, 1925): 627-640.)

34. Elin Anderson, *We Americans* (Cambridge: Harvard University Press, 1938), p. 126.

35. W. Lloyd Warner and Paul S. Lunt, *The Social Life of a Modern Community* (New Haven: Yale University Press, 1941) p. 242.

36. C. Wendall King, "Branford Center: A Community Study in Social Cleavage "(Ph.D. dissertation, Yale University, 1943). Cited in C. H. Anderson, *White Protestant Americans,* p. 23.

37. C. H. Anderson, *White Protestant Americans,* p. 26. Anderson compiled his figures from the following studies: Julius Drachsler, *Intermarriage in New York City* (New York: Columbia University Press, 1921); Edmund DeS. Brunner, *Immigrant Farmers and Their Children* (Garden City, New York: Doubleday, 1929); Bessie Bloom Wessel, *An Ethnic Survey of Woonsocket, Rhode Island* (Chicago: University of Chicago Press, 1931); Milton Barron, *People Who Intermarry* (Syracuse: Syracuse University Press, 1946); Lowry Nelson, "Intermarriage Among Nationality Groups in a Rural Area of Minnesota," *American Journal of Sociology* 48 (March, 1943): 585-592; Ruby Jo Kennedy Reeves, "Single or Triple Melting Pot"; and from studies conducted by Anderson himself.

38. C. H. Anderson, *White Protestant Americans,* p. 25.

39. The religious census of 1957 reported that 91 percent of marriages involving a Protestant were religiously endogamous with the lowest exogamic marriage rate occurring among the elite. See Anderson, *White Protestant Americans,* p. 133.

40. Edwin Laumann, "The Social Structure of Religion," *American Sociological Review* 34 (April, 1969): 187.

41. See Baltzell, *Philadelphia Gentlemen,* Chapter 10, for a more extended discussion of this point. See also Robert K. Merton, *Social Theory and Social Structure* (Glencoe, Illinois: Free Press, 1957) for a theoretical discussion of the reference group phenomenon eluded to here.

42. James McLachlan, *American Boarding Schools: A Historical Study* (New York: Scribners, 1970), p. 218.

43. As late as 1890, only about 1.5 percent of the population was attending public and private secondary schools. Total number of students in high schools increased by 250 percent during the next decade, but the secondary school population only constituted 10.2 percent of the youths aged fourteen to seventeen at that time. See Edward A. Krug, *The Shaping of the American High School, 1890-1920* (New York: Harper and Row, 1964), pp. 11, 172.

44. McLachlan, *American Boarding Schools: A Historical Study,* p. 195; Krug, *The Shaping of the American High School, 1880-1920;* Stephen Thernstrom, *Poverty and Progress* (Cambridge: Harvard University Press, 1964), pp. 50-51.

45. McLachlan, *American Boarding Schools: A Historical Study,* p. 194; See also Michael B. Katz, *The Irony of Early School Reform* (Cambridge: Harvard University Press, 1968); Krug, *The Shaping of the American High School, 1880-1920;* Michael B. Katz, "The 'New Departure' in Quincy, 1873-81: The Nature of Nineteenth Century Educational Reform," *The New England Quarterly* 40 (March, 1967): 3-20; David Tyack, "Bureaucracy and the Common School: The Example of Portland Oregon, 1851-1913," *The American Quarterly* 19 (Fall, 1967): 475-498; Joel H. Spring, *Education and the Rise of the Corporate State* (Boston: Beacon Press, 1972) for more extended discussion of aspects of this issue.

46. McLachlan, *American Boarding Schools: A Historical Study,* p. 195.

47. Barbara Miller Solomon, *Ancestors and Immigrants,* pp. 45-46.

48. Baltzell, *Philadelphia Gentlemen,* pp. 328-329.

49. McLachlan, *American Boarding Schools: A Historical Study,* pp. 213, 218.

50. Baltzell, *Philadelphia Gentlemen,* p. 343.

51. McLachlan, *American Boarding Schools: A Historical Study,* p. 136.

52. This analysis is based largely upon material in McLachlan, *American Boarding Schools: A Historical Study.* By 1890-91, one-third of the students were from New York, and the next largest proportion (15 percent) were from Pennsylvania. Only 12 percent were from Massachusetts (p. 159). See also Lawrence B. Fuller, "Private Secondary Education: The Search for a New Model, 1880-1913," *Foundational Studies* 2 (Spring, 1976): 10-21.

53. McLachlan, *American Boarding Schools: A Historical Study,* p. 169.

54. *Ibid.,* p. 171.

55. From 1881 to 1905 and onward, the great majority of St. Paul's graduates became businessmen, increasingly disdaining the professions and other activities. See McLachlan, *American Boarding Schools: A Historical Study,* p. 197.

56. McLachlan, *American Boarding Schools:* p. 197.

57. *Ibid.,* pp. 197-199.

58. *Ibid.,* pp. 221-240.

59. *Ibid.,* pp. 213ff.

60. *Ibid.,* pp. 269-297. Of 2,517 students who graduated from Groton from 1920 to 1929, 25.3 percent held elective or appointive office in federal, state and local governments.

61. Baltzell, *Philadelphia Gentlemen,* p. 357.

62. McLachlan, *American Boarding Schools,* p. 216.

63. See Lawrence Veysey, *The Emergence of the American University* (Chicago: University of Chicago Press, 1965) for a more extended discussion of this phenomenon.

64. W. Bruce Leslie, "A Comparative Study of Four Middle Atlantic Colleges, 1870 to 1915: Bucknell University, Franklin and Marshall College, Princeton University, and Swarthmore College," (Ph.D. dissertation, Johns Hopkins University, 1971), p. 129.

65. Percentages compiled from raw figures supplied by W. Bruce Leslie on religious preferences of the Princeton student body between 1875 and 1933.

66. A more definitive key to social status at these schools were the social and eating clubs. They served as more accurate barometers of relative social standing. See Baltzell, *Philadelphia Gentlemen,* pp. 330-332. This information, however, was not available on a large enough proportion of the members of the iron and steel families to be functional in the present analysis.

67. Dixon Wector, *Saga of American Society* (New York: Scribners, 1937), pp. 257, 253.

68. Alexis de Tocqueville, *Democracy in America,* 2 vols. (New York: A. A. Knopf, 1945), I, pp. 198-199.

69. Murray Hausknecht, *The Joiners: A Sociological Description of Voluntary Association Membership in the United States* (New York: Bedminster Press, 1962), p. 18. See Louis Wirth, "Urbanism as a Way of Life," *American Journal of Sociology* 44 (July, 1938) for a theoretical discussion of the impelling forces behind the associational activity on the urban scene. In brief, Wirth states: "Reduced to a stage of virtual impotence as an individual, the urbanite is bound to exert himself by joining with others into organized groups" (p. 22).

70. Walter S. Glazer, "Participation and Power: Voluntary Associations and Functional Organizations of Cincinnati, in 1840," *Historical Methods Newsletter* No. 4 (September, 1972): 150-168.

71. "No matter what index of social stratification is used, the higher the class position, the greater the rate of voluntary association membership." Hausknecht, *The Joiners: A Sociological Description of Voluntary Association Membership in the United States,* p. 17. Comments based upon 1954 National Opinion Research Center and 1955 AIPO surveys of American Society.

72. Wector, *Saga of American Society,* p. 257.

73. Baltzell, *Philadelphia Gentlemen,* p. 338.

74. *Ibid.,* p. 340.

75. Wector, *Saga of American Society,* p. 270.

76. Domhoff, *The Higher Circles* (New York: Random House, 1970), p. 76.

77. Floyd Martinson, *Family in Society* (New York: Dodd, Mead, 1972), p. 219.

78. Talcott Parsons, "The Kinship System of the Contemporary United States," *American Anthropologist* 45 (1943): 22-38; Louis Wirth, "Urbanism as a Way of Life."

79. See Marvin B. Sussman and Lee G. Burchinal, "Kin Family Network: Unheralded Structure in Current Conceptualizations of Family Functioning," *Marriage and Family Living* 24 (August, 1962): 231-240; Marvin B. Sussman, "The Help Patterns in the Middle Class Family," *American Sociological Review* 28 (1953): 22-28; Marvin B. Sussman and Lee G. Burchinal, "Parental Aid to Married Children: Implications for Family Functioning," *Marriage and Family Living* 24 (November, 1962): 320-332; Bert N. Adams, *Kinship in an Urban Setting* (Chicago: Markham Press, 1968); Eugene Litwack, "Occupational Mobility and Extended Family Cohesion," *American Sociological Review* 25 (1960): 385-394.

These views have recently been criticized by Geoffry Gibson, "Kin Family Network: Overheralded Structures in Past Conceptualization of Family Functioning," *Journal of Sociology* 47 (1961): 312-322. Also, Frank F. Furstenberg, "Industrialization and the American Family: A Look Backward," *American Sociological Review* 31 (1966): 326-337.

Excellent historical anthologies on the American and European family are: Theodore K. Rabb and Robert I. Rothberg, eds. *The Family in History: Interdisciplinary Essays* (New York: Harper and Row, 1973; *Journal of Urban History* 1, no. 3 (May, 1975). A useful sociological text on the family is F. Ivan Nye and Felix M. Bernardo, *The Family: Its Structure and Interaction* (New York: Macmillan, 1973).

80. Sussman and Burchinal, "Kin Family Network" p. 233.

81. Parsons, "The Kinship System," pp. 28-29.

82. See Edwin N. Saveth, "The American Patrician Class: A Field of Research," *American Quarterly* 15 (Summer Supplement, 1963): 235-252. Baltzell's *Philadelphia Gentlemen,* although alluding to marriages and families, never covers the topic in systematic fashion. Nor does Domhoff in *Higher Circles,* even while he stresses its great importance. Nathaniel Burt's, *First Families: The Making of an American Aristocracy* (Boston: Little, Brown, 1970) is a disappointing attempt to analyze a few leading families. Lawrence Rosen and Robert Hall, in "Mate Selection in the Upper Class," *The Sociological Quarterly* 7 (Spring, 1966): 157-196, present an interesting but limited analysis of Philadelphia *Social Register* marriages. Clyde Griffen and Sally Griffen, in "Family and Business in a Small City: Poughkeepsie, New York, 1850-1880," *Journal of Urban History* 1 (May, 1975): 316-338, present an interesting analysis demonstrating nuclear family and extended kinship ties among middle echelon businessmen. The present author has published: "The American Urban Upper Class: Cosmopolitans or Locals?" in *Journal of Urban History* 2 (November, 1975); and "Rags to Riches Revisited: The Relation of City Size and Related Variables to the Recruitment of Business Leaders," in *Journal of American History* (December, 1976).

83. McLachlan, *American Boarding Schools,* p. 339.

84. Robert K. Merton, "Intermarriages and the Social Structure: Fact and Theory," *Psychiatry 4* (August, 1941): 368.

85. George Peter Murdock, *Social Structure* (New York: Free Press), pp. 17, 62.

86. Alwyn D. Rees, *Life in a Welsh Countryside: A Social Study of Llanfihangel yng Ngwynfa* (Cardiff: University of Wales Press, 1950), p. 80.

87. J. A. Barnes, "Social Network," *An Addison-Wesley Module in Anthropology* (n. publ., 1972), pp. 26-31.

88. J. Clyde Mitchell, "The Concept and Use of Social Networks," in *Social Networks in Urban Situations: Analysis of Personal Relationships in Central African Towns.* (Manchester, England: Manchester University Press, 1971), p. 49.

89. *Ibid.,* pp. 12-29.

90. J. A. Barnes, "Networks and Political Process," in Mitchell, *Social Networks in Urban Situations: Analysis of Personal Relationships in Central African Towns,* p. 64.

91. Greeley, *Denominational Society,* p. 2.

92. For an analysis of these values, see Nye and Bernando, *The Family,* p. 66, and Baltzell, *Philadelphia Gentlemen,* Chapter 4.

4

Institutions of an Urban Upper Class: The Pittsburgh Model

Pittsburgh will serve as the principal model of the developing upper-class system of the late nineteenth and early twentieth centuries. Each of the major upper-class institutions, generally delineated in Chapter 3, shall be examined in some detail in the case of Pittsburgh, demonstrating their function and historical development. This should allow for a better understanding of the importance of these institutions for the cohesion and permanence of an upper-class system within a city, while also providing a relatively clear mechanism for rank ordering citizens of wealth and economic power by social status.

Since the older families of Pittsburgh were confronted by a formidable challenge from newer elites on the economic scene, it was natural that this struggle would carry over into the social arena. Analysis of the ramifications of this social phenomenon should be clarified by an understanding of the nature of the upper-class institutions within the environment and the network of relationships which resulted. In addition, much of the ultimate credit for the ability of these older families to withstand the challenge of newer elites must be assigned to the relative strength and viability of the various upper-class institutions and networks.

NEIGHBORHOOD

The first area which attracted large numbers of the pre-Civil War upper class in Pittsburgh was in what is now the central business district of the city. A significant number during these early years also lived just across the river in Allegheny City. Others were scattered more widely, tending to settle within walking distance of the iron mills, since transportation was still rudimentary.

In the 1870s and 1880s, rapid changes began to take place in elite living areas. The downtown area began a precipitous decline; having contained 24 percent of the iron and steel elite within its boundariesin 1874, this fell to 14 percent by 1887. By this date Allegheny City had become the choice living area, holding 29 percent of the iron and steel families. It maintained that percentage for the next quarter century.

At the same time, however, the geographic locus of elite residents shifted to the eastern edges of the city, with the development of Oakland and the East End as prime living areas. Although Oakland never became more than a transitional zone, the East End became the most popular of the elite areas. While Oakland fluctuated between 3 and 9 percent of the steel elite families throughout the late nineteenth century, the East End experienced a phenomenal boom. In 1874, the East End was just beginning to attract monied and high-status families, having only 13 percent of the total. Four years later, it had surged to 21percent, and by 1887 to 35 percent. Throughout the 1890s, the area maintained percentages in the high forties. Then, in the first two decades of the twentieth century, it climbed above the sixtieth percentile. Although a decline had set in during the 1930s, even as late as 1963 the East End still contained some 38 percent of the iron and steel elite families.

Perhaps the most glamorous of the twentieth-century Pittsburgh residential areas was Sewickley—a suburb of the "Main Line" type, which began to attain prominence in the 1920s. By 1933, it had 21 percent of these families, and this increased to over 30 percent in the 1950s. It still remained, in the mid-1960s, "the" Pittsburgh residence for the socially prominent. Other high-status living areas developed in the 1950s included Ligonier and Fox Chapel; but neither challenged the preeminence of Sewickley as an upper-class community. Table 17 indicates the percentage of iron and steel elite families living in each of the urban and suburban residential areas from 1874 to 1963. A more detailed analysis of each of these elite neighborhoods follows.

Since the downtown area in Pittsburgh, as an area of elite residence, declined rapidly after 1870, only a brief analysis of it will be undertaken. Prior to the Civil War this area contained a large number of elite domiciles, but was hardly an "elite" neighborhood in the conventional sense. Although a few streets, such as Penn Avenue and Duquesne Way, contained a disproportionate number of elite residences, they were liberally mixed with commercial establishments and lower-class homes. By 1895, the only iron and steel elites remaining in the downtown area were bachelors who lived at the Pittsburgh or Duquesne clubs. Although no evidence presently exists on the reasons for this rapid exodus in the late nineteenth century, it may be assumed that it rested upon a desire for more neighborhood homogeneity, coupled with the improved transportation methods which made it possible to live further from one's place of business.[1]

Insofar as the ethno-cultural composition of its dwindling elite population is concerned, downtown Pittsburgh was characterized by a large German group in 1874, which rapidly moved to other areas by 1892. The second largest group in 1874, the Scotch-Irish, had more staying power—comprising 47 percent of the total in 1892. The English remained essentially static. In religious terms the area's elite was predominantly Presbyterian, as were all of the other upper-class neighbor-

TABLE 17

Residential Areas of Pittsburgh Iron and Steel Manufacturers and Their Families

Area	Percentage of Families Residing in Area													
	1874 N=224	1878 N=263	1882 N=378	1887 N=257	1892 N=339	1895 N=336	1900 N=490	1908 N=384	1915 N=357	1921 N=334	1933 N=275	1943 N=264	1953 N=227	1963 N=188
Downtown	24	14	19	9	5	2	1	1	1	1	0	0	0	0
Allegheny	29	26	28	29	28	25	22	21	12	11	6	—	—	—
Oakland	3	4	5	4	6	7	9	8	3	3	4	6	8	4
East End	13	21	22	35	43	47	49	55	64	63	60	49	41	38
Hazelwood	6	7	7	4	4	4	2	—	0	0	0	0	0	0
Oakmont	0	0	0	0	0	1	3	3	3	1	1	2	2	2
Sewickley	1	2	2	4	4	3	6	8	10	14	21	26	30	32
Ligonier	0	0	0	0	0	0	0	0	0	—	0	1	2	3
Other, within City Limits	21	18	16	7	3	3	3	1	2	1	2	1	2	7
Other, including suburbs	4	7	8	7	8	8	6	3	5	5	7	15	15	14
TOTALS	100	100	100	100	100	100	100	100	100	100	100	100	100	100

hoods in Pittsburgh. The vast majority were members of families which were of elite status prior to the Civil War, and most had come to America between 1750 and 1850. In social and cultural terms, then, the elite in downtown Pittsburgh did not differ greatly from those in other high-status ateas of the city.

The other important pre-Civil War elite residential area was in Allegheny City. Across the river from downtown Pittsburgh, it had long contained elite residences; but it was in the 1820s that two avenues, Ridge and Western, began to develop as separate and homogeneous elite neighborhoods. By the 1870s Allegheny was the most prestigious haven of the rich and prominent. Decline did not really begin to commence until the 1920s, and even as late as the 1930s, a significant number of the oldest and most prestigious families continued to maintain residence there.

A key fact about Allegheny is that it was urban, as opposed to the later favored neighborhoods. The urban nature of the area was demonstrated in its relative density, the number of people in each residence, the closeness of the residences, and the size of the lots. It's elite nature was defined by the relative homogeneity of the area. Unlike downtown Pittsburgh, and even some of the later suburban developments, Allegheny's elite neighborhoods were peopled almost exclusively by elite families of high status. Some sense of both the compactness and homogeneity of Allegheny can be gained from Table 18, showing elite residences in the area in 1900.

The close-knit characteristic of the Allegheny elite neighborhood was reflected by the existence of both the *extended,* and, more often, *expanded* family structures.[2] The presence of even a relatively small number of extended family households is significant, according to the prevailing opinion of sociologists on the nature of the American kinship system.[3] Extended families did not exist in America, according to this opinion; yet several prominent examples may be found in Allegheny. A good illustration of this extended family relationship was the Byers-Lyon home on Ridge Avenue. Built as a double home, with fifty to sixty rooms, it was intended to house several conjugal units of the family. Other extended family units included: the John U. and Curtis C. Hussey home at 308 Cedar Ave.; the B. F. Jones, Jr. and Alexander Laughlin, Jr. home at 801 Irwin Ave.; the Horne, Sproul, and Wilson home at 835 Lincoln Ave.; the John W. Chalfant and George W. McKee home at 308 North Ave., East; the Henry W. Oliver, Jr., and Henry R. Rea home at 845 Ridge Ave.; the Friend family home at 950 Ridge, which housed the conjugal families of Henry T., Porter C., James K., and James W. Friend; and the C. C. and J. V. Scaife home at 1135 Western Avenue.

More typical, however, was the expanded family structure. Table 18 illustrates how closely proximate the residential units of the various kinship groups tended to be. As sons grew to manhood, as daughters married, they usually purchased homes a few doors from—or, at most, a few blocks from—their parents. As the years progressed, this produced a tightly knit kinship system whereby most were living in individual residences, but were able to have continual contact with parents and other relatives.

TABLE 18
Elite Residences in Allegheny City, 1900

Ridge Avenue		Western Avenue		Lincoln Avenue	
House No.	Family	House No.	Family	House No.	Family
701	C. L. Fitzhugh	934	W. H. Singer	826	F. W. Severance
705	Malcomb Hay	939	Joshua Rhodes	827	J. M. Bailey
707	Benj. Bakewell	948	C. Y. Wheeler	828	H. Holdship
713	Matilda Denny	1003	T. J. Graff	832	H. J. Miller
717	Annie Byers	1027	B. H. Painter	835	Horne, Sproul &
807	C. H. Fitzhugh	1029	C. A. Painter		Watson Fam.
811	H. D. Denny	1109	Herbert DuPuy	841	G. H. Hoffstot
823	W. P. DeArmit	1122	Wm. Walker	842	W. G. Wilkins
827	S. C. Walker	1136	Scaife Family	847	J. W. Scully
829	P. F. Smith	1231	John Walker	849	Kirkpatrick Fam.
845	H. W. Oliver, Jr.			851	W. H. Singer, Jr.
	& H. R. Rea			928	Calvin Wells
846	J. S. Hays	Allegheny Avenue		930	W. Thaw, Jr.
850	Park Painter			931	W. McCandless, Jr.
854	R. G. Wood	609	W. M. Orr	936	T. Ewing
901	J. D. Lyon	615	J. H. Ricketson, Jr.	937	Wilson Miller
905	A. M. Byers	617	T. G. McCutcheon	940	J. W. Rhodes
911	Sellers McKee	621	George Shiras	942	Hay Walker
919	Thomas McKee	1119	J. F. McCord	948	J. J. Donnell
921	Chas. Hays			949	D. H. Stewart
928	J. J. Moorhead			1006	Jas. Laughlin, Jr.
931	J. H. Ricketson	Bidwell Avenue		1010	J. H. Dalzell
937	J. W. Dalzell				
939	Stuart McKee	925	G. Pennock	Irwin Avenue	
950	Friend family	1019	W. B. Schiller		
1001	O. O. Phillips	1036	L. F. Demmler	701	B. F. Jones
1006	T. W. Bakewell			705	W. W. Willock
1021	J. H. Lindsay			709	J. N. McCullough
		Fayette Avenue		717	Caldwell Family
				721	H. Darlington
		1212	B. F. Jennings	801	B. F. Jones, Jr. &
					H. Laughlin, Jr.

The relative social and class homogeneity of Allegheny prior to 1908 is more difficult to establish. In broad terms, a large minority—nearly a majority in some years—of the iron and steel elite inhabitants were of Scottish or Scotch-Irish ancestry. They were supplemented by significant minorities of families with English and German ancestors. In religious heritage, the great majority were Presbyterians, and a minority were Episcopalian. There were very few of any other religious persuasion, though some Jews and Catholics were represented. The vast majority of the iron and steel elite in Allegheny derived from the pre-Civil War economic elite, and the same statement could be made for those living in other elite neighborhoods. Similarly, the greatest number were from families who had arrived in America between 1750 and 1805, but this was also generally true of the Pittsburgh iron and steel elite. Although quite socially homogeneous, the iron and steel elite in Allegheny did not differ greatly from their counterparts in other elite areas of the city. Its distinction lay in the nature of its physical environment, rather than in the people who resided there.

Allegheny was Pittsburgh's premier, elite urban neighborhood. Like elegant Rittenhouse Square in Philadelphia, or Boston's Beacon Hill, it was urban, in contrast to Pittsburgh's suburban East End and Sewickley. As such, it represents the city's most glamorous inner-city neighborhood. Professor Baltzell's reference to Rittenhouse Square could well be applied to Allegheny: "At no other time in the city's history, before or since, have so many wealthy and fashionable families lived so near one another."[4] The high comparative social prestige of the Allegheny area is indicated by Table 19, which shows the neighborhood having between 90 and 100 percent of its iron and steel elite inhabitants listed in the Social Register in the representative years. This was higher than for any other Pittsburgh elite area except Sewickley, which had about the same percentage. Even when the number of elite families began to decline in Allegheny, it still maintained a high prestige factor.

Thus, despite the fact that in ethnic, religious or economic backgrounds, Allegheny's iron and steel elite did not differ greatly from those in other preferred areas, they were more highly ranked in terms of relative social status; at least 93 percent of the iron and steel elite family members in the neighborhood were listed in the Social Register for each given year.

In the ethno-cultural composition of its elite iron and steel families, the East End resembled Allegheny. Although a larger percentage here were of English background, nearly as large a number during the years from 1874 to 1900 were Scottish or Scotch-Irish. An increasingly larger percentage over the years were of Germanic origin. In religious affiliation, the iron and steel elite in the East End were predominantly Presbyterian, with the largest minority being Episcopal. As in Allegheny, the majority were from pre-Civil War elite families, and most came to America between 1750 and 1850.

This cultural similarity of the East End's iron and steel elite with those in Allegheny belies some important spatial differences between the two. Whereas Allegheny was compact and concentrated, the East End was diffuse. Unlike Allegheny, the East End was principally a suburban development. In the mid-nineteenth century it was primarily farm land, decorated with the occasional country homes of several

TABLE 19
Neighborhood and Social Register Listings of Pittsburgh Iron and Steel Elite, 1908-1963

Neighborhood	1908		1915		1921		1933		1943		1953		1963	
	*N**	%**	*N*	%	*N*	%	*N*	%	*N*	%	*N*	%	*N*	%
Upper Class														
Allegheny	81	95	44	100	37	95	15	93	1	100	1	100	–	–
East End	210	83	230	79	212	74	165	84	130	84	94	81	71	86
Sewickley	31	84	36	92	47	96	58	97	68	100	69	100	61	97
Ligonier	–	–	–	–	1	100	–	–	1	50	4	75	6	100
Transition														
Oakland	29	59	9	56	11	73	10	100	17	77	17	77	8	50
Other Suburbs	10	40	17	53	16	50	18	78	39	62	33	70	24	75
Élite Areas														
Downtown	5	80	3	100	4	100	–	–	–	–	–	–	–	–
Other/City	6	50	7	14	2	0	6	33	2	0	5	0	14	21
Oakmont	12	17	11	9	4	50	3	33	5	0	4	25	4	25
TOTAL	384	76†	375	78	334	82	275	86	264	82	227	82	188	86

**N* refers to the total number of members of iron and steel elite families living in neighborhood in year indicated.

**% refers to the percentage of those iron and steel family members living in neighborhood who are also listed in Pittsburgh *Social Register.*

† Totals for percentages are the average percentage of iron and steel family members living in *all* neighborhoods in year indicated.

of Pittsburgh's more prestigious families. Only in small, isolated villages such as East Liberty were there such concentrations of elite families, such as the Negleys, Aikens, McClintocks, Baileys, and Mellons. The area was remembered by William G. Johnston:

> The road (Penn Avenue) ran through the strictly rural district into narrow limits, and it was scarcely more than a bridal path, where winding around the hill it led up to Morningside, when a scene yet one of great beauty burst into view. Far below the Allegheny wound among the hills like a silver thread, and the blue smoke from the cottages nestled there in the quaint valleys, curled gracefully above the tops of the forest trees.[5]

By the 1870s parts of the area, particularly around East Liberty and Oakland, began to coalesce into definite suburban neighborhoods. Unlike Allegheny, it was a broad, sprawling scape, providing much expanse for large estates with rolling lawns and natural woods. This allowed the building of larger homes and estates, but also dispersed the elite population far more than in Allegheny. This made for greater social and cultural heterogeneity than existed in Allegheny.[6] The East End was, in fact, a series of suburban neighborhoods of varying economic position and social prestige, held together in the early years by the railroad. Since the Pennsylvania railroad meandered through the area, with stations at Shady Side, East Liberty, and Homewood, this did much to dictate the area's development. It also helps to explain the lower percentage of Social Register listees here, as compared to Allegheny: it was large enough to contain the "best" families, the newly rich, and a fair number of middle-class and upper-middle-class families.

For example, far out on Penn Avenue—at the intersection of Homewood and Lexington Avenues—grew what was to be called the Carnegie Colony. Once a part of a large estate owned by Judge Wilkins, Andrew and Tom Carnegie bought a home there while Wilkins still ruled the suburb (known as Homewood) like a feudal baron.[7] Also living there at the time were: David Stewart of the Pennsylvania Railroad; William Coleman, a Carnegie partner and Tom Carnegie's father-in-law; and Thomas N. Miller, another Carnegie partner. In later years, other Carnegie men also built homes in the vicinity: Henry Clay Frick, at Penn and Homewood; Alexander Peacock, at Penn and Lexington; William W. Blackburn, at Penn and Homewood; Henry W. Borntrager, at the same place; Robert B. Brown at Penn and Lexington; and George Lauder, at Penn and Homewood.

Shadyside was another of those semiautonomous suburbs within the East End. Although more prestigious in terms of family status, it was not as uniformly wealthy as the "Carnegie Colony." The area ran from the intersection of Penn and Fifth avenues, west to the intersection of Fifth and Morewood, including intersecting streets and several parallel streets. A large number of upper-class families lived there, many continuing to do so into the 1960s. Although the prestige of Shadyside rivaled that of Allegheny, the elite families were much more widely scattered.

Despite a couple of pockets—such as Woodland Road—where several families lived in close proximity, the tendency in Shadyside was for greater dispersion than in Allegheny. This is characteristic of a suburban as opposed to an urban upper-class neighborhood.

Although there were some examples of extended family units in the East End (the kinship cluster on Woodland Road, with the Bissell, Brown, Howe, Laughlin and Rea families), and although a fairly well-developed expanded family system functioned, the greater distance between the homes of most kin probably made familial ties less strong than they were in Allegheny. For continual family visiting and mutual involvement in one another's affairs, a mile or even a half mile between family residences in the days before automobile made daily contact less probable.

Thus the East End, though of great wealth and generally high prestige, had neither the homogeneity or the cohesion of Allegheny. It was far more diverse, with extremes of great and small wealth more liberally intermixed. Its boundaries were less well defined; but it was able to maintain a definite prestige even down to the mid-1960s. Although an average of only 80 percent of its iron and steel elites were listed in the Social Register over the years (less than either Allegheny or Sewickley), it remained a solid upper-class area in many respects. Many of the old mansions had been destroyed by the mid-1960s; but several remained, most still inhabited by the old elite families.

Like the East End, Oakland was "out in the country" in the mid-nineteenth century: it was a rural area with a sprinkling of country estates. In the late nineteenth century Oakland attracted more elite families, but this never came to more than a small minority of the total—3 percent in 1874, and a high of 9 percent in 1900. Some of these families, such as the Zugs, lived in large homes and estates in the area; but many others, particularly in the twentieth century, were elderly inhabitants of the area's hotels and apartment houses. The Schenley Hotel, King Edward Apartments, Ruskin Apartments, and several others were very popular lodgings, especially for the elderly women.

Culturally, the iron and steel elite in Oakland differed from those in Allegheny and the East End—primarily in its larger percentage from Germanic origins. Evidently, many of those Germans who once resided in downtown Pittsburgh had migrated to Oakland, an area of diverse land-use patterns (similar to the downtown area, in that respect). Most of the iron and steel elite in Oakland were Presbyterian, though there was also a significant Quaker group. As in the other elite neighborhoods, the great majority in Oakland were members of pre-Civil War elite families; but a larger percentage were from families which had come to America in the earlier eighteenth century. In fact, a majority arrived *before* 1800, averaging nearly fifty years earlier than their counterparts in the East End or Allegheny.

Although an important elite area, Oakland never acquired the structure of an urban or suburban neighborhood. Being more of a transitional zone —particularly with the location of the University of Pittsburgh and other civic institutions there, it was a rather crowded and heterogeneous place: thus most elite families settled a mile or so further east, in Shadyside or East Liberty.

Lying southeast of Oakland was the Hazelwood area. It had been popular as an elite area during the earlier nineteenth century, when it was still rather rural and located high above the Monongehela River and the factory smoke. In addition, it was within walking distance of several iron mills on that side of the river. Thus, it was able to combine, in those early years, a rural atmosphere with convenience. Before the appearance of street railways, this was especially valuable. The largest estate in the area belonged to Hill Burgwin, and several other iron manufacturers made their homes there—between 6 and 7 percent of the elite in the 1870s and 1880s.

In ethno-cultural terms, Hazelwood's small iron and steel elite colony was primarily Scotch-Irish, with a large minority of English origin. Most were Presbyterians, though a large number were Episcopalian. In the early years, the area seemed to attract a larger percentage of men from recent immigrant backgrounds than did the East End or Allegheny. A larger percentage of the iron and steel elite in Hazelwood came to America *after* 1800, and relatively few had come during the eighteenth century.

Sewickley became Pittsburgh's premier suburban development for elite families in the twentieth century, surpassing the East End in opulence and rivaling—if not surpassing—Allegheny in status. As Herbert Casson has remarked:

> Highest of all Pittsburgh heavens is Sewickley Heights. All homes are built after the fashion of baronial castles with imposing entrances and winding roadways from gate to house. Fortunes have been spent in landscape gardening. Most of the owners of this smokeless, slumless Eden are steel millionaries.[8]

Throughout the nineteenth century, Sewickley had been an isolated, rural village, remote from Pittsburgh, with its own indigenous upper class and a sprinkling of summer homes of Pittsburgh elites. The Irwins, Nevins, and Browns had long lived in the village, where they functioned partially within the Pittsburgh social system and partially within their local social circles.

Prior to 1900, there was little that was unique about the ethno-cultural composition of Sewickley's iron and steel elite: the great majority were Scotch-Irish, Presbyterian, and had attained elite status before the Civil War. Most also had come to America between 1750 and 1850. It was after 1900, especially after 1920, that the relative status of Sewickley began to change. By 1900 Sewickley still held only 6 percent of the iron and steel elite, but a steady growth ensued from that time onward. Most of this growth seemed dependent upon the automobile. Although the Pennsylvania Railroad tracks had long passed through Sewickley, the great expansion of the suburb did not come until the 1920s—when it was conveniently connected to Pittsburgh by auto routes. The auto seemed necessary due to the fact that most homes were located a long distance from the railroad terminus in the village: it became easier to reach the city by car.

Many of the families who moved to Sewickley after the 1920s were former residents of Allegheny. They had maintained summer homes in the village for several years and—following the lead of B. F. Jones, Jr.—they later built palatial residences on vast estates in the sprawling area known as Sewickley Heights. Most of these homes cost hundreds of thousands of dollars, and were in the finest "English country estate" tradition. By 1933, 21 percent of the iron and steel elite were living in Sewickley; this was increased to 30 percent in 1953, and 32 percent in 1963. Only recently has the area shown hints of possible decline, with the demolition of the 100-room, B. F. Jones Jr. mansion.

The social prestige of Sewickley has been uniformly high over the years, with the proportion of Social Register listees among its elite families ranging between 95 and 100 percent. It has been Pittsburgh's version of Philadelphia's wealthy, sprawling suburbs on the "Main Line." It was, and remains, the most homogeneous and exclusive of Pittsburgh's upper-class suburbs.

Among other suburbs which developed in the twentieth century, was Oakmont. Several miles up the Allegheny River from Pittsburgh, it also began to develop in the 1920s, but it never captured the fancy of more than 3 percent of the iron and steel elite families. Most of those who moved there were of generally lower social prestige than those who moved to the East End or Sewickley. Only one-quarter to one-third of the iron and steel elites in Oakmont were listed in the Social Register; and the suburb itself remained primarily an upper-middle-class area.

The most recent elite suburb to develop is Ligonier. The brainchild of the Mellon family, it was developed in the mid-1950s on the order of Sewickley—with huge mansions set on vast, rolling acreage—in Westmoreland County, east of Pittsburgh. Although only 3 percent of the iron and steel elite families were living there in 1963, it appeared to be the next major upper-class suburb for Pittsburgh.

The elite neighborhoods of Pittsburgh, then, reflected a structure stratified to some degree by ethno-cultural origins, but were primarily delineated according to social class standing. The three upper-class neighborhoods, as defined by their percentage of Social Register listings, all had an ethno-cultural makeup similar to that of the iron and steel elite in the city as a whole. The more transitional areas in terms of social class, such as Oakland, differed more substantially from the whole number of iron and steel manufacturers' neighborhoods in terms of their ethno-cultural composition. Although neighborhood was the least selective institution of upper-class life, it did tend to group persons of relatively similar class and cultural backgrounds together. Pittsburgh's social clubs were to perform the same function in a more rigorous and evident manner.

SOCIAL CLUBS

Related to neighborhood as an indicator of social status, but far more precise in its rankings, was the system of urban and suburban clubs. Neighborhood was a generalized ranking, since if one had enough money to buy a home in a particular area, it was difficult to keep that person out. With clubs, however, there was greater selectivity: an "undesirable" person could be blackballed from membership in the more exclusive clubs. So, the gradations in rank among the social clubs were more minute and precise than the ranking system of neighborhood.

The first social clubs to develop in Pittsburgh were the men's luncheon clubs in town. The most exclusive of these was the Pittsburgh Club—which had grown out of membership split in the six-year-old Duquesne Club, in April of 1879. The popular tale of this split claimed that it was based upon the desire of the younger members of the Duquesne Club to escape the scrutiny of the boss's eye while at lunch or relaxing.[9] This seems more apocryphal than true. In fact, the situation seems to have developed out of a desire on the part of those men who formed the Pittsburgh Club to create a more socially exclusive organization than the older Duquesne Club.[10]

The later history of the Pittsburgh Club would seem to bear this out. As the city's leading society newspaper commented: "The Pittsburgh Club is Pittsburgh's fortress of conservative social prestige. It is comparable to Washington's Metropolitan and Boston's Somerset."[11] Beginning in 1884, the Pittsburgh Club hosted the annual cotillions—the most prestigious social event in the city, and the mark of "arrival of status" similar to Philadelphia's Assembly Balls.

The club's founders in 1879 were Malcomb Hay, William G. Park, Francis H. Denny, George C. Burgwin, Harry Darlington, Sr., and Henry Graham Brown, all members of some of the oldest and most prestigious families in the city. It met in a small, three-story brick building at 259 Penn Avenue—until 1884, when John H. Shoenberger donated his town home at 425 Penn Avenue, the most luxurious residence remaining in the downtown area. The club remained at this location until 1942, when it moved to the William Penn Hotel and ceased most of its functions.

The membership started at about twenty-five, and reached a peak of about 300 during its halycon days. The men selected for admission to the club reflected the cream of the upper class of the city, as evidenced by the roster of club presidents: Hill Burgwin, James W. Brown, William N. Frew, Walter Mitchell, Wynn Reeves Sewall, Henry R. Rea, and John F. Byers.[12] The relative social standing of the club can be seen by measuring the percentage of its iron and steel family members who were also listed in the Social Register, as shown in Table 20. This high percentage of members who were listed in the Social Register (the only intercity upper-class ranking system available) corresponds exactly to the ranking of the upper-class Philadelphia Club.[13] Thus, Pittsburgh's most prestigious urban club had roughly the same social ranking as the most prestigious club in Philadelphia.

In ethno-cultural respects, the Pittsburgh Club did not vary greatly from the broader iron and steel elite in the city. Of the members in 1910, there were nearly equal numbers from English and Scotch-Irish origins, and significant minorities with Scottish and German ancestry. A majority were Presbyterian; but there was a larger group of Episcopalians than among the iron and steel elite as a whole.

TABLE 20

Pittsburgh Club Iron and Steel Members, Related to Pittsburgh Social Register Listings

1910			1925 (New Members)		
Total Members	Total in Social Register	% in Social Register	Total Members	Total in Social Register	% in Social Register
124	122	98	28	28	100

SOURCE: Pittsburgh Social Register, published annually in New York by the Social Register of America.

Eighty-five percent were members of pre-Civil War elite families. Of the new iron and steel family club members in 1925, a majority were Scotch-Irish, with English and German forming the two principal minorities. Most were still Presbyterian, and only 14 percent Episcopalian. Of importance is the fact that only 57 percent of the new members in 1925 emanated from pre-Civil War elite origins: 29 percent were from the native American middle class, and 14 percent from working-class and middle-class immigrant families. Thus, although the social prestige of this new group of members was uniformly high in 1925 (as indicated by their Social Register listings), it does represent the movement to respectability of men and families from less "desirable" social and economic origins in the nineteenth century.

Pittsburgh's first club in town was the Duquesne Club, organized in 1873 by several of the city's iron and steel men. Although representing several of the city's older families, the club also included in its early membership many younger iron and steel men from less auspicious backgrounds. This was to set the tone of the club throughout its history, and it led to the creation of the more socially exclusive Pittsburgh Club in 1879. The Duquesne Club functioned primarily as a luncheon gathering place for the city's economic elites, many of whom were of the highest social ranking, but it also included men who were, for various reasons, excluded from the highest prestige rankings. Some sense of this can be gained by looking at the Social Register listings of the club's iron and steel family members, and comparing it to the Pittsburgh Club.[14] Thus the Duquesne Club, with only about 78

TABLE 21

Duquesne Club Iron and Steel Members, Related to Pittsburgh Social Register Listings, 1909

Total Members	Total in Social Register	% in Social Register
205	159	78

percent of its iron and steel members listed in the Social Register, showed a significantly lower social rank than the Pittsburgh Club, corresponding to its concentration upon economic elites rather than on the purely social upper class.

This differentiation in social status between the Duquesne and Pittsburgh Clubs was also reflected partially in the ethno-cultural origins of their respective iron and steel elite memberships. Although there was little variation in either ethnicity or religion (with the Duquesne having slightly more Scotch-Irish and Episcopalians among its members), the major difference was in the economic backgrounds of the members. Although a substantial majority (68 percent) of the Duquesne members were from pre-Civil War elite families, this figure was well below the 85 percent recorded at the Pittsburgh Club at the same time. Accordingly, the Duquesne Club contained higher percentages of men from native American and immigrant middle-class and working-class origins. In all areas of analysis, then, the Duquesne Club members would appear to reflect a less exalted status than their counterparts in the Pittsburgh Club. Fewer of its members were listed in the Social Register, and a larger number were members of families which had not been of elite status prior to the Civil War.

A more recent urban men's club was the Union Club. The origins of the club are a little obscure, but it seems to owe its birth to the feud between Andrew Carnegie and Henry Clay Frick in the mid-1890s. The club was organized by Frick in 1902 as a luncheon club, with offices in the First National Bank Building. The year before, Frick and Andrew Mellon had organized the Union Steel Company (to provide direct competition for Carnegie Steel), so the coincidence of the names and dates would seem to lend substance to the rumors concerning the nature of the club's origin.

The Union Club had about 600 members in its heyday; but a complete list of its membership was difficult to obtain.[15] Those memberships which could be traced made it evident that the Union Club was of a primarily elite nature, like the Duquesne Club, and that it was not on the same prestige level as the Pittsburgh Club. Table 22 shows these figures for the Union Club.

The Union Club also resembled the Duquesne Club in the cultural and economic backgrounds of its iron and steel members, although the proportion of men from

TABLE 22
Union Club Iron and Steel Members, Related to Pittsburgh Social Register Listings

1912			1921 (New Members)		
Total Iron & Steel Members	No. in Social Register	% in Social Register	Total Iron & Steel Members	No. in Social Register	% in Social Register
42	36	88	28	22	79

Germanic background was almost double that in either of the other clubs. It was, however, dominated by Presbyterians, as were its two sister clubs. Similar to the Duquesne Club, the Union Club drew only 65 percent of its members from pre-Civil War elite families. Just as the Union Steel Company was organized to compete with Carnegie Steel, so the Union Club seemed to have been organized to provide direct competition for the Duquesne Club, perhaps owing to the large number of Carnegie men who were members of that latter club.

When the Union Club was disbanded in 1932, its 402 active members were absorbed into the Keystone Athletic Association, which had been organized in 1925. With club rooms at the old St. Charles Hotel in downtown Pittsburgh, it had an active membership of reportedly 4,000.[16] Since no membership list was available, it was impossible to ascertain the precise social rankings of the club in relation to the other Pittsburgh clubs; but its high membership limit, along with the general nature of athletic associations in other cities, make it most likely a less prestigious organization. The Pittsburgh Athletic Association, on which little information was gathered, would seem to have had a similar ranking.

In addition, there were a couple of more specialized urban clubs in Pittsburgh: the Junta Club and the Americus Club. The Junta Club had been organized in 1883 as an intellectual, rather than social club. Limited to thirty members drawn from the business and intellectual communities, its prestige was more along academic lines than upper-class ones.[17] The Americus Club was principally a political organization of wealthy Republican business leaders. With high yearly dues of $1,000, it was designed to provide monetary and moral support to various Republican candidates and platforms.[18]

There was also a variety of clubs for the various ethnic and religious elite groups in the city. There was a Columbus Club for prominent Catholics, but little information could be found concerning it. Of the Catholic steel makers in the study, Leopold Vilsack belonged to the Columbus Club, but Francis Keating apparently did not, although he retained memberships in the Duquesne and Union clubs. For Jewish businessmen, there was the Concordia Club, which had been organized in 1874, with its club house located first in Allegheny and later in Oakland. Its members included most of the prominent Jewish leaders of the city, including Joseph and Emanuel Kaufman, the only two Jewish steelmakers in the study. Neither of these two were listed in the Social Register, nor did they belong to any of the other social clubs in the city.

During the late nineteenth and early twentieth centuries, a series of suburban, or "country," clubs were also organized in Pittsburgh. Intended to fulfill the recreational and social needs of the whole family, they became important cogs in the upper-class system of the city. The "queen" of Pittsburgh's country clubs was the Allegheny Country Club. Organized in Allegheny in 1895, it purchased 200 acres in Sewickley in 1900. Building a club house and golf course there, the club moved its 110 members to the facility in 1902. The Allegheny Country Club's prestige ranking among the other suburban clubs was similar to the position of the Pittsburgh Club among the town clubs; its charter members were from the most socially prominent families of the city.[19] Comparing the club's membership in 1911 with Social Register listings indicates its high-ranking status, as demonstrated in Table 23.[20] This high social status of the Allegheny Country Club not only equals that of the Pittsburgh Club in the city, but also reflects a percentage similar to that of the Radnor Hunt and Gulph Mills Golf Clubs in Philadelphia—which Baltzell found to be the most prestigious country clubs in that city.[21]

TABLE 23
Allegheny Country Club, 1911

Total Iron and Steel Family Members	Number Listed in Pittsburgh Social Register	% in Pittsburgh Social Register
128	125	98

In other respects, the Allegheny Country Club also replicated the Pittsburgh Club's membership. Predominantly Scotch-Irish and Scottish, it had a large minority of men from English backgrounds. Nearly two-thirds were Presbyterian, and the vast majority came to America between 1750 and 1850. In the important area of family economic background, 77 percent of Allegheny Country Club's iron and steel family members emanated from the pre-Civil War elite—slightly less than the 85 percent in this category in the Pittsburgh Club, but well ahead of the 68 percent at Duquesne and 65 percent at Union Club. In nearly all areas, then, Allegheny Country Club was the Pittsburgh Club's suburban counterpart.

The Pittsburgh Golf Club was organized in 1896. The club had a prestigious, though somewhat strange career. It was organized by several prominent Pittsburgh businessmen living in the East End area of the city, who had found it inconvenient to travel to Allegheny or Sewickley for their golf and other social activities. The clubhouse and golf course were located on the Schenley estate for many years—well after the entire estate was donated to the city for use as a public park. Some years afterward the private use of park lands by the club was challenged, and the club's golf course was converted to public use. It remained an important social club, however, and in later years, after the decline of the Pittsburgh Club, it became one of the most prestigious of the town clubs. Comparing the Pittsburgh Golf Club's iron and steel family members to the Social Register, Table 24 indicates its high relative social standing.

Thus, the only discernible difference between the Allegheny Country Club and the Pittsburgh Golf Club was geographic rather than one of class. With equal social rankings, according to the Social Register, the Pittsburgh Golf Club served those upper-class East End families who preferred a club more accessible than the Allegheny Country Club.

TABLE 24
Pittsburgh Golf Club, 1912 and 1938 (New Members)

1912			1938		
Total Iron & Steel Family Members	No. in Social Register	% in Social Register	New Iron & Steel Family Members	No. in Social Register	% in Social Register
124	118	95	44	43	98

This compatibility was also reflected in the cultural and economic (as well as the social status) backgrounds of the club's iron and steel members. Exhibiting almost no variation from Allegheny Country Club in ethnicity or religion, Pittsburgh Golf drew 83 percent of its iron and steel family members in 1912 from pre-Civil War elite backgrounds.

Also located in the East End was the Pittsburgh Country Club. Founded in 1889, it was located near the "Carnegie Colony" in Homewood. This was sociologically significant, since the Pittsburgh Country Club tended to draw its membership more heavily from the newly wealthy, less socially secure men of the Carnegie ilk.[22] The "nouveau riche" leanings of the club are reflected in the percentage of its iron and steel members who were listed in the Social Register, as shown in Table 25.

This relatively diminished social status of the Pittsburgh Country Club was also reflected in the cultural and economic backgrounds of its iron and steel members. More heterogeneous ethnically than either Allegheny Country or Pittsburgh Golf clubs, it contained a large percentage of men of Germanic background (a cultural minority at the time). A significantly lower proportion of the men were from pre-Civil War elite origins, with Pittsburgh Country Club admitting to membership larger numbers of "new men" on the economic scene. Finally, their families generally arrived in America at a later date, with 54 percent (of those for whom information was available) coming after 1800.

Thus, although the Pittsburgh Country Club counted among its members several individuals from older, more prestigious families (Mellons, Laughlins, and Childs), there was a larger number of newly emergent "self-made" men, particularly those who rose from within the ranks at the Carnegie plants. They found

TABLE 25
Pittsburgh Country Club, 1901

Total Iron and Steel Family Members	Number in Social Register	% in Social Register
53	38	72

this club the most congenial of the suburban clubs, and its resulting social prestige was significantly lower than that of the Allegheny or Pittsburgh Golf Clubs.

A few years after the Pittsburgh Golf Club lost its eighteen-hole golf course to the city, the Fox Chapel Golf Club was organized to fill the void. As the club's publication stated:

> From the day in 1910, when Mayor Magee decided to take over and make public the course in Schenley Park . . . a hungry and dissatisfied feeling was in the hearts of many of those who for many years played there. Some joined Oakmont, more joined Allegheny . . . but [many felt] they should have a course of their own.[23]

In 1922, William Larimer Mellon and George M. Laughlin, Jr., purchased property in the suburb of Fox Chapel for a new club. A dinner was held at the Pittsburgh Golf Club in 1923 to raise over $150,000 to build a new clubhouse on the acreage. The first officers of the new club were old Pittsburgh Golf Club members: Mellon, Laughlin, Francis S. Guthrie, William Frew and John C. Dilworth. With the demise of Pittsburgh Golf as a suburban club, and with the remoteness of the Allegheny Country Club for these East Enders, they felt the need of a new country club located near the East End; and neither the Pittsburgh Country Club nor the Oakmont Country Club had sufficient prestige to fit their needs. This new club was intended to recapture the allure of the old Pittsburgh Golf Club.

This venture was only partially successful, since Fox Chapel was never able to attract more than a small minority of the iron and steel families onto its membership rolls. Those who did join were of high social status, as indicated by the comparison to Social Register listings in Table 26; but large enough numbers from this group were never persuaded to join.

TABLE 26
Fox Chapel Golf Club, 1939

Total Iron and Steel Family Members	Number Listed in Social Register	Percentage in Social Register
50	50	100

Examination of the economic and social backgrounds of these Fox Chapel Golf members reveals a basic similarity with Allegheny Country Club and Pittsburgh Golf in the important categories. The great majority were Scottish, Scotch-Irish or English, were Presbyterian, and came to America between 1750 and 1850, with a majority of those for whom information is available arriving before 1800. Of greatest significance, fully 82 percent of the men were descended from pre-Civil War economic elites. Few new men from disadvantaged economic or cultural origins in the nineteenth century were admitted as members to Fox Chapel, even by 1939.

The problem with Fox Chapel Golf, then, had to do with its inability to attract sufficient numbers of the older iron and steel families as members. Those who did join were of uniformly high social prestige, but for some reason, its popularity remained below that of the Allegheny Country Club and the old Pittsburgh Golf Club. Because of this, William L. Mellon, a few years later, organized the Rolling Rock Club in a second attempt to provide a high-status suburban club for East Enders.[24]

Rolling Rock Club, unlike Fox Chapel Golf, was completely financed and organized by the Mellon family. Membership was strictly by invitation from the Mellons, and until 1934 no dues were charged for membership. After that, a nominal $25 per year was assessed. All other operating costs were absorbed by the Mellons. It had started as a hunt club in 1917, on the family's vast properties near Ligonier, Pennsylvania. Soon afterward, a golf course was completed and an all-purpose clubhouse was constructed in 1921. It was not until the 1930s, with the difficulties of the Fox Chapel Golf Club in attracting upper-class members, that Rolling Rock began vigorously recruiting members into its ranks.[25]

Although the club was just beginning to grow in popularity in the 1940s, an examination of its membership list indicates that it was not only of uniformly high social prestige, but was also more successful in attracting larger numbers of iron and steel elite families than was the Fox Chapel Golf Club.[26] Of its 116 members from iron and steel families in 1947, 99 percent were listed in the Social Register. Like Allegheny Country Club, Rolling Rock was successful in combining popularity with high social selectivity.

As with Allegheny Country, Pittsburgh Golf and Fox Chapel Golf, Rolling Rock's membership derived from preferred social and economic origins. Predominantly Scotch-Irish, English and Scottish in ancestry, most were Presbyterians or Episcopalians. Fully 85 percent emanated from pre-Civil War elite families, and well over one-half were members of families who had come to America prior to 1800. Even as late as 1947, Rolling Rock counted few men from disadvantaged nineteenth-century social origins among its membership. As Allegheny Country Club reposed as an anchor of upper-class respectability for the western suburbs, Rolling Rock played a similar role in the East.

The Oakmont Country Club was founded in 1903 by Pittsburgh steel men, Henry C. Fownes and Lawrence C. Dilworth. An outgrowth of the Highland Golf Club and the Westmoreland Country Club, it was also located in the East End, serving many of the businessmen and their families from that area.[27] The Oakmont Club, like Pittsburgh Country Club, was primarily elite rather than upper class, though several members of older families held memberships. The comparative social standing of the Oakmont Club may be gauged from Table 27, which shows the iron and steel family members and the percentages who were listed in the Social Register. Like the Pittsburgh Country Club and the Duquesne Club, its percentages hovered in the high 70s and low 80s, indicating its basic elite orientation.[28]

The somewhat lower status of the Oakmont Country Club was particularly evident in the economic backgrounds of these families, where only 67 percent

TABLE 27
Oakmont Country Club, 1909 and 1919 (New Members)

Total Iron & Steel Family Members, in 1909	No. in Social Register	% in Social Register	New Members in 1919	No. in Social Register	% in Social Register
52	43	82	63	44	70

in 1909 and 68 percent in 1919 were descended from the pre-Civil War elite. In addition, one-half in 1909 and slightly more than that in 1919 came to America after 1800, with a large minority arriving after 1850. Overall, then, Oakmont was much like Pittsburgh Country Club—a haven for men of new wealth and their families.

The Edgewood Country Club was also located in Pittsburgh's East End. Organized in 1898, it was chartered in 1907; but it did not have a clubhouse until 1927, when one was built in Churchville Borough.[29] A decidedly upper-middle-class club, Edgewood Country Club had little attraction for Pittsburgh elite and upper-class families from the iron and steel industry. In 1909 only two members of these families belonged to the club: John M. Irwin and Charles E. Dinkey. Its attraction grew little in succeeding years.

On the other hand, the Edgeworth Country Club was able to attain fairly high social prestige. Organized in Sewickley in 1887, it functioned primarily as an elite club for those families in the Allegheny and Sewickley areas who were not of sufficient prestige for membership in the Allegheny Country Club.[30] Lending somewhat higher status were some of the older Sewickley families, who had belonged to the club since the days before the Allegheny Club had moved to their village. Analysis of the membership rolls in 1909 reveals that Edgeworth greatly resembled Fox Chapel Golf in its later period: although it was able to attract members of high social status, it was not able to attract sufficient numbers of them to assume the same predominant role of Allegheny Country Club.[31] Of twenty-eight iron and steel family members in 1909, 86 percent were listed in the Social Register, giving the club a comparative status only slightly below that of the Allegheny Country Club and well above Pittsburgh Country and Oakmont. This was also reflected in the social and cultural composition of its membership, with 85 percent from pre-Civil War elite families. A large majority were of Scotch-Irish or Scottish ancestry, and were Presbyterians, though nearly one-half came to America after 1800. On balance, then, the major social difference between Edgeworth and its neighboring club, Allegheny Country, was a slightly smaller percentage of men from colonial families. In large measure, however, they tended to complement one another as attractions for the upper classes in the western suburbs.

In addition to the above clubs, there were several others of varying importance, although no detailed analysis of them will be presented. The Pittsburgh Field Club had been organized in Brushton, in the East End of Pittsburgh in 1889. The land for this golf and cricket club was donated by Henry Clay Frick, and it attracted primarily the new elite families of the area. In 1913, Frick sold the land to his coal company, and the club was relocated in O'Hara Township.[32] Although no membership lists were available, the club is now popularly assumed to be made up largely of wealthy Roman Catholics. There was also the Sportsmen's Association of Western Pennsylvania, a riding and hunt club. Organized in 1874, it had a large membership of both old and new families, but it is difficult to make exact comparisons with other clubs, since its membership lists ceased to be published some twenty years before the appearance of the Social Register.[33] Similar was the Sportsmen's Association of Cheat Mountain, which had been formed in 1886 on land purchased for hunting purposes in West Virginia. Fewer members of older, more prestigious families belonged to this club.[34]

The final social club to be considered in Pittsburgh, the Twentieth Century Club, was of seminal importance. Unlike the other clubs considered thus far, this was neither a men's club nor a club for the whole family, but a literary and social club for women. As such it attracted large numbers of wives and daughters in the most prestigious iron and steel families. With 86 percent of its iron and steel family members in 1905 listed in the Social Register, the Twentieth Century Club ranked slightly below the august Pittsburgh and Allegheny Country Clubs, yet was above the Duquesne Club and several suburban country clubs. The cultural and economic backgrounds of its members also reflected this orientation. Eighty percent were of English, Scotch-Irish or Scottish ancestry, and 83 percent were Presbyterian or Episcopalian. More significantly, nearly 80 percent descended from pre-Civil War elite families, while 63 percent of the families for whom information was available arrived in America prior to 1800. The Twentieth Century Club assumed a position of social importance among upper-class women rivaling that of the Pittsburgh Club among men.

The club structure of Pittsburgh, then, hewed closely to the image of urban clubs on a national level. With a full range of both urban and suburban clubs, graded and ranked according to social prestige, it was an effective instrument for assimilating newer elites into the older family structure. In a city like Pittsburgh, where so many newer elites rose to wealth and power, these upper-class clubs performed a yeoman service, providing a sense of tradition and stability in a frenetic age.

MARRIAGE

> In the first generation thee must do well, in the second, marry well, in the third breed well, then the fourth will take care of itself.[35]

More intimate and important than the clubs of Pittsburgh as urban upper-class institutions, were the intermarriage patterns. Whereas families might be willing, albeit grudgingly, to share their social clubs and neighborhoods with those whom they considered inferior, the final barrier to fall to these new families was marriage itself. For complete social acceptance a newly rich family must, of necessity, include marriage into older upper-class families. This important area of social contact, however, has been given little systematic investigation by the leading social commentators on the upper class.[36] The principal reason for this probably has to do with the difficulty in collecting comprehensive data on marriages and then analyzing the information properly.

It was decided, for the purposes of this study, to allow the families to group themselves, on the basis of their own marriage choices, into four basic groups: *core families,* who had at least four endogamous marriages among themselves; *non-core upper-class families* who had from one to three marriages into the core families; *marginal upper-class families* who had no marriages into the core families, but married into the non-core upper-class families or into prestigious families from other cities; and *non-upper-class or elite families,* who for a variety of reasons had no significant marriage pattern.

After allowing the families to group themselves by a somewhat independent variable—marriage—these self-defining categories were checked against other variables (Social Register listings and club memberships) as supportive evidence. The result is a rather clear social class demarcation within the economic upper class—the iron and steel elite—with the core families at the top and the elite families at the bottom of the pyramid.

THE CORE FAMILIES

There is a rather famous doggerel rhyme on Philadelphia's upper classes, called the "Philadelphia Rosary":

> Morris, Norris, Rush and Chew
> Drinker, Dallas, Coxe and Pugh,
> Wharton, Pepper, Pennypacker,
> Willing, Shippen and Markoe.[37]

These names refer to what was, at one time, a group of upper-class Philadelphia families who belonged to the same clubs, married with one another, and were the "core" families of that city's early-nineteenth-century upper class.

In Pittsburgh, there were some sixty-eight families, forty-three of them steel families, who belonged to the same clubs and intermarried extensively with one another. Generally the oldest families in the city, along with several of the newer ones who had risen to prominence in the middle and late nineteenth century, were Pittsburgh's core upper-class families.

Two important related characteristics of the phenomenon of endogamy are the relative frequency and density of these marriages. Each measures a slightly different aspect of the various families' relationships to one another. Within the group of forty-three core iron and steel families, there were significant variations in the relative frequency of endogamous marriage. Although each family had to average a minimum of one endogamous marriage for each of the four generations considered, one family averaged as many as six endogamous marriages per generation. Table 28 shows the average frequency of endogamous marriage per generation for each of the core families.

TABLE 28
Frequency of Endogamous Marriages for Pittsburgh Core Families

6 Endogamous Marriages per Generation		*2 Endogamous Marriages per Generation*	
Robinson		Bailey	Painter
		Burgwin	Richardson
5 Endogamous Marriages per Generation		Herron	Singer
Laughlin		Howe	Smith
Brown		Mellon	Verner
		Metcalf	
4 Endogamous Marriages per Generation			
Bakewell			
Blair		*1 Endogamous Marriage per Generation*	
Childs		Allderdice	Moorhead
Dilworth		Bissell	Neale
Oliver		Cassidy	Nimick
		Chalfant	Park
3 Endogamous Marriages per Generation		Dickson	Phillips
Irwin	Scully	Lockhart	Walker
Jones	Speer	Lupton	Zug
Miller	Wood	Lyon	Black
Rea		Kennedy	

As is evident from Table 28, some of the core families were more essential to the maintenance and functioning of the upper-class kinship system than were others. The Robinson, Laughlin, Brown, Bakewell, Blair, Childs, Dilworth and Oliver families, having between sixteen and twenty-four endogamous marriages over the four generations considered were obviously a core group within the core families. On the other hand, those with between four and eight endogamous marriages were more clearly on the outer fringes of these core families.

Yet, the large number of endogamous marriages of some of these core families was a direct result of the fact that they operated with far larger families and kinship units (or that the present investigator was unable to find more marriage and kinship information on some of the families). Of importance, then, is the question of density. That is, given the number of possible marriages for each family, what percentage of these were endogamous? This is important since it indicates the degree to which a family facing a marriage choice will opt for endogamy—regardless of whether that family has one child or a dozen children to marry. Table 29 shows some surprising results. The Bailey and Lupton families, at the fringe of the core families in terms of frequency of endogamous marriage, were at the very core in terms of density, with over 60 percent of the marriages to other core families. Whereas the frequency of endogamous marriages measures the relative importance of that particular family to the broader upper-class marriage system, density measures the rather opposite aspect of the importance of the upper-class kinship system for each family.

Of those families with over sixteen endogamous marriages, one family, the Robinsons, had more than 50 percent of their total marriages within the endogamous system. Most ranged between 30 and 50 percent endogamous marriages, with two families below that percentage (Dilworth and Oliver). Since most of those families with a high frequency of endogamous marriage generally had less than one-half of their total number of marriages within the core upper-class system, the question remains as to the nature of these exogamous marriages. Some of these were to non-core upper class families in Pittsburgh; others were cosmopolitan marriages to upper-class families in other cities. Before considering the phenomenon of these exogamous marriages more closely, however, it is necessary to establish the relative social standing of the core upper class group vis-à-vis the other marital groups in Pittsburgh.

The first important variable is Social Register listings, followed by club memberships, which show a pattern establishing the upper-class nature of these core families. They not only had a significantly higher percentage of their families

TABLE 29
Density of Endogamous Marriage in Pittsburgh Core Families

60% Endogamous		*20-29% Endogamous*	
Lupton	Bailey	Bissell	Moorhead
		Chalfant	Oliver
50-59% Endogamous		Dilworth	Scully
Dickson	Robinson	Lockhart	Verner
Richardson	Speer		Zug
40-49% Endogamous		*10-19% Endogamous*	
Black	Irwin	Herron	Neale
Blair	Jones	Kennedy	Park
Cassidy	Lyon	Mellon	Walker
Howe	Phillips		
	Wood	*Less than 10% Endogamous*	
30-39% Endogamous		Nimick	
Bakewell	Metcalf		
Brown	Painter		
Burgwin	Rea		
Childs	Singer		
Laughlin	Smith		

listed in the Social Register than did the other family groups (100 percent); but in those clubs with the highest relative social ranking (as determined by percentage of members listed in the Social Register) the core families consistently had higher rates of membership than the other family groups in the city. The three most prestigious clubs in the city showed the core families with significantly higher percentages of membership than the other family groups. Table 30 demonstrates the percentage of the various family groups holding memberships in the major clubs of Pittsburgh, along with the percentage listed in the Social Register.

Viewed in comparative fashion with the other family groupings, the core families would appear to be rather solidly at the apex of Pittsburgh's upper class. With percentages of listing in the Social Register and membership in prestigious clubs consistently above those of the other groups, there would seem to be little question that these forty-three families, along with twenty-five or so non-steel families, were the city's social upper class. It was into this group of families that new elites must marry if they wished to become an intimate part of the upper class of Pittsburgh.

What about the relative social status within the core families themselves? Did some families, especially those with a high frequency of endogamous marriage, enjoy a higher relative social status? Or was their endogamous marriage frequency merely idiosyncratic? The same questions must be addressed in terms of those families with a high density of endogamous marriage.

The figures in Table 31 indicate that those families with the highest frequency of endogamous marriage among the core families (sixteen to twenty-four marriages) were, in fact, of significantly higher social status than the other two groups. In the most prestigious clubs (Pittsburgh, Pittsburgh Golf, Allegheny Country Club, Rolling Rock, and Duquesne), all of the families with the greatest frequency of endogamy held memberships. Although their percentages of membership were lower in clubs of lower status, it was still generally above that of the other two family groupings. The degree of social difference between those families with eight to fifteen endogamous marriages and those with four to seven is less clear. In general, however, those with eight to fifteen endogamous marriages have slightly higher relative social status, particularly when viewing their membership in Allegheny Country, Pittsburgh Golf and Rolling Rock clubs.

Analysis of relative social status by the density of endogamous marriage, however, produces a nearly inverse relationship of these core families. Those families with the highest density of endogamous marriage have a markedly lower percentage of membership in prestigious clubs than do the other two family groups. Although the status relationship between those with 30 to 49 percent endogamous marriages and those with 10 to 29 percent is less uniform, generally those with the lowest density of endogamous marriage have a slightly higher relative social status. This reflects the accuracy of the proposition, stated above, that those families with the highest density of endogamous marriage find marriage to another core family to be of great importance to their own family—while those with the

TABLE 30
Endogamous Marriage Groups as Related to Social Register and Club Membership

Family Group		Social Register, %		Club Membership				
				Pittsburgh Club, %	Pittsburgh Golf, %	Allegheny Country C., %	Duquesne Club, %	Union Club, %
Core	*N*=43	43	100	91	81	88	97	77
Non-Core	*N*=60	60	72	57	45	35	83	52
Marginal	*N*=33	33	55	24	15	15	82	19
Elite	*N*=71	71	28	10	10	10	59	23
TOTAL	*N*=207							

Family Group		Club Membership					
		Rolling Rock, %	Oakmont Country C., %	Edgeworth, %	Edgewood, %	PAA, %	Pittsburgh Country C., %
Core	*N*=43	65	51	58	5	28	63
Non-Core	*N*=60	30	24	17	5	30	40
Marginal	*N*=33	9	18	15	3	15	39
Elite	*N*=71	7	14	6	4	13	23
TOTAL	*N*=207						

TABLE 31

Social Status as Related to Frequency of Endogamous Marriages Among Core Families

Family Group by No. of Endogamous Marriages		Pittsburgh Club, %	Pittsburgh Golf, %	Allegheny Country, %	Duquesne, %	Union, %	Rolling Rock, %	Oakmont, %
16-24	(*N*=8)	100	100	100	100	88	100	88
8-15	(*N*=18)	83	83	100	89	73	67	56
4-7	(*N*=17)	94	71	65	100	76	47	35

Family Group		Edgeworth, %	Edgewood, %	PAA, %	Pittsburgh Country, %
16-24	(*N*=8)	88	0	25	75
8-15	(*N*=18)	50	5	33	56
4-7	(*N*=17)	47	6	24	71

TABLE 32
Relative Social Status as Related to Density of Endogamous Marriage Among Core Families

Family Group by Density		Pittsburgh Club, %	Pittsburgh Golf, %	Allegheny Country, %	Duquesne, %	Union, %	Rolling Rock, %
50% & more	(*N*=6)	67	67	67	80	67	50
30-49%	(*N*=19)	95	79	95	100	85	74
-10-29%	(*N*=16)	94	88	100	95	75	69

Family Group		Oakmont, %	Edgeworth, %	Edgewood, %	P.A.A., %	Pittsburgh Country, %
50% & more	(*N*=6)	50	33	17	17	67
30-49%	(*N*=19)	42	63	–	26	58
-10-29%	(*N*=16)	69	69	6	44	69

greatest frequency of endogamous marriage are more important to the kinship system as a whole and reflect a higher relative social status within that system.

As Table 33 indicates, there was a rather high degree of correlation between those families with a high frequency of endogamous marriage among the core families, and those with a high frequency of marriage to non-core families. Sixty-four percent of those families with two to seven marriages to non-core upper-class families, also had sixteen to twenty-four endogamous marriages to core families. At the same time, 75 percent of the core families with a high frequency of endogamous marriage also had two or more marriages to non-core families. Conversely, nearly three-quarters of those families with only one or no marriages to non-core families also had the lowest frequency of endogamous marriages to core families (four to seven endogamous marriages). Thus, it is important to reanalyze the forty-three core families in terms of their relative importance to the upper-class kinship system in Pittsburgh.

TABLE 33
Number of Endogamous Marriages Among Core Families as Related to Number of Non-Core Marriages

X	16-24 Endogamous Marriages *N*=8	8-15 Endogamous Marriages *N*=18	4-7 Endogamous Marriages *N*=17	Totals
4-7 Non-Core Marriages	25%	6%	12%	
N=5	40%	20%	40%	100%
2-3 Non-Core Marriages	30%	33%	47%	
N=18	24%	33%	44%	100%
1 Non-Core Marriage	25%	39%	12%	
N=11	18%	64%	18%	100%
0 Non-Core Marriages	0%	22%	29%	
N=9	0%	44%	56%	100%
TOTALS	100%	100%	100%	X

The core families may be conveniently grouped into four separate categories in relation to their importance to the upper-class system. The first, and most important, group of six families are those with *both* sixteen to twenty-four endogamous marriages *and* two or more marriages to non-core families. The second group of five families are those which have *either* sixteen to twenty-four core marriages *or* four or more non-core marriages. The third group of nineteen families had *either* eight to fifteen core marriages *or* two to three non-core marriages. The fourth and final group were those with four to seven core marriages and one or less non-core marriages.[38]

As Table 34 indicates, there were subtle, but real, social gradations among the four groups of families. Groups I and II were highest in status, with the next two groups ranked below them. This may be seen more clearly by reanalyzing the figures presented in the table. The average percentage of membership of families in Group I in those clubs with the highest social prestige was 90 percent. The average percentage of membership in these clubs for families in Group II was 86 percent; of Group III, 80 percent; and Group IV, 71 percent. Yet, even when all clubs are included, those families in Group I showed the highest percentage of membership (71 percent), compared to 70 percent for those in Group II, 65 percent in Group III and 56 percent in Group IV. As befitted the status of families in Groups I and II, they not only possessed the highest relative social status, but were also the most gregarious, marrying and clubbing extensively, not only with other core families, but also with those of more marginal status.

Thus, if marriage into the core families was generally the apex of Pittsburgh's social upper class, it was essentially a group of eleven iron and steel families which served as principal social arbiters. These families provided the essential cement which held the system together and allowed it to function—combining high social status and frequency of endogamy; they had a marked propensity to reach out to the most deserving of the new men and families for admission into the highest reaches of the social upper class in the city.

NON-CORE UPPER-CLASS FAMILIES

The non-core upper-class families had at least one, but less than four marriages into these core families. The guiding principal here is that one marriage by a non-core family into a core family—since it was the most intimate form of social contact—should be sufficient to establish that a non-core family had become part of the upper class (though they would generally be newer to the scene than the core families, and consequently less highly regarded). This conclusion was borne out by an analysis of the social and cultural backgrounds of these families, and by their Social Register listings and club memberships.

There were significant social, cultural and economic distinctions between the core and non-core upper class families in Pittsburgh. The most important area of difference was in the nineteenth-century economic backgrounds of these families. Where 91 percent of the core families emanated from pre-Civil War elites, only 58 percent of the non-core families did so. Twenty-seven percent of the latter group came from nineteenth-century native American middle-class origins, while 10 percent were from immigrant working-class and middle-class families, and 5

TABLE 34

Social Status as Related to the Importance of Core Families to Upper-Class Kinship System*

Family Group by Importance to System		Percentage of Group Holding Membership in Club					
		Pittsburgh Club	Pittsburgh Golf	Allegheny Country	Duquesne	Union	Rolling Rock
Family Group I	(*N*=6)	100	83	100	100	100	83
Family Group II	(*N*=5)	100	80	100	100	100	67
Family Group III	(*N*=19)	84	84	89	95	63	72
Family Group IV	(*N*=13)	92	62	77	100	77	54

Family Group		Oakmont	Edgeworth	Edgewood	P.A.A.	Pittsburgh Country
Group I	(*N*=6)	67	67	0	17	67
Group II	(*N*=5)	50	50	0	33	83
Group III	(*N*=19)	56	72	0	39	67
Group IV	(*N*=13)	31	38	8	23	54

*"Importance of core families to upper-class kinship system" has been defined as follows: Family Group I, sixteen to twenty-four endogamous core marriages ***and*** two or more marriages to non-core families. Group II, ***either*** sixteen to twenty-four endogamous core marriages ***or*** four or more marriages to non-core families. Group III, ***either*** eight to fifteen endogamous core marriages ***or*** two to three non-core marriages. Group IV, four to seven endogamous core marriages and one or fewer non-core marriages.

percent derived from poverty backgrounds. More significantly, a larger number of the non-core families, although having been in America for several generations, did not arrive in Pittsburgh until the later nineteenth century. Thus, these non-core families were in several senses "new" families of lesser longevity in the Pittsburgh area when compared to the core families.

Although ranking lower in most club memberships and Social Register listings than the core families, they were consistently above the percentages for the marginal and elite families. Many of the non-core families who lacked Social Register listings, or who did not belong to the more prestigious clubs of the city, were from families who had left Pittsburgh for other cities. Thus, although solidly upper class, these latter families were no longer indigenous to Pittsburgh, and they no longer retained local standing and importance.

The relatively high social standing of the non-core families was also demonstrated by their ability to marry into upper-class families of other cities: the Morris, Bingham, Biddle, Drexel and Robertson families of Philadelphia; the Schley, Rhinelander, Grace, Perkins, Rockefeller, Mills, Astor, Aldrich and Livingston families of New York; the Crosby and Merrick families of Boston; and others. The non-core upper-class families, then, were solidly upper class—though somewhat less important and prestigious than the core families, at least on the Pittsburgh scene.

In general terms, the social status of the non-core families was acquired through marriage with core families. On that basis it is possible to categorize and rank order these sixty non-core families according to the frequency of their marriages to core families. Similarly, these non-core families played an important social arbiter role of their own with regard to marginal upper-class families, although this was less clearly defined than among their core family counterparts. Just as several core families functioned as social arbiters at the top of the status pyramid in Pittsburgh, several non-core families performed a similar service at the middle echelons.

As Table 35 indicates, those non-core families with three marriages to core families (that is, those closest to categorization as core families themselves) had far higher percentages of membership in the leading social clubs of Pittsburgh. The non-core families with two core marriages tended generally to have higher membership totals than those with only one marriage, but were substantially below the first group. Thus, the principle of endogamous marriage to core families would appear to provide a sensitive and accurate barometer to rank non-core families according to social status.

In addition to their "mobile" marriage pattern of ties with core upper-class families, the non-core upper class also played an important role in the upper-class system as a bridge between the core, non-core and marginal upper-class families. Thus, some families had marriages to core families, to other non-core families, and also to the marginal upper-class group below them. The non-core families were thus arranged according to the importance of each family to the functioning of the entire upper-class system, ranking them according to the frequency of their

TABLE 35
Social Status as Related to Frequency of Core Marriages for Non-Core Families

Family Group by Number of Core Marriages	Percentage of Group Holding Membership in Club					
	Social Register	Pittsburgh Club	Pittsburgh Golf	Allegheny Country	Duquesne	Union
Group I (3 core marriages) N=19	75	74	74	53	79	63
Group II (2 core marriages) N=21	67	52	38	33	81	48
Group III (1 core marriage) N=20	70	45	25	20	90	45

Family Group	Oakmont	Rolling Rock	Edgeworth	Edgewood	P.A.A.	Pittsburgh Country
Group I (N=19)	26	47	21	16	37	47
Group II (N=21)	29	19	19	0	29	33
Group III (N=20)	25	25	10	0	25	40

marriages to these three groups.[39] After arranging them into three groups according to marital frequency, this was compared to Social Register listings and membership in social clubs. The results, although somewhat uneven, are basically similar to those found for core families.

All of those families with five or more total upper-class marriages were listed in the Social Register (compared to 61 percent of those with two or three marriages and 73 percent of those with only one or two). A clearer pattern emerges, however, when we look at the average membership for each family group in the social clubs. The group with the most frequent upper-class marriages averaged 51 percent memberships in the seven most prestigious clubs and 44 percent in all eleven clubs. Those with two to three marriages averaged 48 percent in the former and 41 percent in the latter. Finally, the group with the lowest frequency of upper-class marriage was also lowest in average membership, averaging 43 percent in the seven prestigious clubs and 36 percent in all eleven clubs.

The non-core upper-class families, then, although demonstrably lower in social status and prestige than the core families, performed a similar role and function within the upper-class system. In both groups, those families which tended to participate most fully in upper-class marital endogamy were also those which participated most fully in other upper-class social institutions and could be clearly rank-ordered as to social status according to their marital choices.

MARGINAL UPPER-CLASS FAMILIES

The first two family groups would appear to be clearly represented in the Pittsburgh upper-class system. The third group, the marginal upper-class families, are precisely what the name implies—marginal to that indigenous system. It is much less clear the extent to which they actually did function within the upper class of Pittsburgh. The makeup of this marginal group, however, is complex and somewhat difficult to analyze. In practice, the marginal families would seem to break down into about three subgroups. Those with the highest prestige, at least outside the community, were those who married with upper-class families from other cities. At the next level were those upwardly mobile families who, in the third and fourth generations, married into a non-core family which itself was just moving into marriage alliances with the core families. Finally, there were those families who had married one of the non-core families in the first or second generation, when both families were of relatively low prestige.

Many of those marginal families in the first subgroup did not remain long in Pittsburgh. For example, the Abbott, Bache and Converse families were all old, prestigious east coast families. Although they did not remain in Pittsburgh, they married very well in their home areas: these included the Vauclain and Bingham families of Philadelphia, the Crosby and Peabody families of Boston, the Worrall and Morgan families of New York and the Chisholm and Hanna families of Cleveland. They appeared to have high prestige, but did not stay in Pittsburgh long enough to establish marital alliances there.

TABLE 36

Social Status as Related to the Importance of Non-Core Families to Upper-Class Kinship System*

Family Group by Number of Upper-Class Marriages	Percentage of Group in					
	Social Register	Pittsburgh Club	Pittsburgh Golf	Allegheny Country	Duquesne	Union
Group I (5-6 upper-class marriages)						
N=7	100	57	71	43	86	43
Group II (2-3 upper-class marriages)						
N=23	61	61	43	39	78	65
Group III (1-2 upper-class marriages)						
N-30	73	53	37	33	90	47

Family Group	Rolling Rock	Oakmont	Edgeworth	Edgewood	P.A.A.	Pittsburgh Country
Group I (*N*=7)	43	14	14	14	57	43
Group II (*N*=23)	35	39	13	9	26	30
Group III (*N*=30)	20	20	20	0	27	43

*"Importance of non-core families to upper-class system" is defined according to the total number of marriages to upper-class families (core, non-core, and marginal upper class). They are then ranked according to the number of these marriages for each family.

On the other hand, there were several rather old Pittsburgh families who never married into the core families, though they seemed to have had all the other requirements for upper-class status. These families would include the Hussey family (who were married to several non-core families, and who belonged to all the best social clubs), the Darlington family (who did not marry Pittsburghers, but belonged to all the "right" clubs in the city), and several others.

The final group of marginal families would seem to be of lower overall prestige. Although a few had marriages to fairly prestigious families outside of Pittsburgh (the Martin and Grace families of New York, the Osborn and Edson families of Cleveland, the Glass family of Wheeling), their club membership patterns and Social Register listings would indicate a less-than-solid upper-class standing. Thus the group as a whole must be considered marginal. As such, its overall prestige (reflected in Social Register listings and club memberships) in addition to the marriage pattern, places them significantly below the core and non-core upper-class families, but markedly above the elite families.

In their social and cultural backgrounds, the marginal upper-class families were dramatically different from the core and non-core upper-class families. They differed most substantially from the core families, but were also at striking variance in many ways from the non-core group. Whereas the Scotch-Irish had been the dominant group with both the core and non-core families, with the English the next largest group, this situation was reversed among the marginal families—with the number of English nearly twice that of Scotch-Irish.

In religion, the difference was less striking: Presbyterians were the largest denomination in all three groups. The ratio of Presbyterians among the marginal group, however, was somewhat less than among the non-core families and substantially less than the core families. The time of family arrival in America also revealed important variations. Whereas none of the core families and only 9 percent of the non-core families had arrived after 1850, fully 24 percent of the marginal families for whom information was available had done so.

Finally, the family economic backgrounds of the three groups was quite different. The dichotomy was most striking with the core families, where 91 percent emanated from pre-Civil War elites, compared to only 50 percent of the marginal families in this category. Although the non-core families contained 58 percent from elite origins, the major variation with the marginal families occurred in the native and immigrant categories. Whereas 27 percent of the non-core families came from the native American working class and middle class, and only 10 percent were immigrants, the marginal families had 29 percent in the immigrant category and 21 percent native.

The social and cultural distinctions between the marginal families and the core and non-core families, however, become more graphic if the marginal families are divided into two groups: indigenous Pittsburghers and late nineteenth-century migrants. Two-thirds of the marginal families were rooted in the local area. In ethnic and religious terms, as might be expected, they correlated closely to the core and non-core families—with 60 percent Scottish or Scotch-Irish, and Presbyterian. In family economic background and arrival in America, however, they deviated widely. Only 39 percent were from pre-Civil War elite origins, with another 39 percent from the immigrant working and middle classes and 22 percent from the native American middle class. Correspondingly, nearly 70 percent arrived during the nineteenth century. Thus, although sharing similar cultural and religious origins with the older Pittsburgh upper-class families, they were newer to America and they achieved wealth and position at a later date.

Those marginal families who migrated from elsewhere in the late nineteenth century were more similar to the core families in economic background, but differed significantly in cultural areas. Seventy-eight percent of this group were of English origin, and only 11 percent were Scotch-Irish, while 40 percent were Episcopalian and only 10 percent were Presbyterian. Nearly two-thirds of these families had arrived in America before 1750, well before the bulk of the Pittsburgh upper-class families had immigrated to America. In economic background, however, 70 percent were from pre-Civil War elite families, comparing favorably with the core and non-core families. The marginal families, then, comprised at least two separate and distinctive groups. In order to fully understand their place and role in the Pittsburgh upper-class social system, it will be necessary to continue to separate the two groups for analytic purposes.

The social class differences between the two groups of marginal families appears somewhat surprising at first glance. The indigenous Pittsburghers, despite newer wealth and more recent immigration to America, showed generally higher percentages of both Social Register listings and club memberships. However, it should be recalled that many of these elite migrants either did not establish residence in Pittsburgh or they lived there for only a short period (never relinquishing their social ties and status in their former areas). The Pittsburgh Social Register and the city's social clubs are an indigenous listing; when families are mobile, they escape classification. The large number of marriages of this migrant group to families listed in the Social Registers of their home communities, however, would imply that they were of ultimately higher social prestige than the indigenous group. When an elite migrant family, such as Allderdice, chose to establish permanent residence in Pittsburgh, it was able to move rapidly into core family status. The marginal families, as the name implies, were truly marginal to Pittsburgh's upper-class system, some because of their late arrival to elite status, others because of their geographical mobility and lack of propinquity.

ELITE, NON-UPPER-CLASS FAMILIES

The group of families classified as "elite, non-upper class" number seventy families who do not have the formal marital requirements for any of the foregoing three categories. We assume that they are not in the upper-class social group in Pittsburgh. In all but a few cases, the outside data from Social Register listings

TABLE 37

Social Class as Related to Indigeneous and Migrant Marginal Family Groups in Pittsburgh

	Percentage of Group in					
Family Group	Social Register	Pittsburgh Club	Pittsburgh Golf	Allegheny Country	Duquesne	Union
Group I: Indigenous N=21	62	29	19	14	81	52
Group II: Migrant N=11	45	9	9	18	73	18

Family Group	Rolling Rock	Oakmont	Edgeworth	Edgewood	P.A.A.	Pittsburgh Country
Group I: N=21	14	24	19	0	14	48
Group II: N=11	0	0	9	9	27	27

and club memberships would support this assumption. The overall percentages for the elite families were significantly below those of the core, non-core and marginal upper-class family groups in the city.

There were a few families placed in this category, however, whose marriage patterns could not be discerned, or who simply did not produce a family. On balance, this subgroup (which included the Hammond, McCandless, Buchanan, C. L. Taylor, Quay and Rhodes families, among others) seemed to possess upper-class standing. Their club memberships indicate high prestige, and all were listed in the Social Register. Thus, in their case, the marriage patterns were perhaps somewhat deceiving. A few other families, more nouveau riche, seemed to be marginally upper class. They belonged to a fair number of the better clubs, but had only recently risen to this status; and marriages to core and non-core upper-class families were probably at least a generation away. Outside of these fifteen or so families, though, the elite families were outside even the margins of the upper class.

Analysis of the social and cultural backgrounds of these elite families makes clear their nearly total variance with Pittsburgh's upper-class families. In ethnicity, there was a disproportionate number of Germans among this group, while the Scotch-Irish were drastically reduced. If Pittsburgh was a relative haven of social acceptance for a former cultural minority like the Scotch-Irish, this evidently did not transfer as easily to the Germans. Although a large number were able to rise to elite status in the city, relatively few having German ancestry were accepted as social equals.

In religion there was less variation, with a substantial number of Presbyterians among the group. Of significance, however, was the higher percentage of Catholics included here and the only Jewish steel-making family. Just as Germanic ethnicity appeared to limit one's chances for social advancement, so did adherence to a non-Protestant religion. This is, of course, not surprising, given the general tenor of nineteenth-century society; yet it is significant to note that even after four generations of elite status there was little movement to fully accept the descendants of these families.

In economic background, only 23 percent were from pre-Civil War elite families (many German in ethnicity), while most of the rest were either native or among the immigrant working or middle classes. The vast majority came to America after 1800, with 35 percent arriving after 1850. Although there were many families of fairly recent arrival in America among this group, there were not many more than among the marginal families. Ethnicity and religion appeared to be a more dominant inhibiting factor than was recency upon the American scene.

Since these elite families were such a diverse group, and since their general social class standing was so low, it is difficult to determine much else from their data. It is possible, however, to divide them into three groups, which will give some indication of the upper-class social selection process: The German group, consisting of eighteen families; the pre-Civil War elite group, excluding the Germans, consisting of ten families; and the remaining forty-two families.

TABLE 38

Social Status of Three Family Subgroups Within the Elite, Non-Upper-Class Families

Family Group		Percentage of Group in					
		Social Register	Pittsburgh Club	Pittsburgh Golf	Allegheny Country	Duquesne	Union
Group I: Germans	*N*=18	11	6	0	0	72	11
Group II: Pre-Civil War	*N*=10	80	10	40	40	80	80
Group III: Other	*N*=42	24	10	7	5	31	10

Family Group		Rolling Rock	Oakmont	Edgeworth	Edgewood	P.A.A.	Pittsburgh Country
Group I:	*N*=18	11	17	0	11	28	22
Group II:	*N*=10	20	30	10	10	40	60
Group III:	*N*=42	2	7	2	0	2	12

In Social Register listings, the Germans, with only 11 percent being listed, were well behind the pre-Civil War elite families (which had 80 percent) and even behind the other assorted forty-two families (which had 24 percent). In club memberships, the Germans lagged significantly behind the pre-Civil War elite families, averaging 14 percent membership in the most prestigious clubs and 16 percent in all clubs, compared to 40 percent and 38 percent, respectively, in these categories by the pre-Civil War elite group. In this category the Germans were, however, well ahead of the remaining forty-two families, (who ranked, respectively, 8 percent and 9 percent). Many of these latter families, however, had not remained in Pittsburgh long enough to have attempted admission.

In summary, then, the position of the elite, non-upper-class families vis-à-vis the three upper-class family groups would appear to fall into three categories: those, like the Germans and Catholics (oftentimes embodied in the same person), who were denied admittance to the upper class on the basis of ethnic and religious prejudice; the old, pre-Civil War elite families whose failure to marry into the system was not consistent with other social factors concerning them (so that it must be termed idiosyncratic); and finally, a third group which either arrived in Pittsburgh late in the nineteenth century, left Pittsburgh after a few years of economic success, or both.

With only a few exceptions, then, an analysis of 2,525 marriages among the iron and steel elite in Pittsburgh indicates a fairly strong four-part division of the 207 families involved in the industry. When rank ordered on the basis of status, endogamous marriage patterns correlate strongly with other social variables to provide a more intricate and accurate structure of upper class in the city.

THE PITTSBURGH IRON AND STEEL ELITE—LOCALS OR COSMOPOLITANS?

To what degree did these Pittsburgh iron and steel elites (most of whom became members of that city's upper class) begin to exhibit more cosmopolitan traits in the late nineteenth and early twentieth centuries? Baltzell, in his book on the Philadelphia upper classes, feels that they became part of a "national aristocracy" by the end of the nineteenth century. Can the same thing be said about the Pittsburgh upper classes who derived from iron and steel backgrounds?

Throughout most of the nineteenth century, there was relatively little contact between elite and upper-class groups across city lines. Most of those connections which did exist were of a business nature. It would be too much to list or specify all the various outside business connections of the Pittsburgh iron and steel families, but a few examples of these intercity business connections should indicate what was involved: the Wood family of Pittsburgh owned several mills in Philadelphia and Delaware; the Shoenberger family started iron mills all over Pennsylvania and in Wheeling and Cincinnati; the Eaton family owned an oil well supply business in New York City; the Flagler family of Boston had iron interests in Pittsburgh and Connecticut; the Converse family of Boston had interests in that city and in Pittsburgh and New York City; the Woodside family owned a large snuff-manufacturing business in Philadelphia.

The bulk of the families involved in the iron and steel industry in Pittsburgh during the late nineteenth century, however, remained strictly provincial, with few marital or business connections outside the city. The coming of the twentieth century heralded a pronounced loosening of this parochialism. Several factors played an important part in creating this new atmosphere, the most important of which were business, schooling, and summer resorts.

An important new factor with the dawn of the twentieth century was the extensive nationalization of business, occuring in particularly pronounced fashion in the steel industry. The process by which this occurred along with its detailed effect on the steel families, will be discussed in a separate study. At this point, only the main features of the change and its effect on the steel families will be analyzed. A critical result of this nationalization of the steel industry was the degree to which the older iron and steel families lost much of their earlier day-to-day control of the industry. In the case of those families who did retain a strong management interest in their twentieth-century firms, they found themselves becoming increasingly cosmopolitan in their social relationships. Extensive intercity business relations demanded a more extensive series of intercity social connections.

Tied to the consolidation of businesses was the corresponding nationalization of several social institutions, including schools and summer resorts. The general national development of boarding schools and universities was discussed above. Here, attention will be focused on their impact on the Pittsburgh iron and steel families, and on its relationship to cosmopolitan marriage patterns. Because of the lack of consistent data, summer resorts will not be considered in any organized fashion.

Among the core families of Pittsburgh there was a rather high dispersion of attendance at the major educational institutions, along with continuing attendance at local schools. There was a definite shift in the educational pattern for the core families' children, beginning in the late nineteenth century—a shift away from local academies, such as Sewickley and Shadyside, and toward the newly nationalized eastern prep schools. St. Paul's, in Concord, New Hampshire, became the special preserve of Pittsburgh's core families, with at least one-third of them sending sons there. None of the other prep schools even approached this high percentage, and if information were more readily available, St. Paul's percentage would probably be even higher.

At the college level, Yale ranked as the favorite among these core families, with 70 percent sending sons there. Following Yale were Princeton with 49 percent, Harvard with 33 percent, and Penn with 16 percent. Other schools, including local ones, attracted some 87 percent of the core families at one time or another. These figures, however, tend to mask an important generational pattern. In the first generation, that of the family founders, few attended college. Those who did obtain some college education generally did so either at a local college, or at one of the specialized technical schools—such as Lehigh, Renssaeler, or the Sheffield School at Yale. Only a few, such as the Browns, Burgwins and the Bissells, attended the more elite, ivy league schools.

In the second generation, among those who came of age in the 1870s and 1880s, most went to college—but primarily to local schools of one kind or another. The first major shift towards prestige national schools began in the 1890s, when second and third generation sons began attending Yale University. There was a twofold purpose in this. In the first place, it was an emblem of national prestige sorely desired by the core families, many of whom were of Scotch-Irish background. Second, the Sheffield Scientific School at Yale provided a fine technical education needed by families who still controlled their steel mills, a type of education not given at other prestige institutions.[40]

A second important shift took place around World War I, accelerating into the 1920s and beyond. This shift saw the general replacement of Yale by Princeton as the principal status school for upper-class families in the city. Several factors initiated this change, including the financial problems of Princeton, the low social standing of Sheffield School at Yale, and the mediator role of the Laughlin family. The relatively low social status of Sheffield School at Yale was due to its special status as a three-year course outside the regular school curriculum. In no sense was Sheffield a part of the Yale social environment. The situation was best portrayed by Marcia Davenport, in her novel, *Valley of Decision.* The protagonist, Paul, was attending Sheffield School at Yale, and wrote his family concerning his experiences: "There was a big crowd of men out for the tryouts [rowing crew] . . . and I didn't think I had much of a chance. They don't notice us much over at Sheff, you know. They leave us pretty much to ourselves, which suits us all right."[41]

The Pittsburgh boys from core families who went to Sheffield were not able to participate fully in Yale's social life, and, most critically, were not eligible for membership in the more prestigious eating clubs. For families intent upon establishing a parity with families from seacoast cities, this was a serious problem. It was made doubly serious by the fact that a technical education for their sons was no longer of utmost necessity. With less influence in the direct management of the steel companies, the technical expertise supplied by Sheffield could scarcely supplant the desire for high social status in these families.

This desire to secure a "gentleman's education" for their sons corresponded with unfolding financial problems at Princeton. Long a strongly denominational college dominated by upper-class Presbyterian families from New York, New Jersey and Philadelphia, Princeton experienced the first stirrings of dissatisfaction by elite families from other areas in 1900.[42] On April 27 of that year, the Western Association of Princeton Clubs was formed, made up of alumni groups from cities west of the Alleghenies, including Pittsburgh.[43] The purpose of this movement was to gain more influence for western alumni on the board of trustees of the university.

Prominent at this meeting was James Laughlin Jr. of Pittsburgh, who had graduated from Princeton in 1868. As a result of the drive spearheaded by Laughlin and other western alumni, he and four other westerners were elected alumni trustees of Princeton in June of 1901.[44] This marked a profound shift in the direction of the university, as Howard Maxwell has stated: "Possibly the first election of alumni trustees marks the end of denominational control of Princeton University. A year later, this Board was to elect a new president (Woodrow Wilson) who would be the first layman to hold this position."[45] Wilson's candidacy for the presidency of Princeton was opposed by the older New York, New Jersey and Philadelphia alumni groups, but was strongly supported by the western alumni, including the Pittsburghers.[46]

Upon entering office, Wilson announced ambitious plans for Princeton to become a prestigious institution of national ranking, on the order of Harvard and Yale. To accomplish this, vast sums of money were needed. An alumni trustee, James W. Alexander, said of Wilson: "There is only one thing he lacks, and that is cash."[47] It was this scarce resource that the wealthy elites of Pittsburgh and other western cities were willing and able to provide. Thus, soon after assuming the presidency, Wilson began his appeals to the western alumni groups for money. In November of 1902, he announced plans for his new praeceptor system at the Princeton Club in Pittsburgh, and requested twelve million dollars to carry it out.[48] Cleveland H. Dodge (of New York, but related to the Laughlin and Rea families of Pittsburgh) was appointed chairman of this fund committee by Wilson.

The appeal was well heeded by Pittsburgh alumni and other elite families, as they donated millions to Princeton's endowment and building funds. Although exact totals are not available, the Laughlin family gave land and money to the college, as did the Jones and Carnegie families, among others. In response to this monetary support, the Pittsburgh core families received many concessions from Wilson and the university. First of all, the eating clubs were abolished. Though a highly controversial issue, and not supported by all western alumni, the Pittsburgh group strongly supported Wilson, feeling that this bastion of social prestige at Princeton was dominated by coastal upper classes.[49] The most important concession to the Pittsburgh upper classes, however, was the appointment of Ledlie Laughlin as dean of admissions of the university (in the second decade of the century). This was a highly sensitive and important position, allowing Pittsburgh upper-class boys to receive preferential treatment over eastern seacoast families; it helped to begin the shift of most Pittsburgh core families from Yale to Princeton in the 1920s and 1930s.

By World War II, then, the Pittsburgh core families were an intimate and important part of one of America's leading social institutions, Princeton University. One of the main reasons the core families sent their sons to institutions such as Princeton was to ensure that they mixed with the "right" sort of people from other cities. In theory, at least, this should be reflected in more cosmopolitan marriages for this core group. What does an analysis of their marriage patterns reveal in this regard?

The answer is a bit surprising. Only 3 percent of the core family marriages were to readily recognizable upper-class families in other cities—though another 7 percent were married into families from other cities and not listed in their respective Social Registers. A large number of other marriages were not traceable. At the very most, 10 percent of the core family marriages were to social elites of other cities. Though it is difficult to know what a statistically significant percentage would be, this 10 percent does seem rather low, given the large percentage of sons and daughters attending national prep schools and colleges. The answer would seem to be that the core families, as the hub of the Pittsburgh upper class, had a role as social arbiters in their own local community which was too encompassing to allow the luxury of extensive marriage to families outside of the city. This leads one to surmise that the core families, the most important social elements of the city's upper class, were more provincial than cosmopolitan, precisely because their principal social interests always remained local rather than national. It was more important for them to maintain prestige at home than to marry into more glamorous New York or Philadelphia families.

The school attendance patterns for the non-core upper-class families resembled that of the core families, though their percentages of attendance were slightly lower. They started in local colleges, then went to Yale, and finally began switching to Princeton in the 1930s. On the prep school level, most went to local academies, but they were increasingly switching to St. Paul's—Pittsburgh's favorite prep school—in the twentieth century.

Although a distinctly lower percentage of the non-core families attended prestigious eastern prep schools and colleges, twice as high a percentage (6 percent) married with recognizable upper-class families of other cities. Although most of these more cosmopolitan families were among those who had sent their sons to the national upper-class institutions, some did not; and many of those who availed themselves of these institutions did not marry non-Pittsburgh upper classes.

The higher percentage of non-core family marriages to upper-class families outside of Pittsburgh seems due to the fact that these families were more free to marry exogamously than were the core families, since they had fewer of the social burdens normally imposed upon the latter group. Most were on their way up the social ladder; and marriage to upper-class families in other cities could help build their prestige at home, easing acceptance by the local core families. Thus, although more cosmopolitan than the core families, their goals were similarly provincial—acceptance in their home community.

The marginal upper-class families in Pittsburgh had by far the highest percentage of cosmopolitan marriages (16 percent), despite the fact that their percentages of attendance in national prestige schools were quite low. To some degree, this higher percentage was due to the fact that the "marginal family" category was partially created out of family groups who married to non-Pittsburgh upper classes. Even discounting for this, the degree of exogamous marriage is impressive. For many of these families it is clear that they had chosen to seek their marriages and ultimate prestige in areas other than Pittsburgh. This was true particularly of a group of families from eastern seacoast cities, who had preferred to retain their social connections and marriages in that area rather than Pittsburgh. Another group of Pittsburghers, of long standing in the city, chose for some reason to develop cosmopolitan rather than local marriage relationships. The Darlington family was a good example of this phenomenon. With great prestige in Pittsburgh, belonging to all of the right clubs, all of their marriages were to upper-class families in other cities. Thus, the marginal upper-class families were the most cosmopolitan of the Pittsburgh groups; and, by the mid-twentieth century, few chose to maintain a residence in the city.

The elite, non-upper-class Pittsburgh families had the lowest percentage of attendance at prestigious eastern schools—which corresponded to a low percentage of marriages to upper-class families outside of Pittsburgh. Some of these families left Pittsburgh rather early, and therefore might be considered more cosmopolitan; but many stayed on in the city for several generations. For ethnic, cultural, religious, or purely personal reasons, they did not become members of the local upper class; nor were they accepted by upper-class families in other areas.

The whole phenomenon of the relatively low percentage of exogamous marriages for Pittsburgh core families raises some questions concerning Baltzell's claim that the Social Register is a "national upper-class index".[50] Of the 235 individuals descended from nineteenth-century iron and steel families listed in the 1963 Pittsburgh Social Register, 170, or 72 percent, were members of core families. Thus, it is apparent that the Social Register measures the local upper class of the city—which, despite its membership in national clubs and attendance at ivy league schools, remained fundamentally provincial in nature. The usual pattern for a family with extensive exogamous marriages was to move to another city. Thus, the Pittsburgh model would indicate that the Social Register measured a series of local upper classes which were marginally connected by marriage, but hardly measured a cohesive, national upper class. It is possible, of course, that Pittsburgh was unique in this and other aspects of its elite and upper-class structure. To determine this, a comparative analysis of the upper-class systems in other cities will be presented in Chapter 5.

THE PITTSBURGH UPPER-CLASS SOCIAL NETWORK

Implicit in the above discussion is the concept of a viable, functioning social network system at the upper-class level in Pittsburgh, with marriages, families and kinship systems lying at its very core. As Table 52 indicates, the extent of intermarriage among these iron and steel elite families was extensive and comprehensive. The marital connections formed a web of interaction which included the vast majority of these upper-class families in its net.

In fact, 72 percent of all Pittsburgh iron and steel families were integrated into this kinship network. Some, as noted above, were more integral to the system than others; but all of these 72 percent were bound in a permanent and, at that time, nearly irrevocable manner to one another—marriage.

Of the 28 percent who were not included in the network by marriage, the majority were united by common club memberships. Only twenty families, less than

10 percent of the total, were not connected to the upper-class system by either marriage or common social club membership. Of these twenty families, 60 percent remained in Pittsburgh only a short time, spending a few years in the iron and steel industry and then moving on to other environments and ventures. The remainder (40 percent), although remaining in the city, were aloof or excluded from upper-class social participation. Several were German families, one was Jewish, and many were of more recent immigration to America.

The Pittsburgh model, then, reveals a well-organized, highly articulated and complex social network at the upper-class level. This system, composed of marital connections, clubs, neighborhood and schools, was able to include nearly all of the elite families in some manner in its operation, while at the same time ranking them in fine gradations according to social status. It is this model which shall be tested in the four other cities under study, in order to determine its general applicability to the upper-class levels.

NOTES

1. This conclusion is based partially on observations of the kind of neighborhods these elites moved into after leaving the downtown area, and on an application of the concepts developed by Sam Bass Warner, Jr. in his ***Streetcar Suburbs: The Process of Growth in Boston*** (Cambridge, Mass.: Harvard University Press, 1962); see especially pp. 11-14.

2. "Extended Family" is a term in common use among sociologists and anthropologists, denoting a kinship group extending beyond the nuclear family, all living under the same roof. "Expanded Family" is a term used by Herbert Gans in his ***The Urban Villagers: Group and Class in the Life of Italian Americans*** (New York: Free Press, 1962), pp. 45-56. In the expanded family, although extremely close kinship ties are maintained through proximity and frequent visiting, each nuclear unit maintains a separate residence.

3. Talcott Parsons, ***The Social System*** (Glencoe, Ind.: Free Press, 1951), p. 27.

4. E. Digby Baltzell, ***Philadelphia Gentlemen*** (New York: Free Press, 1958).

5. William G. Johnston, ***Life and Reminiscences From Birth to Manhood*** (Pittsburgh: privately printed, 1901) pp. 284-286.

6. Some sense of the intimacy of the neighborhoods in Allegheny as compared to other developments can be gained from looking at lot sizes. Following are the lot sizes of several homes in Allegheny (keep in mind that these lots all contained extraordinarily large houses which covered much of the square footage):

J. F. Jennings	Ridge & Allegheny	200′ x 400′
J. M. McCutcheon	47 Irwin Ave.	250′ x 50′
B. F. Jones	52 Irwin Ave.	100′ x 250′
Henry Irwin	54 Irwin Ave.	200′ x 200′
A. D. Smith	Park Street	200′ x 400′
James Park Jr.	North Ave.	200′ x 1000′
Jacob Painter	Liberty Street	50′ x 400′
A. E. W. Painter	Liberty Street	50′ x 400′
B. H. Painter	Ridge Ave.	200′ x 1000′
George Black	Ridge Ave.	400′ x 100′
Jos. Horne	Bidwell	200′ x 300′

By contrast, the S. McKee estate in Oakland was 2100′ x 600′; the A. P. Childs estate at Forbes and Halkett was 1200′ x 300′; John Moorhead's estate at Fifth and Darragh was 600′

x 1200'; and Christopher Zug's estate in Oakland was 1200' x 2400'; John Shoenberger's estate near Allegheny Cemetery, on 46th Street, was 1000' x 1000'; E. W. Shenley's estate at Stanton Avenue in the East End was 5000' x 4000'; and C. G. Hussey's estate in Shadyside was 1200' x 600'. In Hazelwood, close to downtown Pittsburgh, Hill Burgwin's estate was 600' x 900', as was Henry W. Oliver Sr.'s. Thomas S. Blair's lot was 900' x 900'. (Source: ***Atlas of the Cities of Pittsburgh and Allegheny and the Adjoining Boroughs*** (Philadelphia, 1872).

7. Joseph Frazier Wall, ***Andrew Carnegie*** (New York: Oxford University Press, 1970), p. 146.

8. Herbert Casson, ***Romance of Steel*** (New York: A. S. Barnes, 1907), p. 275.

9. Henry O. Evans, ***Iron Pioneer: Henry W. Oliver 1840-1904*** (New York: E. P. Dutton, 1942) p. 70.

10. ***Pittsburgh Press,*** May 29, 1932, and November 24, 1934.

11. ***Pittsburgh Bulletin-Index,*** July 23, 1942.

12. Members had to be twenty-one years of age and recommended for admittance by two members not on the Board of Governors. The initiation fee was $100, the yearly dues, $150. ***The Pittsburgh Club*** (Pittsburgh: privately printed, 1910). The list of iron and steel families who were members of the club was compiled from the Pittsburgh club directories printed in 1910, 1919, and 1925.

13. Baltzell, ***Philadelphia Gentlemen,*** p. 384. Out of fifty-seven men who reported membership in the Philadelphia Club, Baltzell found fifty-six, or 98 percent, who were also listed in the ***Social Register.***

14. Information was compiled from the Duquesne Club directories, which were privately printed in Pittsburgh for the years, 1881, 1890, 1909, 1915, 1924, 1928, 1945, 1955 and 1957.

15. A partial list was obtained from a club directory, ***The Union Club of Pittsburgh*** (Pittsburgh: privately printed, 1921). This was supplemented by lists from the ***Social Register*** and ***Blue Books*** of Pittsburgh. Additional information was also secured from the ***Pittsburgh Press,*** September 22, 1929, and the ***Pittsburgh-Gazette,*** February 9, 1932.

16. ***Pittsburgh Post,*** June 28, 1925.

17. ***Pittsburgh Bulletin-Index,*** November 2, 1936.

18. ***Pittsburgh Chronicle-Telegraph,*** October 16, 1922.

19. ***Pittsburgh Press,*** May 19, 1933.

20. Membership lists were derived from the ***Constitution, By-laws and List of Members of the Allegheny Country Club, Sewickley, Pa.*** (Pittsburgh: privately printed, 1911).

21. Baltzell, ***Philadelphia Gentlemen,*** p. 395.

22. The club was founded by Andrew Carnegie, Andrew Mellon, William B. Schiller, George Westinghouse, William B. Scaife Jr. and Henry Clay Frick. ***Pittsburgh Dispatch,*** May 1, 1904, and August 30, 1908; The ***Pittsburgh Bulletin-Index,*** September 17, 1936.

23. ***Fox Chapel Golf Club*** (Pittsburgh: privately printed, 1939), p. 1.

24. Membership lists were taken from a privately printed club directory, published in 1939.

25. J. Blau Van Urk, ***The Story of Rolling Rock*** (New York: Scribners, 1950), p. 79.

26. Membership list was derived from the ***Rolling Rock Club Directory*** (Ligonier, Pa.: privately printed, 1947).

27. ***Pittsburgh Press,*** October 1, 1904; ***Pittsburgh Post,*** October 2, 1904.

28. Membership list derived from the club's directory: ***Oakmont Country Club—Constitution and By-laws*** (Pittsburgh: privately printed, 1919).

29. ***Pittsburgh Post-Gazette,*** January 30, 1964.

30. ***Pittsburgh Bulletin-Index,*** September 17, 1936.

31. Membership list derived from ***Pittsburgh Blue Book,*** 1907.

32. ***Pittsburgh Sun-Telegraph,*** May 9, 1937; ***Pittsburgh Gazette-Times,*** November 23, 1924.

33. Information and membership lists were derived from ***Charter of Incorporation and***

By-Laws of the Sportmen's Association of Western Pennsylvania (Pittsburgh: privately printed, 1882 and 1886).

34. *Sportsmen's Association of Cheat Mountain* (Pittsburgh: privately printed, 1889).

35. Quoted in Nathaniel Burt, *The Perennial Philadelphians* (Boston: Little, Brown, 1963), p. 41. The saying is attributed to the Quakers.

36 Baltzell, for example, only mentions marriage occasionally, as supportive evidence for other information on clubs. Burt discusses marriages more often, but not in a systematic fashion.

37. Burt, *Perennial Philadelphians,* p. 44.

38. Following are the families ranked according to importance to the upper-class kinship system in Pittsburgh:

1. Most important (six families): Blair, Childs, Bakewell, Brown, Dilworth, Robinson;
2. Second in importance (five families): Laughlin, Oliver, Miller, Nimick, Black;
3. Third rank (nineteen families): Irwin, Jones, Rea, Scully, Speer, Bailey, Bussell, Dickson, Herron, Lockhart, Lyon, Mellon, Neale, Painter, Park, Singer, Walker, Zug, Wood;
4. Least important (thirteen families): Allderdice, Howe, Kennedy, Metcalf, Richardson, Smith, Verner, Burgwin, Cassidy, Chalfant, Lupton, Moorhead, Phillips.

39. Following are the non-core families ranked according to their total marriages within the upper-class system in Pittsburgh:

Group I (five or six upper-class marriages)—Lloyd, Carnegie, Leech, McCutcheon, Gillespie, Everson.

Group II (three or four upper-class marriages)—Snyder, Wainwright, Byers, Forsythe, Jennings, Schiller, Howard, Loomis, Porter, Phipps, Curry, Kelly, Lazear, Stewart, Rowe, Shoenberger, Wade, Clark, Lewis, Lee, Tinker, Johnston, Kirkpatrick.

Group III (one or two upper-class marriages)—Friend, Hemphill, Tener, McClure, Travelli, Donnell, Fitch, Clarkson, Baken, Blackburn, Clapp, Shinn, Spang, Frick, Hugus, Wightman, Mackey, Coleman, Browne, Binns, Brackenbridge, Bradley, DeArmit, Donnelly, DuPuy, Fitzhugh, Jamison, Keating, Stevenson, Tindle.

40. Sheffield Scientific School was established at Yale in 1860 as a three-year course, specializing in applied chemistry. It was not integrated into Yale proper until the twentieth century. See Russell H. Chittenden, *History of the Sheffield Scientific School of Yale University: 1846-1922* (New Haven: Yale University Press, 1928).

41. Marcia Davenport, *Valley of Decision,* p. 55. It was not until well into the twentieth century that Sheffield actually became part of Yale, having been a special three-year course before then. See Chittenden, *History of Sheffield.*

42. The following material is based largely upon an unpublished Ph.D. dissertation by Howard Bowden Maxwell, "The Formative Years of the University Alumni Movement, as illustrated by Studies of the University of Michigan, and Columbia, Princeton and Yale Universities, 1854-1918" (University of Michigan, 1965). Some information was also taken from Henry Wilkinson Bragdon, *Woodrow Wilson: The Academic Years,* (Cambridge: Harvard University Press, 1967).

43. Maxwell, "Formative Years at the University Alumni Movement", pp. 188-189.

44. *Ibid.,* pp. 192-193, 199.

45. *Ibid.,* p. 200.

46. Bragdon, *Woodrow Wilson,* pp. 373-378.

47. Maxwell, "Formative Years at the University of Alumni Movement," p. 201. Quoted from Princeton *Alumni Weekly* III (December 15, 1902): 195-196.

48. *Ibid.,* pp. 203, 216.

49. *Ibid.,* pp. 234-235.

50. Baltzell, *Philadelphia Gentlemen,* p. 33.

5

Comparative Analysis of Upper-Class Institutions

Pittsburgh provides a basic model of the upper-class institutions instrumental in the formation of an upper-class system around the nucleus of iron and steel elites. Though the other cities in the study shared the basic outlines of this model, they did differ from Pittsburgh, and from one another, in significant respects. The cultural background of the city, the role of the iron and steel industry within the city, the kind of iron and steel firms developed there, the age and cohesion of the social system and the later economic vitality of the city, all had profound implications for upper-class institutions. In order to understand these differences, each of the other cities in the study will be examined in some detail.

PHILADELPHIA

In his pioneering study of the upper-class system of Philadelphia, E. Digby Baltzell made several seminal observations.[1] The "ideal-typical" proper Philadelphian of 1940 was said to possess the following attributes:

(1) Of English or Welsh descent, his great-great-great-grandfather would have been a prominent Philadelphian in the great age of the new republic. Somewhere along the line an ancestor would have made money, or married wisely. And along with money and social position, some good Quaker ancestor would have preferred the Episcopal Church, or have been banished from the "Society of Friends" for marrying "out of meeting."

(2) His family would have been listed in the *Social Register* at the turn of the nineteenth century.

(3) He would have been born on Walnut Street, facing Rittenhouse Square.

(4) After an early education at the Episcopal Academy or some other private school in that city, he would have gone away to one of the fashionable Episcopal boarding schools in New England.
(5) Unless his parents felt an unusual loyalty and pride in local institutions, he would have gone to either Harvard, Yale, or Princeton where he would have belonged to one of the more exclusive clubs.
(6) After attending law school at the University of Pennsylvania, this young Proper Philadelphian would enter one of the fashionable and powerful law firms of the city and eventually become a partner . . .
(7) Finally, the Proper Philadelphian would live either in Chestnut Hill or the Main Line in 1940, attend the Episcopal Church, be married with three or four children, and walk either up or down Walnut Street to lunch with his peers at the Rittenhouse, or preferably the Philadelphia Club.[2]

As should be evident, this "ideal-typical"Proper Philadelphian of 1940 differs little in broad outlines from the typical upper-class iron and steel core family member from Pittsburgh. Two aspects must be investigated further. First, how do the iron and steel elite fit into this picture of the Philadelphia upper class painted by Baltzell? Second, how does the resulting upper-class system in Philadelphia differ from the model developed in Pittsburgh?

NEIGHBORHOOD

As Baltzell has noted, Proper Philadelphians living within the city "have always lived south of Market, between Chestnut and Pine Streets. Meanwhile the elite, but unfashionable, Philadelphians lived north of Market Street, and along Broad Street."[3] From the colonial period to 1840, the upper-class areas in Philadelphia had been on the east side of the city, around Independence and Washington Squares. By the 1880s these families had moved west, to an area around Rittenhouse Square, still south of Market Street.

Of the eighty-two Philadelphia iron and steel men on whom information could be found for 1883-1884, 34 percent lived south of Market Street. True to form, they were generally members of the oldest and most prestigious families among the iron and steel men. Only a few of the newer elite families lived in this area. An additional 32 percent of the iron and steel families lived in the elite (non-upper-class) area north of Market Street—either out Broad Street, or around Franklin and Logan Squares. Nearly all of these men were members of newer elite families. The remaining 34 percent of the steel families lived scattered in the suburbs of Germantown, Frankford, and further out in Montgomery, Delaware and Bucks counties. Since this was still prior to the development of the "Main Line" suburbs, most of these outlying families were simply living contiguous to their family iron mills.

An analysis of the social and cultural backgrounds of these iron and steel entrepreneurs in 1883-1884 indicates the extent of homogeneity in each neighborhood, and the degree to which the neighborhoods differed from one another. The area south of Market Street was almost completely dominated by iron and steel men of English and Welsh origins. They were largely Episcopalian, with minorities of Presbyterians and Quakers. All were members of pre-Civil War elite families. Of those for whom information was available, nearly all came to America prior to 1800. As befit Philadelphia's most prestigious neighborhood, they were uniformly of the preferred social origins in the city.

Although the Philadelphia iron and steel elite was, overall, the most culturally homogeneous of any of the cities under investigation, there were significant variations in the cultural stamp for the neighborhoods studied. The area north of Market Street differed in important respects from the area south of Market. Virtually all of the iron and steel elite living north of Market were English, and the proportion of Presbyterians was much higher than among those south of Market. In addition, there were no Quakers, an important minority in the south of Market neighborhood. More significantly, only 80 percent of the iron and steel men living north of Market were of pre-Civil War elite backgrounds, compared to 100 percent living in the south of Market area. Although 75 percent of the north of Market group were members of families which had come to America during the seventeenth century, the other 25 percent had arrived during the nineteenth century. Thus, although the iron and steel men living north of Market street were highly homogeneous, they reflected social origins which were somewhat newer and less preferred in Philadelphia.

Those living in various outlying areas around Philadelphia were the most heterogeneous, reflecting their dispersion in ten widely separated, scattered communities. While a slight majority were English, there were significant minorities of Scotch-Irish, Germans and Welsh. A similar variety existed in religious affiliation. Although 88 percent were from pre-Civil War elite families, 17 percent had come to America after 1800, and only one-half had arrived during the seventeenth century. Thus, in most respects, this group of suburban iron and steel men represented the most heterogeneous backgrounds among the steel men in Philadelphia; yet, when compared to those in Pittsburgh, they appear much more homogeneous.

By 1899, of the ninety-six iron and steel manufacturers on whom information could be found, 40 percent lived in the central city, south of Market Street. At this time, only 27 percent of the iron and steel families made their residences in the elite area north of Market Street in the center city. Some of those had moved south of Market, but others had gone to the suburbs, especially to the newly developed Chestnut Hill area. In 1899, 30 percent of the families still lived in outlying suburbs, a decline from 1883 and 1884; but this figure conceals some important changes in suburban development.

Much of the suburban loss from 1884 to 1899 entailed the movement of families from isolated, outlying areas near their iron and steel plants to the center city, south of Market. They were actually moving to a well-defined upper-class residential area for the first time. Meanwhile, those remaining in the suburbs, along with some expatriots from the city, were beginning to coalesce into fairly identifiable upper-class and elite suburbs for the first time—Germantown, Chestnut Hill and Mt. Airey. The remaining 3 percent of these families had recently moved to the "Drexel Colony" in West Philadelphia, near the University of Pennsylvania.

By 1899 the social and cultural makeup of the iron and steel men living south of Market had undergone only minor changes. The percentage of men from English origins had increased from 58 percent to 74 percent, while the Welsh had dropped from 31 percent to 12 percent. Ninety-six percent of the families had arrived in America prior to 1750, compared to "only" 88 percent in 1883. All were descendants of pre-Civil War elite families. In its principal outlines, then, the south of Market neighborhood in 1899 remained similar to 1883—English, Episcopalian, colonial family, and pre-Civil War elite status.

The area north of Market in 1899 remained similar to 1883 also, but had become somewhat more diverse and heterogeneous. Only 83 percent of the families were now English, compared to 96 percent in 1883, and a fairly large Welsh contingent (17 percent) now resided there. The percentage of Episcopalians had declined sharply, now sharing almost equal status with Presbyterians. Most significant was the growth of Baptists, Quakers and unspecified Protestant groups—from 5 percent to a total of 31 percent. There were also more families of recent immigrant status, since the number of colonial families declined from 75 percent to 57 percent. Thus, the neighborhood north of Market continued as a haven for newer families—who now displayed more heterogeneous cultural origins than they had in 1883.

The suburban areas by 1899, on the other hand, were becoming more culturally homogeneous. Where there was a substantial dispersion of ethnic stocks in 1883, by 1899 95 percent were of English origin, with only one Scottish family to add variety. Episcopalians were also becoming increasingly dominant, with 50 percent of the total, while 80 percent of the families now had origins in the seventeenth century. The suburban areas were evidently moving toward a more homogeneous cultural norm, as they began to replace the central city areas as the preferred domicile for upper-class families.

By 1907, 49 percent of the eighty iron and steel families located through city directories lived in the south of Market Street area; and it was during this time that the area reached its apex as a center of upper-class residence. Although a classically urban upper-class living area, the clustering of upper-class iron and steel families was less dense than in Pittsburgh's Allegheny. Part of this was due to the fact that the iron and steel elite made up a smaller portion of the entire upper class in Philadelphia than in Pittsburgh. But even adding to the iron and steel list the residences of other Philadelphia upper-class families, as revealed in Baltzell's book, indicates a somewhat less compact arrangement. Table 39 illustrates the more expanded nature of the south of Market residential area as compared to Allegheny.

In 1907 only 20 percent of the iron and steel families lived in the north of Market Street elite area. Many of the former residents had moved to the suburbs, which claimed 30 percent of the families by this time. Ten families now resided

TABLE 39
Philadelphia Center City Upper-Class Residences, South of Market

Spruce Street		Walnut Street		Locust	
No.	Family	No.	Family	No.	Family
1016	Howard and Alan Wood	1701	C. J. & C. J. Wurts, Jr.	1221	R. H. Smith
1033	H. L. & Jos. Carson	1706	Daniel, S. J. & W. H. Reeves, Jr.	4160	Ed., H. C. & H. L. Townsend, Jr.
1101	S. M. Felton				
1313	R. D. Wood	Pine Street		Chestnut Street	
1420	C. N. & J. L. Welsh	1830	E. J. Sellers	3635	C. S. Hinchman
1422	E. L. & J. L. Welsh, Jr.	4430	R. J. Johnson		
1508	Edward S., Edward S., Jr. Edward S. III, Daniel & Richard V. Buckley				
1533	Gecrge C. & G. A. Carson				
1535	G. C. Carson				
1903	E. Y. & H. T. Townsend				

in Germantown, a suburb of elite status; four lived in neighboring Chestnut Hill, a more opulent suburb for the very wealthy of newly arrived status; and three lived in Bryn Mawr, the first of the Main Line suburbs. Another seven were scattered in other outlying areas.

The relative social status of these elite residential areas by 1907 can be partially gauged by an analysis of the Social Register listings of iron and steel families living there. The south of Market area had 95 percent of its thirty-nine families so listed, compared to 88 percent of the sixteen families in the north of Market neighborhood and only 67 percent of those living in the various suburban areas.

By 1930 the elite area north of Market Street had disappeared entirely, as far as the iron and steel families were concerned, and the area south of Market had significantly deteriorated as an upper-class domicile. By that year, only 19 percent of the eighty-six families lived in the south of Market area, these being primarily widows and older couples living out the balance of their lives in the old family mansions. The principal living area for the Philadelphia iron and steel elite had now shifted to the suburbs. Eighty-one percent of these families resided there. The Main Line suburbs were most popular with 34 percent of the total; Chestnut Hill was second with 15 percent. Another 19 percent lived in a variety of outlying suburban areas.

The relative social position of these various Philadelphia living areas can be assessed by viewing Table 40—adapted from Baltzell—which relates Philadelphians

TABLE 40
Neighborhood as Related to Social Class, Philadelphia, 1940

	Percentage of Neighborhood Families	
Neighborhood	In Social Register	Not in Social Register
Upper Class		
Penllyn-Whitemarsh	86	14
Chestnut Hill	78	22
Main Line	48	52
Transition		
Rittenhouse Square	40	60
Jenkintown	27	73
Elite		
Germantown	15	85
West Philadelphia	9	91
Swarthmore	6	94
Other		
North Philadelphia	0	100
South Philadelphia	0	100
Outside Metropolitan Area	10	90
Average, all areas	29	71

SOURCE: E. Digby Baltzell, *Philadelphia Gentlemen* (New York: Free Press, 1958), p. 178.

listed in *Who's Who in America in 1940* with neighborhood and Social Register listings.[4] As the table indicates, the areas with the highest social status in 1940 were all suburban developments—Penllynn-Whitemarsh, Chestnut Hill, and the Main Line Suburbs. Befitting their status, the majority of iron and steel families had also made their exodus to the suburbs. Of those who had not moved, most lived in the Rittenhouse Square area (defined as "transitional" by 1940) and Germantown (which still retained its "elite" status). The other, less prestigious, areas of the city, felt little influence from the iron and steel families.

In comparison to Pittsburgh residential areas, one fact is most striking: whereas by the 1930s some 72 percent of the iron and steel elite in Pittsburgh continued to live in the city, less than 20 percent of the Philadelphia iron and steel elite did so. Although Allegheny had virutally disappeared by that time, the East End was in its full flower and represented a stronger sense of persistence by the Pittsburgh upper-classes in urban living. Perhaps this also explains the more active role taken by the Pittsburgh upper-class families in the civic and political life of their community. Two factors seemed to have hastened the exodus of the Philadelphia upper class to the suburbs: the increasing number of immigrants flocking into the city; and the increasing commercialization of the center city area. Although Baltzell stresses the first factor, the second would seem to be more germane. As Sam Bass Warner Jr. has shown, the downtown area experienced a sharp drop in population from 1860 to 1930 (from 137, 756 to 55,859), as the area became the home of office buildings: Walnut Street itself became Philadelphia's "Wall Street"—the center of the financial district.[5] Since Pittsburgh's East End was far enough removed from the downtown center, it faced little commercial competition for its residential land.

SOCIAL CLUBS

Philadelphia's upper-class social clubs are among the oldest and best known in America. It was here, as in Boston and New York, that the basic model for town and suburban upper-class clubs was refined. The major town clubs to be analyzed in this study are: the Philadelphia Club; the Rittenhouse Club, the Union League, Franklin Inn, the Racquet Club, and the Penn Athletic Club. The principal suburban clubs are: Radnor Hunt, Merion Cricket, Philadelphia Country Club, Philadelphia Cricket, and Germantown Cricket Clubs. Baltzell has provided a general ranking of the relative social status of these town and suburban clubs, according to Social Register listees:

Of the town clubs, the Philadelphia Club was the most prestigious, with 98 percent of its members listed in the Social Register of 1940. Comparable to the Pittsburgh Club, it had been organized in 1835, and remained Philadelphia's oldest and most revered town club. With its percentage of Social Register listees comparable to that of the Pittsburgh Club, it performed a similar function within the upper-class institutional framework of Philadelphia. Which of the Philadelphia iron and steel families, and how many, were members of the Philadelphia Club?

TABLE 41
Philadelphia Town and Suburban Clubs as Related to Social Class

Town Clubs	Members Listed in Social Register, %	Not Listed in Social Register, %	Suburban Clubs	Members Listed in Social Register, %	Not Listed in Social Register, %
Philadelphia	98	2	Radnor Hunt	100	0
Rittenhouse	88	12	Merion Cricket	72	28
Union League	42	58	Philadelphia C. C.	38	62
Racquet Club	80	20	Philadelphia Cricket	86	14
Penn Athletic	29	71	Germantown Cricket	70	30

SOURCE: E. Digby Baltzell, *Philadelphia Gentlemen* (New York: Free Press, 1958), pp. 344, 356.

Between 1899 and 1930 the Philadelphia Club claimed the membership of fifty-five individuals from iron and steel families. More important than individual membership, however, was family membership. For example, in 1899, although there were fifteen individual iron and steel men in the club, they represented only eight different families. By 1907, the number of iron and steel families represented had risen to eighteen, reflecting the influence of the growth of new fortunes in the late nineteenth century. Twenty-three years later, in 1930, just three more families had been added to its rolls, making a total of twenty-one different families holding membership over this period. These families hypothetically can be considered as the most exclusive of Philadelphia iron and steel upper-class families. The validity of this conclusion will be checked later against intermarriage patterns.

During the generation under study, from 1899 to 1930, the iron and steel men in the Philadelphia Club displayed fairly homogeneous and highly preferred social and cultural origins. Of these fifty-five men, the majority were English, with minorities of Welsh and Scotch-Irish. The largest number were Episcopalian, with large minorities of Presbyterians, Quakers and unspecified Protestants. Ninety percent were members of colonial families, with 68 percent having arrived during the seventeenth century. Finally, 98 percent were descended from pre-Civil War elite families. Eighty-five percent of the iron and steel members in 1907 were listed in the Philadelphia Social Register, while 100 percent of the 1930 members were so listed.

The Rittenhouse Club was somewhat less exclusive than the Philadelphia Club. Only thirty-seven individual iron and steel men were members between 1899 and 1930. These men represented twenty different family units. Thirteen of the twenty families represented in the Rittenhouse Club were also members of the Philadelphia Club; so only those members who were not in the latter club would constitute a group of possibly lower social prestige. The social and cultural beckgrounds of the iron and steel family members of the Rittenhouse Club were, overall, quite similar to their counterparts in the Philadelphia Club. Of the thirty-seven members from iron and steel families between 1899 and 1930, 60 percent were of English ancestry, compared to 69 percent in the Philadelphia Club. There were similar proportions of Scotch-Irish and Welsh in each club, although the Rittenhouse Club had a significant minority of men of Germanic background. There were also comparable patterns of religious affiliation. The greatest number at Rittenhouse were Episcopal, followed by unspecified Protestants, Quakers and Presbyterians. All of the Rittenhouse iron and steel family members were from colonial families, with 72 percent coming to America during the seventeenth century, compared to 68 percent in this category among their counterparts at the Philadelphia Club. Finally, 97 percent were descendants of pre-Civil War elites, matching almost exactly the 98 percent found at the Philadelphia Club. Thus, in overall cultural terms, the differences between the two clubs were slight. In terms of social status, though, Rittenhouse ranked somewhat below the Philadelphia Club, with only 78 percent of its iron and steel members listed in the Social Register.

The Union League was the least prestigious of the three major town clubs. Forty-five individuals from nineteen iron and steel families were members. Of these, fourteen also belonged to either the Philadelphia or Rittenhouse Clubs. Only four families did not belong to these clubs: they were possibly of a lower social category, elite rather than upper class. The social and cultural origins of the iron and steel members of the Union League Club corresponded in many ways to those of the two clubs previously analyzed. A larger percentage (86 percent) were of English ancestry, with Welsh being the only significant minority. About the same proportion were Episcopalian, but a larger number were Presbyterian. Although a majority were members of colonial families which had arrived in America prior to 1800, it was significant that fully 23 percent had immigrated during the nineteenth century. This figure was well above those found in that category in the Philadelphia and Rittenhouse clubs. Like those two clubs, however, 98 percent were descended from pre-Civil War elite families. Thus, these were "new men" in only one sense. Although sharing nearly identical cultural and economic backgrounds with their counterparts in the two more prestigious clubs, their families were generally later arrivals to America. Although of relatively "old" wealth, many were not of "old" family. This was reflected in the 1907 Social Register listings of the iron and steel family members, where only 67 percent were so listed. Thus, a fairly clear rank ordering on the basis of social status existed among the three clubs, despite a striking overall similarity in social and cultural origins.

A prestigious town club, the Racquet Club, was a special interest athletic club. Of slightly less status than the Rittenhouse, it ranked well above the Union League. Thirty-six members of iron and steel elite in the city belonged to the Racquet Club from 1899 to 1930, representing fourteen different families. The Racquet Club memberships, however, do not seem to fit the "lock-step" patterns of the other three, men's town clubs. For example, the Disston family were Racquet Club members in 1899, but not members of the Philadelphia Club until 1907. Conversely, the Morris family, charter members of the Philadelphia Club, did not have a membership in the Racquet Club until 1907.

The social origins of the thirty-six iron and steel family members of the Racquet Club differed little from the other three town clubs thus far considered. The great majority were English, with minorities of Welsh and Scotch-Irish. The largest group of religious adherents were Episcopalian, with most of the rest Presbyterian or unspecified Protestants. Eighty-five percent were descendants of colonial families, 64 percent arriving during the seventeenth century. All were members of pre-Civil War elite families. As befit a group from such uniformly preferred social origins, all the iron and steel members of the club in 1907 were listed in the Social Register.

Of the Philadelphia suburban clubs, Radnor Hunt was socially the most exclusive. Only twelve members of iron and steel families were members of the club, and they represented nine different families. The correlation of these families to the town club memberships was not always close. Generally, however, the club ranked on a social level with the Philadelphia Club. As such, it was a haven of Philadelphia core family members, and comparable to the Allegheny Country Club in Pittsburgh. The social origins of the twelve iron and steel family members of Radnor Hunt were distinct replications of the four town clubs. The great majority were English, with the largest minority Welsh. There was an even larger proportion of Episcopalians, with Presbyterians accounting for 17 percent. All were members of colonial families, with 83 percent (the largest percentage for any of the clubs) deriving from the seventeenth century. All were also members of families with elite status prior to the Civil War, and all were listed in the Social Register. Although of limited appeal because of its specialized activities, Radnor Hunt was of obviously high social status.

Ranking next in prestige among the suburban clubs was the Philadelphia Cricket Club. Thirty-one members of iron and steel families belonged to the club between 1899 and 1930, and they represented only eleven separate families. Of these, seven families were not members of Radnor Hunt, and generally represented a slightly lower social position. But since Radnor and Philadelphia Cricket clubs were of rather specialized interest—cricket and the hunt—it is a little difficult to create a neat categorization between the two. The social origins of the thirty-one iron and steel members of the Philadelphia Cricket Club differed in only one important respect from those at Radnor Hunt, and in that manner, more resembled the members of the Union League. Predominantly English, with a minority of Welsh and German, the largest number were Episcopalian, followed by Presbyterians and unspecified Protestants. All were of pre-Civil War economic elite status. Thirty-one percent, however, were members of families who had come to America during the nineteenth century. The social status of the members of Philadelphia Cricket was higher than those in the Union League, however, with 85 percent in 1907 listed in the Social Register. Thus, Philadelphia Cricket was a club which attracted and admitted a significantly larger proportion of newer families; but these families had all achieved wealth and position prior to the Civil War—this being reflected in the high percentage who were listed in the Social Register.

Next in rank were two clubs of nearly equal prestige: Merion Cricket and Germantown Cricket. Since their recreational interest was identical to that of Philadelphia Cricket, it is possible to gauge their relative social status. Merion Cricket enrolled forty-two different individuals from the iron and steel industry—making it a clear favorite over Germantown Cricket, since the latter had only eight individuals as members. Analysis of the social origins of the fifty iron and steel family members of these two cricket clubs fails to substantiate the lower social status observed by Baltzell. These men were preponderantly English, but somewhat more diverse in their religious affiliation—though 56 percent were either Episcopalian or Presbyterian. Ninety-four percent were members of colonial families, and all had attained elite status prior to the Civil War. Furthermore, 93 percent of the iron and steel family members were listed in the Social Register in 1907. In every respect, then, these two cricket clubs appear to reflect high cultural, social and economic prestige.

The final suburban club to be analyzed, the Philadelphia Country Club, was primarily elite. It counted forty-three iron and steel individuals among its members, from seventeen different families; only two did not hold membership in suburban clubs with greater prestige. Examination of the cultural backgrounds and social status of the forty-three iron and steel family members of Philadelphia Country club fails to substantiate the elite status of the club. A majority of its members were English, with minorities of Welsh and Scotch-Irish. Religious adherence was more mixed, but 56 percent were either Episcopalian or Presbyterian. Ninety-eight percent were members of families which had attained elite status before the Civil War. Only in the times of arrival of their families in America do the members of the Philadelphia Country Club appear more similar to the members of Union League and Philadelphia Cricket, with 19 percent coming to the United States during the nineteenth century. Most were of high social status, however, with 87 percent of the thirty members in 1907 being listed in the *Social Register.*

The analysis of club data for Philadelphia iron and steel families presents a less clear picture than in Pittsburgh. With a group of iron and steel manufacturers from older and more prestigious origins, and with a higher degree of homogeneity among them, the clubs in Philadelphia reflected this bias. They were in general, however, even more homogeneous and selective than the iron and steel elite as a whole. Whereas 65 percent of the Philadelphia iron and steel entrepreneurs were of English ancestry, three-quarters of those holding membership in the eight most prestigious clubs were so. There were about the same percentage of Episcopalians in both groups, but fewer of the club members came to America during the nineteenth century (14 percent, compared to 18 percent). A slightly larger percentage of the club members were also from seventeenth century families (66 percent, compared to 61 percent). Of greatest significance, however, is the fact that, whereas 20 percent of the Philadelphia iron and steel men were from non-elite origins, only 10 percent of the club members emanated from these origins. Thus, among an iron and steel elite which was already highly restricted to men from homogeneous cultural backgrounds and elite origins, the social clubs of Philadelphia selected only those from the most prestigious stock. Unlike the social clubs of Pittsburgh, they were more exclusive and acted less as an escalator for once deprived groups to move into the social upper class.

MARRIAGE AND KINSHIP PATTERNS

Since the information on marriage patterns for the Philadelphia iron and steel elite is less complete than for Pittsburgh, and, since they formed a less central part of the older upper class of the former city, Philadelphia's figures on marriage patterns are somewhat less conclusive. Nonetheless, an analysis of these patterns can provide some insight.

Using the same marriage criteria as for the Pittsburgh iron and steel families, the following breakdown results: Thirteen families, representing 17 percent of the total were core upper class; another 17 percent were non-core upper class; 25 percent were marginal upper class, and 40 percent were classified as elite, non-upper class. These totals showed some significant variation from endogomic marriage groups in Pittsburgh—where one-half the families were core or non-core upper class, and only about one-third were elite, non-upper class. On the surface, at least, this would indicate that the process of social selection was more rigorous than in Pittsburgh, despite the fact that Philadelphia's iron and steel elite was from even more restricted social origins.

If these family groupings, as revealed by intermarriages, are then correlated to Social Register and social club listings, the groupings are generally verified. As was the case in Pittsburgh, the core families have the highest percentage listed in the Social Register (100 percent), and have significantly higher percentages than the other family groups in the most prestigious clubs of the city (71 percent average membership in the most prestigious clubs, and 69 percent overall). Generally rank ordered below the core families with decreasing percentages, came the other three family groups. The non-core upper-class families had 69 percent listed in Social Register, and averaged 21 percent membership in the four most prestigious clubs, and 22 percent overall. The marginal upper-class families had 58 percent listed in the Social Register, and averaged 17 percent membership in the prestigious clubs, with the same percentage overall. Finally, the elite, non-upper-class families had only 19 percent listed in the Social Register, with 5 percent average membership in the highest rated clubs, and 5 percent overall. Thus the marriage patterns for Philadelphia, as was the case in Pittsburgh, appear to reveal an accurate picture of the nature of the social system at its upper levels.

Analysis of the social and cultural backgrounds of these family groups reveals several areas of social differentiation, which may have been involved in producing the social ranking. The core families were predominantly English, with small mi-

TABLE 42
Endogamous Marriage Groups as Related to Social Register and Clubs

Family Group		Percentage of Family Group in				
		Social Register	Radnor Hunt	Philadelphia Club	Rittenhouse	Philadelphia Racquet
Core:	*N*=13	100	46	84	69	84
Non-Core:	*N*=13	69	8	38	31	8
Marginal:	*N*=19	58	5	21	37	5
Elite:	*N*=30	19	0	3	9	6

Family Group		Merion Cricket	Philadelphia Cricket	Union League	Philadelphia Country
Core:	*N*=13	84	31	92	62
Non-Core:	*N*=13	8	15	46	23
Marginal:	*N*=19	11	21	11	26
Elite:	*N*=30	6	6	9	3

norities of Scotch-Irish, German and Welsh. A majority were Episcopalian, with small numbers of Presbyterians, Quakers and unspecified Protestants. All were from pre-Civil War elite families, and 92 percent were of colonial origin—with nearly 70 percent who had come to America during the seventeenth century.

The non-core families replicated the core families in nearly every social characteristic. The majority were English and Episcopalian, while all were colonial families—three-quarters having immigrated during the seventeenth century. Ninety-two percent were pre-Civil War elite families. Of importance, however, is the fact that a large minority were Quakers. Once the elite religion of Philadelphia, it appeared to fall into disfavor at the end of the Revolution—and perhaps then retarded the progress of many of these otherwise prestigious families from achieving full acceptance.[6]

The marginal upper-class families, although dominated by men of English background, also contained a large minority of Germans. In addition, only 43 percent were either Episcopalian or Presbyterian; the majority emanated from less highly regarded religious affiliations. Their economic origins were also less favorable, with 16 percent deriving from middle-class homes prior to the Civil War. All were members of colonial families, however, and two-thirds of the families had come to America during the seventeenth century. In most cases, though, each marginal family had one strike against it. Either it was not English, or, if English, it was not Presbyterian or Episcopalian. If they satisfied both of these requirements, then they often were of new wealth from after the Civil War.

The elite, non-upper-class families were much more heterogeneous and were from clearly disadvantaged cultural and economic origins. Only 37 percent were English; 26 percent were German, and only small minorities were of Scotch-Irish and Welsh. Just one-third were Episcopalian or Presbyterian, most being unspecified Protestants. Two-thirds emanated from the pre-Civil War working and middle classes, and 36 percent were recent arrivals, having migrated to the United States during the nineteenth century. In every respect, these elite families ran counter to the dominant social and cultural bias among the old Philadelphia families; and their low social ranking is indicative of the reaction of "proper" Philadelphia to men from these origins.

Unlike Pittsburgh, Philadelphia was generally not a benevolent environment for men who emanated from less favored cultural and social origins in the nineteenth century. As it was difficult for these persons to achieve elite status in nineteenth-century Philadelphia, it was apparently nearly impossible for them to gain full acceptance into the social upper classes.

COSMOPOLITANS OR LOCALS

During his analysis of the Philadelphia upper classes, Baltzell reached the conclusion that around the turn of the century, the urban upper classes lost their provincialism and became part of a cosmopolitan, metropolitan upper class.[7] We have seen that Pittsburgh did not fit his model very well, with most of its upper class—particularly the core families—retaining a high degree of their previous localism. Was Philadelphia different? Was it perhaps a unique case as an older seacoast city? Or does the Philadelphia upper class derived from the iron and steel elites seem to correspond to the Pittsburgh model?

As with Pittsburgh's iron and steel elite, several Philadelphia families had fairly cosmopolitan business interests in the nineteenth century. First of all, involvement with the Pennsylvania Railroad, shared by many of these families, was a fairly cosmopolitan venture. The line, with its subsidiaries, reached into many states, resulting in far-flung business and political involvement for these elites. Besides this connection, there were several others, too numerous to mention in detail. Although these business interests were important, in order to have insight into the relative cosmopolitanism of Philadelphia's iron and steel families it is necessary to look at each of the family groups—with reference to attendance at prep schools and ivy league colleges (outside of Philadelphia), and to memberships in national upper-class clubs in other cities, all in conjunction with cosmopolitan marriage patterns.

Two factors make analysis of the cosmopolitan tendencies of Philadelphia core families difficult. First, four of the twelve families defined as "core" were old New England families who had come to Philadelphia in the early nineteenth century. They were rapidly assimilated into the Philadelphia upper classes; and, in terms of marriage patterns and club memberships, were indisputably core families by the early twentieth century. Yet, by their very mobility and family connections with New England, they demonstrated a more cosmopolitan pattern than the older Philadelphia families. This was further complicated by a second factor in the field of education: The fact that Philadelphia possessed a solid, national upper-class educational institution (the University of Pennsylvania) meant that the need to utilize one of the "big three" ivy league schools was lessened for core family Philadelphians, as compared to Pittsburghers.

Looking first at attendance at major, national upper-class colleges, the following pattern emerges: 58 percent of the core families had sons who attended Penn; one-half attended Harvard; one-third Princeton; and one-third Yale. The pattern represents a fairly sharp reversal of the Pittsburgh core family model, where Yale and Princeton were the two leading schools. However, if one separates the old New England families from the old Philadelphia families, a slightly different picture emerges. Of the eight old Philadelphia core families, 63 percent attended Penn, 38 percent attended Princeton and Harvard, and one-half attended Yale. On the other hand, Harvard was a powerful magnet for the old New England families, nearly all of whom sent a son there at one time or another. So, in educational terms, the old Philadelphia core families seemed somewhat more localistic than the Pittsburgh group, with strong attachments to Penn and nearby Princeton, and somewhat less to Yale and Harvard.

In general, however, with the exception of the four old New England families, one can discern a fairly definite generational pattern for the Philadelphia core families in terms of education. In the nineteenth century, Penn was by far the most attractive institution for educating sons. Only Princeton served as a major alternative. As the twentieth century progressed, Philadelphia upper classes increasingly turned to the national ivy league schools of Harvard, Yale and Princeton. The shift was not so great as in Pittsburgh; but this was mainly due to the continuing attraction of Penn, a local institution with high status nationally. As Nathaniel Burt has commented:

> The chances are that from 1880 to 1900, at least, the majority of old Philadelphians actually went there [Penn] . Around 1900, Harvard attracted the fancy (as opposed to the plain). From 1910 on, the drift was overwhelmingly toward Princeton; even the sons of University [of Pennsylvania] trustees went there.[8]

Although the figures are inconclusive, the pattern on boarding schools seems similar to that found by Baltzell.[9] In the nineteenth century, core family Philadelphians overwhelmingly attended private, local academies such as Penn Charter, Episcopal Day and Germantown Academy. In the twentieth century, St. Paul's, St. Mark's and Groton attracted increasing numbers of the young men from core families, with St. Paul's having the definite edge. Thus, by this time the Philadelphia pattern for core families was nearly identical to that of Pittsburgh.

Though the Philadelphia core families were in some respects slightly less cosmopolitan in educational experience than the Pittsburgh core families, their rate of exogamous marriage to upper-class families in other cities was significantly higher. Of the 483 core family marriages on which information could be found, 18 percent were to fairly identifiable upper-class families in other cities. This was at least double the percentage in Pittsburgh. Some of the reason for this larger figure, however, is due to the presence of old New England families with naturally more cosmopolitan marriage patterns. Of the eighty-seven recorded marriages of these New England families, 37 percent were to upper-class families in other areas. If these are subtracted from the core family totals, the old Philadelphia family cosmopolitan marriage pattern drops to 14 percent.

Thus, although the percentage of cosmopolitan marriages of the old Philadelphia core families was higher than that of the Pittsburgh families, it was still rather low. This seems to reaffirm the strong interest and responsibility of these old Philadelphia families to arbitrate the social structure of the city at the upper levels. As in Pittsburgh, they were the local upper class, with only occasional ties to upper classes in other cities.

The Philadelphia non-core upper-class families displayed patterns of school attendance much like those of the old Philadelphia core families, though their percentages were lower. Two-thirds of the fifteen families attended Penn; 40 percent attended Princeton; 27 percent went to Harvard; and 13 percent to Yale. Thirty-eight percent of these families also attended other schools—especially Haverford, a fairly prestigious local college. Like the core families, they attended local colleges almost exclusively in the nineteenth century, but in the twentieth century they began switching to the more prestigious ivy league schools, especially Princeton.

Unlike the non-core families of Pittsburgh, however, these non-core families of Philadelphia did not have a significantly higher percentage of cosmopolitan marriages, as compared to the core families. With only 12 percent of the 160 recorded marriages classified as "cosmopolitan," they ranked slightly lower in this category than the old Philadelphia core families, and significantly lower than the core families as a whole. No definite answer can be offered for this variation, but it might be speculated that the prospect of achieving social success in Philadelphia was of relatively greater attraction to the Philadelphia non-core families, as compared to those in Pittsburgh, that they preferred not to distract themselves from this purpose. Marriage to a wealthy New York family, for example, may have carried far less prestige in Philadelphia circles than in Pittsburgh. As Nathaniel Burt has commented:

> If Philadelphia can be said to be self-conscious about anything . . . it is their desire not to be New Yorkers, or what they think of as New Yorkers. This is more than mere antipathy; New York is too close, and represents too strong an economic threat to be ignored. . . It represents too easy an escape for the rebellious, talented and ambitious youth who finds opportunities there he can't find at home.[10]

Whereas marriage to a prominent New York family could be used as an acceptable alternative means to social status for non-core families in Pittsburgh, in Philadelphia it had the image of disloyalty, of selling out to a cheap commercialized café set.

As in Pittsburgh, the marginal upper-class families of Philadelphia had a high percentage of cosmopolitan marriages to upper-class families in other cities, despite a rather low percentage of attendance at the prestigious national schools. Twenty-seven percent of the 113 marginal upper-class marriages were cosmopolitan. Conversely, none of the families attended Harvard; 16 percent attended Yale; 11 percent went to Princeton; and 16 percent to Penn. One-third attended other colleges, mostly outside of Philadelphia. Not only were these overall college percentages lower, but the pattern of attendance was markedly different from the core and non-core families of Philadelphia. For a variety of reasons, the social connections and prestige of these marginal families lay outside of Philadelphia, in a different set of social institutions than for the more prestigious Philadelphia families.

The elite, non-upper-class families had very low attendance at ivy league schools and a low rate of cosmopolitan marriage to upper classes in other cities. Some of these families left Philadelphia early, and little more was heard of them; but several stayed on in Philadelphia or Bethlehem as upper-middle-class citizens—attending local colleges, marrying other middle-class persons, and never approaching the more rarified atmosphere of the upper classes.

PHILADELPHIA UPPER-CLASS SOCIAL NETWORK

Analysis of 830 iron and steel family marriages in Philadelphia reveals a strong network of interrelationships at the kinship level. The data also demonstrate that those families with the most frequent incidence of endogamous marriage within this kinship system similarly had the highest status ranking, according to Social Register listings and club memberships. Table 52 indicates the basic nature of this kinship and club network among the iron and steel families.

The thirteen core families ranged between four and sixteen marriages each within the kinship network. Three families (Morris, Wharton and Wood) averaged three or four endogamous marriages in each of the four generations under study. As was the case in Pittsburgh, indications are that those families with a high incidence of participation overall in the kinship system were also those with the greatest amount of local prestige. Although these three families had a lower overall level of membership in social clubs, compared to the other ten core families (who averaged one to two endogamous marriages per generation)—51 percent, compared to 72 percent), their average membership in the four most prestigious clubs was higher (75 percent, compared to 70 percent). It was their low average of membership in the nine clubs of lower status (28 percent) which contrasted most sharply with the other ten families (73 percent). In ethnic and cultural terms, there were also some important distinctions. All of the more endogamous families were English, and two-thirds were Episcopalian, with the remaining one-third Presbyterian. All came to America prior to 1750.

Of the ten core families with fewer endogamous marriages, only 60 percent were English, and the remainder were divided among Scotch-Irish, German and Welsh. Thus, if the core families were somewhat diverse ethnically, all were among the less endogamous of the group. Only one-half of these families were Episcopalian, with the rest scattered in several denominations. Finally, although 70 percent of these families came to America during the seventeenth century, 30 percent arrived after 1750. Thus, those core families who participated most frequently and extensively in the endogamous kinship network were in every respect more prestigious and of higher social ranking than those displaying less frequent marital endogamy. The situation was somewhat more complex among the non-core families.

Those non-core families—six in number, with only one endogamous marriage over four generations—generally had the highest prestige, with 25 percent average membership in prestigious clubs and in all the clubs. In addition, 83 percent were listed in the Social Register. On the other hand, those families with at least one endogamous marriage in each of the four generations (five families in number) had less overall prestige, with an average of 20 percent membership in the most prestigious clubs and in all clubs. Only 60 percent were listed in the Social Register. The two families which averaged an endogamous marriage in every other generation had the lowest percentage of membership in the prestigious clubs (13 percent), and had only 50 percent listed in the Social Register.

Those non-core families with only one endogamous marriage over four generations had generally restricted their marital choices to core upper-class families. A highly mobile group, they were near to the margins of the core upper class, and did not luxuriate in marriages to families of inferior standing. The group with one endogamous marriage in each generation were, generally, families of longer standing in Philadelphia. Over the years they progressed by stages from marginal to non-core, to core families in their marital choices. They, too, were near the top of the non-core group, but had progressed to this status by a different path. The marginal upper-class families in Philadelphia, unlike Pittsburgh, had relatively little kinship involvement in the endogamous marriage network. Only seven of the nineteen families had any endogamous marital involvement, with the remainder achieving marginal status via marriage to upper-class families in cities outside of Philadelphia.

In addition to the kinship network, there was a supplementary network of affiliation by common social club participation. This was implicitly recognized in Pittsburgh, but may be viewed more explicitly in Philadelphia—because of the smaller number of families involved in the study. As Table 52 in the appendix indicates, the web of kinship relations was broadened and deepened considerably by a complementary network of family club affiliation.

Here again, the extent and frequency of core family participation in the upper-class network was significantly greater than for the other families studied. Among the core families, the Roberts family had the greatest number of interlocking club affiliations with other iron and steel families (127), and the Wharton family had the least (forty-two). The average number of interlocking club memberships per core family was ninety-three. In the social club network, as in the kinship network, the core families were vigorous and energetic leaders.

The non-core families had significantly less involvement and interconnection with other iron and steel families at the club level. Two non-core families, Buckley and Reeves, had eighty interlocking club memberships with other families, and five non-core families had no recorded club memberships. Thus, the non-core average was significantly lower than for the core families, at thirty-three each. If, however, the five families with no clubs listed are eliminated from the total, the remaining eight families averaged fifty-five interlocking memberships.

The club involvement level of the marginal families was also below that of the non-core families. While they averaged twenty-four interconnecting club memberships per family, this also included eight families who had no clubs listed. When they are subtracted from the total, the remaining eleven families still averaged only forty-four interlocking memberships, well below those of the non-core families.

Finally, the elite, non-upper-class families generally had little involvement in the club network, as they had no involvement in the kinship network. The thirty families averaged only eight interlocking club memberships with other iron and steel families. Of even greater significance, only eight of the thirty families had any club memberships listed at all. Analysis of club memberships, then, would appear to divide these elite families into two groups: those of probable upper-class status, who, for idiosyncratic reasons, had no endogamous marriages (27 percent of the total), and the majority, who were quite obviously excluded from participation in the upper-class system in every respect.

Those eight families probably having upper-class status, however, still ranked below the marginal upper-class families in interlocking club memberships, averaging only thirty-two per family; but their involvement was extensive enough to indicate marginal acceptance in the upper classes. Thus, fifty-two of the seventy-six Philadelphia iron and steel families had some degree of involvement in the upper-class social network in the city. Their participation varied according to class and status; but, significantly, over two-thirds of the elites who emerged in the iron and steel industry in the city in the late nineteenth century were incorporated into the indigenous upper-class social network during the twentieth century. Of the one-third which was not, some were immune to tracing by the present investigator; others achieved status in parallel networks, one example of which was in Bethlehem.

THE BETHLEHEM SUBGROUP

Bethlehem formed a rather unique nineteenth-century entity. Its iron and steel industry was dominated at the topmost levels by absentee Philadelphians . But at the level of middle-management, and sometimes at higher positions, native Bethlehemites played important roles in the industry. Here too, the ethnic and class considerations which had separated elite groups in Pittsburgh and Philadelphia operated. In general, there were two fairly distinct groups of native Bethlehemites. The first were members of the large German-American community which had settled the area in the eighteenth century. The second were members of English families, who occupied a middle ground between the German-Americans and the Philadelphians: they were of the same social and cultural backgrounds as the Philadelphians, but were old families in the Lehigh Valley area, having little prestige or standing among the Philadelphia families.

Among the German-Americans there were men at the middle and lower management levels: John and George Fritz were superintendents; Owen F. Leibert was a superintendent; and Abraham S. Schnapp and Henry S. Snyder were secretaries of Bethlehem Iron. The English group, though not among the owners of Bethlehem Iron, had higher executive positions: Garrett B. Linderman served as vice-president and president; and Albert N. Cleaver was treasurer.

The German-Americans seemed to have had a high standing in the local German-American community. All belonged to the Moravian, German Reformed or Lutheran Church, and participated in a variety of local and ethnic organizations which added to their local prestige and respectability. But they were unable to move among the upper-class Philadelphians who controlled Bethlehem Iron. Their German background and religious preferences operated to their disadvantage in dealing with Philadelphians. The very things which were symbols of belonging, of respect and of continuity with the past in Bethlehem, were also symbols of foreignness and lower-class origins to the upper-class Philadelphians. Of the five native Bethlehemites of German extraction, three were elite, non-upper class by marital patterns, and two were marginal upper class. None belonged to social clubs in Philadelphia, and none were listed in its Social Register. Neither did they belong to the locally prestigious Bethlehem clubs, such as Northampton Country Club. Their affiliations were restricted to ethnic (German) and religious (Moravian) ones. The German-American group in Bethlehem, then, represented the truncated social structure which very early developed in Bethlehem. The firms were controlled by outside financial groups, and the company's top positions went to the outsiders.

The English were more marginal. Although being of the "correct" ethnicity and religion (most were Quaker or Episcopalian), prior to the mid-nineteenth century they had had few social contacts with the Philadelphia upper classes. By the early twentieth century, unlike the German-Americans, they belonged to many of the best Philadelphia clubs, and they married with several of the core and non-core families in that city. Of the six native Bethlehemites of English extraction, three were members of non-core upper-class families according to marital choices; one was marginal upper class and two were elite, or non-upper class. Three were listed in the Philadelphia Social Register and one belonged to the Union League club in that city. More important— two-thirds were involved in the prestigious local social clubs of Bethlehem. They were part of a local aristocracy of indigenous prestige, and were quite separate from the German subgroup in the same city. As such, they were able to transfer their local status to Philadelphia, at least in terms of marital choices. This allowed them to slowly advance within the Philadelphia status system. German-American Bethlehemites, however, remained subordinate to Philadelphia, both economically and socially.

CONCLUSIONS

Philadelphia's upper-class institutions and social network at that level bore considerable resemblance to the Pittsburgh model. The variation from that model served to demonstrate the localistic variety and flexibility of these institutions, rather than serving to invalidate the model itself. Of greatest significance as a part of this difference, was the degree to which the upper-class system in Philadelphia generally appeared to serve as a barrier to exclude men who derived from less desirable social origins. Although this was, to a degree, characteristic of all upper-class systems, it served less of an escalator function than in Pittsburgh.

CLEVELAND

Cleveland was a mixture of the very old and the very new. Although the city did not begin to grow until the 1840s and 1850s, many of its founding fathers and leading citizens, including a large number of its iron and steel manufacturers, were from some of the oldest and most prestigious upper-class families in America. Perhaps this was partially responsible for the failure of Cleveland's upper class to jell successfully. It retained a chaotic quality that seemed to grow rather than diminish with time.

NEIGHBORHOOD

A visitor to Cleveland in the nineteenth century could not help but be impressed and awed by the brilliance of its premier upper-class neighborhood—Euclid Avenue. Running from downtown Cleveland to the east, the avenue, along with surrounding streets, became the city's most oppulent high-status area in the late nineteenth century. William G. Rose, a chronicler of the city, commented on Euclid Avenue: "No avenue in the world presented such a continuous succession of charming residences and such uniformly beautiful grounds for so great a distance. The peak of a Clevelander's earthy ambition was to have a mansion on the Avenue, beyond Erie Street."[11]

In the 1870s and 1880s, Euclid Avenue to East Sixteenth Street, along with Superior and Prospect Avenues, and the area around the Public Square, formed the principal upper-class areas. In the 1890s, with the encroachment of increasing commercialism in these areas, the upper class began to move to the east or—to a lesser degree—west to the area of Franklin Circle. By 1900, the Euclid upper-class area extended to East Ninetieth Street, as commercialism continued to push the wealthy families further from the central city. The Franklin Circle area also declined rapidly when Tom L. Johnson's Forest City Street Railway was run through it in 1907-1908.[12] By the 1920s, most of the elite residences had been pushed east to a neighborhood around Western Reserve College (about 120th Street), or to the new suburbs of East Cleveland, Cleveland Heights, Shaker Heights, or even further to Mayfield Heights, Euclid and Willoughby.

In 1885, 32 percent of the 117 iron and steel families maintaining homes in Cleveland lived on Euclid Avenue, between the Public Square and East Sixteenth Street. Another 18 percent lived on Prospect and Superior avenues—the other two most popular residential streets for upper-class Clevelanders. Living on the nearby streets of Cedar, Case, Sibley, Putnam, Willson and Woodland were another 23 percent of the families. Thus, nearly three-quarters of the Cleveland iron and steel families lived in close proximity to one another in this section just east of downtown Cleveland. Another 5 percent lived in the Franklin Circle area to the west. The remaining 22 percent were more widely scattered. By 1900, 40 percent of the 118 families were living on Euclid Avenue. Another 14 percent lived on Superior and Prospect Avenues, with 8 percent on adjoining streets. This totaled 62 percent of the iron and steel elite families. The remainder were scattered in several areas, with about 7 percent living in the new eastern suburbs.

Euclid Avenue, during its "glory days" of the late nineteenth century, resembled Allegheny in many ways—particularly in its degree of homogeneity and cohesiveness. Some sense of this phenomenon can be gained by looking at Table 43, which indicates area residences in 1885. Several characteristics of the Euclid Avenue area are apparent. First, there was evidence of the extended family and expanded family relationships, as was seen in nineteenth-century Allegheny. Several conjugal family units lived together under one roof (Chisholm and Stone families; Mather and Par-

TABLE 43

Iron and Steel Family Residences on Euclid, Prospect and Superior Avenues, 1885

Euclid Avenue No.	Family	Prospect Avenue No.	Family	Superior Avenue No.	Family
127	H. Chisholm	425	S. A. & H. A. Fuller	640	Tom L. Johnson
174	C. L. Rhodes	515	Jas. & J. B. Savage	649	Henry Wick
496	W. Chisholm & A. A. Stone	542	W. J. Morgan	660	D. B. Wick
514	Amasa Stone & D. Stone	595	F. F. Hickox	1071	H. P. McIntosh
544	S. L. & W. G. Mather	615	S. H. Mather	1075	G. T. McIntosh
615	Ed. Lewis	626	O. G. Kent	1090	Agnes McIntosh
718	Jas. Barnett	720	Edw. Bingham		
726	C. W. Bingham	832	W. C. & G. F. Scofield		
753	H. H. Brown	901	A. G. Stone		
758	C. T. Hickox	953	E. S. Page		
778	Chas. & R. T. Hickox	960	Jay C. Morse		
800	W. Bingham	1065	W. B. Chisholm		
826	S. & H. E. Andrews	1097	Wm. & F. W. Bowler		
831	Jas., W. S. & R. M. Parmelee				
846	W. A. & C. A. Otis				
863	Fayette Brown				
881	Jas. Pickands				
957	S. H. Chisholm				
975	H. C. Rouse				
1082	C. S. Bissell				
1123	W. D. McBride				
1232	A. H. Wick				
1266	L. McBride				
1270	J. H. McBride				
1457	L. W. Bingham				
1486	A. H. & D. W. Stone				
1516	J.W., A. M. & F. W. Britton				
1524	C. B. Lockwood				
1819	F. L. Ford				
2138	L. A. Ford				

melee families) or, more often, in very close proximity. A good example of the latter, an expanded family arrangement, can be seen in the 100 through 700 blocks on Euclid. Nearly all of these families were related by blood or marriage, and they lived close enough to one another to maintain a lively, ongoing expanded kinship relationship. Thus, Euclid Avenue in the nineteenth century appeared every bit as tightly cohesive and homogeneous as Allegheny, as a Cleveland author, George E. Condon, commented.

> In its heyday, between 1875 and 1900, the stretch of Euclid Avenue . . . extended from East 9th Street to East 55th Street must have contained the most overpowering concentration of affluence . . . in America.
>
> To live in the Millionaries Row of Euclid Avenue was to be a member of a private club as exclusive as today's Union Club or Tavern Club . . . All homes were set back from the sidewalk with a pretty expanse of shady parkland for front lawns.[13]

But by the turn of the century, both the relative density and homogeneity of Euclid Avenue began to decline. As upper-class residences began to sprawl for miles, instead of blocks, and as families of more newly acquired status began moving in, Euclid Avenue lost both its urban characterictics and its upper-class homogeneity. A residential sprawl began to ensue, to be followed and replaced by a commercial sprawl.

The social and cultural origins of the iron and steel families in these various neighborhoods in 1885 showed a few interesting variations. Just as the iron and steel elite in Cleveland was predominantly English, with only a minority of Scotch and Scotch-Irish, Euclid Avenue and its allied streets reflected this orientation. Prospect and Superior streets, however, had larger percentages of Scottish and Scotch-Irish; and Franklin Circle area was dominated by those groups. The small numbers of German, Welsh and French were scattered in outlying areas. In family economic background there were some important differences among the three neighborhoods, with Euclid Street containing about three-quarters from pre-Civil War elite origins. All of those on Franklin Circle were from these origins, while only 42 percent of those on Prospect and Superior were so. A majority in the latter area were from middle-class and working-class backgrounds prior to the Civil War.

A similar differentiation existed in terms of family arrival in America. The majority in all areas, except Prospect and Superior streets, were members of colonial families who came to America prior to 1800. Sixty percent of those on Prospect and Superior streets, however, came to the United States after that time. Thus, although the Prospect and Superior neighborhoods were similar to Euclid Avenue in ethnic and religious backgrounds, they did represent the arrival to status of newer men, both in terms of recency of wealth and of family arrival in America.

This *arriviste* status of Prospect and Superior streets was partially reflected in the dramatic decline of iron and steel family members living in the area by 1900. As Euclid Avenue grew in numbers, it also grew slightly in heterogeneity. As it sprawled ceaselessly toward the east, Euclid Avenue evidently was able to assimilate larger numbers of men from less preferred social origins into its midst. By 1911, the Euclid area reached its apex as an upper-class domicile, but the seeds which were to spell its rapid decline in the next decade were already apparent. Although the majority (58 percent) of Cleveland's iron and steel families lived in the neighborhood of Euclid Avenue in 1911, only 78 percent were listed in the city's Social Register. Superior and Prospect streets continued to dwindle, with only 8 percent of the total, but all were listed in the Social Register. The newest elite residential area in Cleveland proper was Lake Shore Boulevard, with 7 percent of the iron and steel families residing there, of whom 71 percent were listed in the Social Register. All told, 84 percent of the iron and steel elites now lived in Cleveland proper, and 80 percent of them were listed in the Social Register.

Of the steel elite living in suburban Cleveland in 1911, 94 percent were listed in the Social Register. It had become apparent, then, as early as the first decade of the twentieth century, that suburban upper-class areas were beginning to grow at the expense of those elite areas in Cleveland proper, especially Euclid Avenue. And, further, it was these new suburban areas which would carry the greatest social prestige among the well-to-do. Euclid Avenue, Cleveland's preferred domicile for a generation, was declining in prestige and attractiveness.

Of the 114 persons descended from the nineteenth-century iron and steel families still living in Cleveland in 1921, 93 percent were now listed in the Social Register. By this time, the disintegration of the once close-knit Euclid Avenue area had become readily apparent. Only 41 percent of the iron and steel families continued to live in the neighborhood, with 91 percent of them listed in the Social Register. Of greater significance, however, is the fact that one-half of all those iron and steel families in Cleveland not listed in the Social Register resided in the Euclid Avenue area. Seven percent continued to live along Lake Shore Boulevard, while 45 percent now inhabited the eastern suburbs, especially Cleveland Heights. All of those in Cleveland Heights, and in all the other major upper-class suburbs, were listed in the Social Register.

By 1931 the flight to the suburbs for upper-class families in Cleveland had become even more pronounced with 61 percent of the 106 families now living in these outlying areas. Less than one-half now resided in Cleveland proper. Of the suburbs, Cleveland Heights was still the most popular for the iron and steel families; and all of those living there were listed in the Social Register. By 1942 the pattern of residence had become even more diffuse. Of sixty-two families remaining in Cleveland, none lived on Euclid Avenue. Further, there was only an insignificant scattering of iron and steel families in the other east-end sections of Cleveland. Most had now moved to the suburbs and exurbs of the city; but even here the pattern was more diffuse than before. Only two families now lived in Cleve-

TABLE 44
Cleveland Elite Neighborhoods as Related to Social Register, 1911

Area	Percentage of Iron and Steel Family Residents in Social Register
Urban Neighborhoods	
Euclid *N*=60	78
Superior & Prospect *N*=8	100
Lake Shore Boulevard *N*=7	71
Other Urban *N*=12	83
Total Urban *N*=87	80
Suburban Neighborhoods	
Euclid Heights *N*=4	100
East Cleveland *N*=7	86
Cleveland Heights *N*=1	100
Other, Suburban *N*=5	100
Total Suburban *N*=17	94
Total City *N*=104	83

TABLE 45
Neighborhood as Related to Social Class, Cleveland Suburbs, 1931

Area	Number of Iron and Steel Families	Percentage in Social Register
Suburban Areas		
Cleveland Heights	20	100
Shaker Heights	4	100
Lakewood	3	100
Chagrin Falls	3	100
East Cleveland	3	100
Other, Suburbs	32	68
Total Suburban	65	85
Urban Areas	41	85
Total City	106	85

land Heights, and no suburb contained as many as 10 percent of the total number of families. Shaker Heights, with 8 percent, had the highest proportion, but was not significantly above the others.

The principal upper-class suburbs, Cleveland Heights, Shaker Heights, Lakewood, Chagrin Falls and East Cleveland, had much greater homogeneity than the old Cleveland urban neighborhoods, since all of their iron and steel residents were listed in the Social Register. Only in more scattered suburban areas, far more diverse in nature, did the suburban percentage fall off significantly. The Cleveland urban areas in 1931 maintained an 85 percent Social Register listing; but the families were much more widely dispersed than they had been twenty years earlier, and one could not really speak of "urban" neighborhoods any longer. Of the sixty-three families still residing in Cleveland in 1942, Cleveland Heights, Shaker Heights, Chagrin Falls and Mentor, all had 100 percent listings in the Social Register. The scattered suburban areas had 85 percent of the families listed. The city of Cleveland showed 90 percent of its widely scattered families listed.

By 1948, 78 percent of the sixty-three iron and steel families listed in the Social Register were living in suburban Cleveland, with Shaker Heights and Cleveland Heights the most popular. Twenty years later, in 1968, only thirty-five iron and steel families still resided in Cleveland, most having moved away to other cities. Of those who remained, nearly all lived in peaceful seclusion in Cleveland's suburbs.

The residential areas in Cleveland, then, were less successful in maintaining themselves as upper-class domiciles for the city's iron and steel elite over time. First Euclid Avenue lost its clientele to the suburbs during the early decades of the twentieth century. Then, after World War II, and particularly during the 1960s, the descendants of the iron and steel elite began leaving the Cleveland suburbs altogether, heading south, east and west for new communities. Unlike Pittsburgh's East End and Sewickley, Philadelphia's Main Line, and Boston's Beacon Hill, Cleveland failed to maintain stable upper-class residential areas.

SOCIAL CLUBS

Cleveland's upper-class social clubs reflect much of the same lack of stability as the residential areas, with great dispersion and diffusion of iron and steel family members, and with a less precise ranking of the clubs by social status than was the case in either Pittsburgh or Philadelphia. Cleveland's principal town clubs were the Colonial, Hermit, Roadside, Rowfant, Tavern and Union Clubs.

The Tavern Club was organized in 1892 by Addison H. Hough, William Cl. Rhodes and Charles A. Otis, Jr. Their first club house was at Case Avenue and Prospect Street, until it was moved in 1898 to 968 Prospect. Then, in 1903, it was moved still farther east to Thirty-sixth and Prospect, reflecting the easterly movement of Cleveland's upper-class neighborhoods. As with the Pittsburgh Club, the popular story concerning the founding of the Tavern Club was that it had been organized as a "rendezvous for gay blades of Cleveland's first families!"[14] However that may be, it is clear that by 1903, when the new club house was built, it served primarily as an "uptown" social club for those who now lived further out on Euclid and Prospect Avenues.[15]

In 1900, there were only ten iron and steel family members in the Tavern Club. Little concerning the social and cultural backgrounds of these men betrayed their relative social status. They were dominated by the Scottish and Scotch-Irish, while a large minority were English. Forty percent were Presbyterian and an equal number were Episcopalian, while 90 percent were from pre-Civil War elite families. Whereas 86 percent were members of colonial families, only one-half of these had arrived during the seventeenth century. Thus, in a city where the preferred social origins appeared to be English, the Tavern Club contained an inordinate number from non-English groups. Eighty-two percent of the seventeen iron and steel club members in 1911 were listed in the Cleveland Social Register.

By 1921 there were fourteen iron and steel family members of the Tavern Club, all listed in the Social Register. Ten years later in 1931, there were ten iron and steel members, and all were again listed. The number climbed to fifteen in 1948; and even with the extensive exodus of old iron and steel families from the city in the next twenty years, by 1968, nine members of iron and steel families still retained memberships. Beginning as an "uptown" club, Tavern appeared to overcome its earlier social disadvantages to become one of Cleveland's premier social clubs. If it never succeeded in attracting a large percentage of the iron and steel elite, those who were accepted were of high status, and maintained their family memberships over a long period of time.

The Rowfant Club was organized in 1892 as an association of men interested in books. The purported objective of the club was the ciritical study of books and the publication of privately printed editions for its members. Like the Tavern Club, it was located on what was then the eastern edge of the city, at Thirtieth and Prospect.[16] As a special-interest club with a limited membership, Rowfant attracted relatively few iron and steel family members. In 1900, only seven men from these families were enrolled. All of those for whom information was available were of English origin and were either Presbyterian or Episcopalian; all but one was a member of a pre-Civil War elite family. Seventy-five percent of the men were from old families who had come to America during the seventeenth century. By 1915, there were thirteen iron and steel members in Rowfant, and all but one was listed in the city's Social Register.

Although the Rowfant Club continued to grow over the years (150 members in 1960), it appeared to have little continuing attraction for iron and steel family members. By 1931, only two still held memberships in the club. Of high prestige and selectivity in the early years, Rowfant apparently was too esoteric for the taste of most iron and steel families, and it failed to replicate even the limited attractiveness and appeal of the Tavern Club.

The Roadside Club at one time was reputed to be Cleveland's most exclusive and prestigious club. A harness racing and driving club, it was organized in 1895 with a club house far to the east on St. Clair Avenue.[17] By 1900, thirty-three members of Cleveland's iron and steel families belonged to the club. An analysis of the ethno-cultural backgrounds of these members, however, fails to support the vaunted exclusiveness of the Roadside Club. Half of the members in 1899 were of English ancestry, while nearly 40 percent were Scottish or Scotch-Irish. Only one-half were either Presbyterian or Episcopalian, while just 71 percent were members of pre-Civil War elite families. Thus, in 1900, Roadside Club, whatever its pretensions, appeared to be less exclusive and less prestigious than either the Tavern or Rowfant clubs.

By 1911 the popularity of the club among iron and steel families had declined considerably, counting only nineteen of these men among its members, exactly one-half of the total a decade earlier. Of them, 85 percent were listed in the Cleveland Social Register of that year. The emergence of the automobile as a principal mode of transportation apparently signaled the final downfall of Roadside. By 1931 there was not a single iron and steel family member in the club; and, after the club house was destroyed by fire in 1935, it ceased to function.

The Hermit Club was another small, town, men's club. Organized in 1904, its purpose was to put on variety shows and to provide a congenial social milieu for its members.[18] The Hermit Club never held much attraction for members of the iron and steel elite. In 1911, only four men belonged, two of whom were listed in the Social Register. By 1921, there were three new iron and steel members, with two of the three listed in the Social Register. In 1942, there was only one new member from these families, and he was so listed.

Another club with a limited, short-term appeal, was the Colonial Club. Organized in 1896, its club house was located on the eastern edge of Cleveland, at 91st Street and Euclid Avenue. A large club, with 350 members in 1897, it appeared to be more inclusive than exclusive in its membership practices. In that year, twenty-two iron and steel men were among its clientele. Although most were of English ancestry, and were either Presbyterian or Episcopalian, a large number were of relatively recent wealth and origin in Cleveland. Only 52 percent were members of pre-Civil War elite families, and almost all of these were elite migrants to Cleveland in the late nineteenth century. Further, one-half of the men were from families who had immigrated to America during the nineteenth century. Since the Colonial Club was founded by the steel man, Henry P. McIntosh, who was himself a recent immigrant, it was perhaps natural that the club had the greatest appeal to men of new wealth and recently acquired social status in Cleveland.[19]

By 1911, twenty-three men from iron and steel families were members of the Colonial Club, but only 61 percent were listed in the Social Register. A few years later, in 1918, the club disbanded. The Colonial Club seemed to attract men from newer families, men on their way up the social ladder. It was the first club membership for many of these newer families, and it had the lowest relative prestige of any of the town clubs in Cleveland. Perhaps this factor caused its early demise; although the fact that the club was "dry", and that it closed on Sunday, did nothing to enhance its long-term popularity.[20]

There were other town clubs with broad elite membership, but all with little attraction for the Cleveland upper classes. The Excelsior Club (later the Oakwood) Club) for Cleveland's Jewish elite, was founded in 1872, with a club house on Superior Avenue. The Cleveland Athletic Club was organized in 1885 in a tailor shop. Later, it moved to a new club house at Euclid and Case Avenues. William

Upson, of a newer iron and steel family, was one of its organizers. The University Club was organized in 1898, for Clevelanders with a college education. Its first club house was on Prospect Avenue; and in 1913 it moved to 3813 Euclid Avenue.

The "queen" of the men's social clubs in Cleveland, however, was the Union Club. It was organized in 1872 as an offshoot of the Cleveland Club (formed earlier in that year). Evidently, the Cleveland Club had not been selective enough for many of its members, since sixty or seventy of them broke away to form the Union Club. William Bingham was the first president of the latter club; a home on Euclid Avenue was purchased as its club house. As William G. Rose has noted, the Union Club became one of the most important social institutions in America, "uniting men of influence and ambition as a social and intellectual force in the community."[21] By 1900, membership in the Union Club had grown to 500, and a new club house was then opened farther east on Euclid Avenue.

Of the original eighty-one members in 1872, nineteen were iron and steel manufacturers in the city, with ten more joining in the following year. Even at its founding, the club appeared to combine, in nearly perfect fashion, the newly arrived and the long established in such a manner that was to serve twin—and somewhat contradictory—functions: it acted as an escalator for the newly arrived families, while at the same time retaining its prestige and relative exclusivity. Of the twenty-nine iron and steel men in the club in 1872-73, 73 percent were of English ancestry, with the remainder being Scottish or Scotch-Irish. Three-quarters were either Presbyterian or Episcopalian; and 83 percent were members of colonial families, nearly two-thirds arriving during the seventeenth century. Added to this old family core, however, were a few new men (since only 88 percent were pre-Civil War elites): 18 percent had immigrated to America during the nineteenth century.

A generation later, in 1900, the Union Club continued to build upon this tradition of prestige and selected openness. Of the sixty-three iron and steel members of the club in that year, two-thirds were of English ancestry, and 29 percent were Scottish or Scotch-Irish. Sixty-one percent were adherents of Presbyterianism or Episcopalianism; but a larger number than before were members of other Protestant denominations. Further, although 72 percent were members of pre-Civil War elite families, this was a substantial decrease from the earlier period. Similarly, 28 percent of the iron and steel members at this later date were from families which had immigrated to America during the nineteenth century, although nearly one-half continued to be derived from seventeenth-century families.

That the Union Club was able to ingest a rather large number of men of new wealth and recent arrival was attested by its Social Register listings of iron and steel family members in 1911. Of the seventy-nine iron and steel men in the club that year, 92 percent were listed in the Social Register. Twenty years later, in 1931, thirty-one additional men from these families had joined the club, and 97 percent of them were so listed.

Thus the Union Club appeared rather enigmatic in some respects. A large club, with a membership of over 1,000 by 1932, it seemed to practice little selectivity; yet it remained highly exclusive and prestigious in terms of the social origins and

Social Register listings of its members. In 1934, after its membership had dropped to a disastrously low point, the club had a membership drive. Of the 250 men suggested for membership, 222 were approved as members. This openness was made even more dramatic by a statement of John R. Kraus, head of the membership drive committee: "If I can get any of these bozos to join, will you approve them?"[22] Evidently they did.

One could logically assume that aggressive selling methods, such as those outlined above, would have diluted the status of the club's membership and rendered it undesirable as an upper-class habitat. Just the reverse seems to have been the case. As late as 1973, twenty-five descendants of iron and steel families still maintained membership in the Union Club, out of a total of over 1,300 members. These twenty-five iron and steel men averaged 23.4 years of membership in the club; but nearly one-third were young men who had joined since 1960. Thus, the Union Club was able not only to retain the loyalty of older members (one of whom had belonged to the club for sixty years and another for fifty-one years), but was also able to attract new generations of young men to its club rooms.[23]

Seemingly, the Union Club combined in one institution the upper-class functions delegated to several clubs in Pittsburgh and Philadelphia. It was an elite club for men of new wealth, similar to the Duquesne and Union League; yet it was also of the utmost prestige and social status in the city, similar to the Pittsburgh Club and the Philadelphia and Rittenhouse clubs.

Cleveland also developed a full range of country and suburban golf clubs. Two of the most prestigious of these clubs were the Mayfield Country Club and the Chagrin Valley Hunt Club. Ranked below these were the Cleveland Country, Cleveland Golf, and Euclid Club. Although there were social distinctions among these clubs, they were never as clear as in Pittsburgh or Philadelphia. No club approached either Allegheny Country Club or Radnor Hunt in its combination of prestige and popularity.

Cleveland Country Club was organized in 1890 by Samuel Mather as a bit and bridle club with a membership of 100. A club house was built on grounds near Lake Erie, where the club remained until 1928—when it was relocated in Pepper Pike Village, a new suburb east of Cleveland which had been financed by the Van Swearingen brothers. Several of the officers during the early years were men from iron and steel families; and, in 1900, twenty-six men from these families held memberships. They were fairly evenly divided between those of English and Scottish or Scotch-Irish ancestry. The majority were Episcopalian or Presbyterian. Though nearly three-quarters were from pre-Civil War elite origins, a rather large minority were from non-elite origins. Similarly, 28 percent immigrated during the nineteenth century, but another 44 percent were members of families which had arrived prior to 1700.

Cleveland Country Club in its early years, then, appeared to be able to combine a prestige and attractiveness to old high-status families, while at the same time admitting significant numbers of new men. In this manner, Cleveland Country seemed to be a suburban counterpart to the Union Club. This was further borne out by the

Social Register listings of its iron and steel members in 1911. Of forty-three such families, 88 percent were listed in the Cleveland Social Register of that year, while all of the thirty-seven new iron and steel family members were listed in 1921.

During the 1930s, however, the club's attractiveness for iron and steel families began to diminish rapidly; and no new men from these families joined its ranks. By 1937, only seven iron and steel descendants belonged; and by 1964 there were only four. It is difficult to ascertain the precise reasons for this decline; but since it was coterminous with the relocation of the club in Pepper Pike, this factor would appear to be germane.

> The old club (in Cleveland) . . . had its own traditions and infinite memories, intangible qualities of slow growth that are not easily moved about from pillar to post. A great many members consequently dropped out entirely and transferred their affections to Kirtland.[24]

During its halcyon days, however, Cleveland Country Club was the premier suburban club in Cleveland.

Cleveland Golf Club had been organized in 1895 by members of the Cleveland Country Club who wished to partake in the popularity of this new pastime. In 1898 it became a totally separate organization, remaining so until 1902 when it was reconsolidated with Cleveland Country Club. There was, naturally, a great deal of similarity in the social characteristics of the iron and steel families who belonged to the two clubs. Of the twenty-five men from these families who were members of Cleveland Golf in 1900, seventeen were also members of Cleveland Country. Of the eight who were not members, five had brothers or fathers in that club. Thus, only three men were members of families which were not represented in Cleveland Country Club. Of the iron and steel membership in 1900, 92 percent were listed in the 1911 Social Register, making Cleveland Golf roughly equivalent to Cleveland Country Club in status—a factor aiding in the merger two years later.

The Euclid Club was organized in 1900 in the eastern Cleveland suburb of Cleveland Heights. Among the founders was Wilson B. Chisholm, member of one of Cleveland's newer elite families not listed in the Social Register until the time around World War I. In 1920 the club was abandoned to a real estate development, and its members joined the newly organized Mayfield Country Club. In 1910, twenty-one members of iron and steel families belonged to the Euclid Club, with 76 percent of them listed in the Social Register. It therefore ranked below Cleveland Country or Cleveland Golf clubs in social status, catering more to the newer elite families of Cleveland.

Chagrin Valley Hunt Club was founded by Charles A. Otis, Jr. in 1908, with grounds situated on his Tannebaum Farm on the eastern edge of Cleveland. Devoted to the classic English-type fox hunt, with other equestrian and sporting activities, Chagrin Valley Hunt enjoyed great prestige among Cleveland's upper classes. Due to the limited appeal of these activities, along with the club's strict selectivity in its choice of members, it remained rather small in total membership for some time. In 1921 there were only eight members of the club from iron and steel families, with all listed in the Social Register. The men for the most part represented Cleveland's oldest and most prestigious families. By 1931 the club had grown only slightly, taking in six new members from these families, all of whom were listed in the Social Register. These six new members represented not only the oldest Cleveland Families, but also the arrival to status of some newer families. The new men had earlier moved up the status ladder of clubs, seemingly reaching a peak at the Chagrin Valley Hunt. In 1945 the status nature of the club continued, taking in only three new members from iron and steel families. Two were from the older families and one was from a newer family. By 1968 five members of iron and steel families belonged to Chagrin Valley. By then all were integral members of the indigenous upper class. Chagrin Valley Hunt appeared to be the most exclusive of the suburban clubs in Cleveland; but unlike similar clubs in Pittsburgh and Philadelphia, it never attracted more than a small minority of the upper-class families.

The Mayfield Country Club was organized in 1910 in the upper-class suburb of Lynnhurst. Most of its early membership core came from the defunct Euclid Club, though the prestige of the Mayfield Country Club seemed to be somewhat higher. In 1911 there were twenty-two iron and steel family members of the club, 86 percent of whom were listed in the Social Register. Growing rapidly during the next ten years, Mayfield enrolled twenty-seven new members from the iron and steel families. All of these new members were listed in the Social Register. The club's popularity declined somewhat in the 1920s, however, as only five new members from the iron and steel families joined. All were listed in the Social Register. By 1942, only three new iron and steel family members had joined, all of whom were listed in the Social Register. The competition from newer suburban clubs, especially Kirtland Country Club, seemed to have diminished the popularity of Mayfield Country Club, though it did not damage its social prestige.

Kirtland Country Club was organized in 1921 near the suburb of Willoughby. Located much further east than the earlier suburban clubs, it was better able to keep pace with the ceaseless, eastward trek of Cleveland's upper-class families. Soon after its founding, Kirtland became the premier Cleveland suburban club in terms of prestige and popularity. In 1931 there were twenty-eight members of iron and steel families who belonged to Kirtland, all of whom were listed in the Social Register. By 1942 five more men from these families were counted among its members, and all were so listed. Of the fifty-five iron and steel descendants listed in the Cleveland Social Register in 1968, thirteen were members of Kirtland Club. Thus, Kirtland was able to maintain its high status and relative popularity over a long period of time, becoming the nearest thing Cleveland had to the Allegheny Country Club or Radnor Hunt.

Although it is possible to delineate, to some degree, the social rankings of Cleveland's club structure by using Social Register listings of its iron and steel members, the general situation was one of considerable shifting of status and less definable stratification over the years than was the case in either Pittsburgh or

Philadelphia. The rather confusing and imprecise nature of the Cleveland club system can be further illustrated by looking at family, rather than individual memberships in each club, broken down by decades, along with the percentage of Social Register listings of these families. Table 46 illustrates at least two characteristics of the Cleveland club system: first, the stratification of the clubs at either the town or suburban level was never enough to rank the clubs according to social status with any confidence; second, this problem was magnified in the mid-twentieth century, when all clubs showed a 100 percent Social Register listing for its iron and steel members. Thus, since both neighborhood and social clubs in Cleveland appear to be a less reliable index of social standing than was the case in other cities, one must turn to marriage patterns, hoping it will provide a clearer guide to the nature of the upper-class system in Cleveland.

MARRIAGE AND KINSHIP PATTERNS

Unfortunately, the marriage patterns for Cleveland's iron and steel elite were nearly as diffuse and indecisive as the neighborhood and club patterns. None of the marriage tests which were applied to Pittsburgh and Philadelphia iron and steel families was able to produce anything approaching clear results in Cleveland. Of 583 iron and steel elite marriages in the city, only 8 percent were endogamous to the group, along with another 6 percent endogamous to a group of non-iron and steel upper-class, Cleveland families. In fact, placing the diffuse marriage patterns alongside the other upper-class, Cleveland institutions calls to question whether the city was able to produce, or at least sustain, a structured upper-class community during the twentieth century.

Using the four endogamous marriages in Cleveland among the sixty-one iron and steel families, along with fourteen other upper-class Cleveland families as an index for inclusion in the core family group, produces just six families as members of this group, only 10 percent of the total. A strong case can be made for these families being among the core families of Cleveland; but the list unfortunately excludes several families which in every other way had the utmost social prestige in the city: Bingham, Otis, Mather, Eells, Barnett, Hough, McBride, Morse, Parmelee, Prentiss, Rockefeller, and Severance. Reducing the number of required endogamous marriages from four to three, however (although including some of these families), would still exclude several of the most prominent. It seemed logical, then, to stay with the endogamous marriage model established for the Pittsburgh Core Families.

The non-core upper class, including most of those prestigious families excluded from the core group, totaled eighteen families. This represented all those who had at least one marriage but less than four marriages to core families. The marginal families, those married to either non-core family members or to recognizable upper-class individuals outside of Cleveland, represented 21 percent of the total (thirteen families). The remainder, the elite, non-upper-class family group was composed of twenty-four families with no significant marriage patterns, representing 39 percent of the total group.

TABLE 46
Family Memberships in Cleveland Social Clubs as Related to Cleveland Social Register

Town Clubs	1900		1911		1921		1942	
	Number of Families	% in Social Register	Number of Families	% in Social Register	Number of Families	% in Social Register	Number of Families	% in Social Register
Tavern	9	89	13	85	13	100	8	100
Roadside	20	85	22	86	23	91	–	–
Rowfant	6	100	9	100	10	100	–	–
Union	29	86	33	85	37	87	36	100
Hermit	–	–	3	67	6	100	7	100
Colonial	12	75	16	63	–	–	–	–
Total Families & Average % for Town Clubs	76	84	96	82	89	93	51	100

Suburban Clubs	1900		1911		1921		1931		1942	
	Number of Families	% in Social Register	Number of Families	% in Social Register	Number of Families	% in Social Register	Number of Families	% in Social Register	Number of Families	% in Social Register
Cleveland	17	88	25	88	27	96	–	–	–	–
Country Club	–	–	–	–	–	–	–	–	–	–
Cleveland Golf	17	94	–	–	–	–	–	–	–	–
Euclid	–	–	16	81	–	–	–	–	–	–
Mayfield	–	–	16	89	22	95	24	92	24	100
Chagrin V.	–	–	–	–	7	100	9	100	11	100
Kirtland	–	–	–	–	–	–	14	100	15	100
Total Families & Average % for Suburban Clubs	34	91	57	86	56	96	47	96	50	100
Total Families & Average % for All Clubs	110	86	151	85	145	95	47	96	101	100

An analysis of the social and cultural backgrounds of the families composing these four endogamous marriage groups gives no clue as to their relative social status. In fact, the core families in many respects appeared to have emanated from more diverse and heterogenous origins than the other groups. This is quite apparent in the area of ethnicity. Where English origins were predominant among Cleveland's iron and steel elite, the core families were evenly divided among English, Scottish, and Scotch-Irish. Further, although two-thirds were from pre-Civil War elite families, one family was from immigrant working-class backgrounds, and one was from poor origins—the only such family in Cleveland. Finally, fully 40 percent were immigrants to America in the nineteenth century, and only 20 percent were from seventeenth-century families. Thus, the core upper-class families in many respects seemed to reflect origins from the newer, non-New England base.

Both the non-core and marginal-upper class families were 80 percent English in ancestry; and nearly two-thirds of each emanated from the pre-Civil War elite. The only difference of any magnitude between the two groups was that a large minority of the non-core families derived from native middle-class roots, while 27 percent of the marginal group were from immigrant middle-class origins. This difference was further reflected in the times of arrival of their families in America. Most of Cleveland's seventeenth-century, old New England families were in the non-core group, comprising 70 percent of the total. None arrived during the nineteenth century. The marginal families contained 40 percent who originated in the seventeenth century, twice as many as among the core group but only 60 percent of the total in the non-core group. Thirty percent of the marginal families arrived during the nineteenth century.

Even the elite, non-upper-class families appeared to reflect more preferred ethnic origins than the core group, with two-thirds of English ancestry. In economic backgrounds, however, they were newer to elite status than any of the preceding family groups, having less than one-third from the pre-Civil War elite. In addition, nearly 70 percent arrived in America during the nineteenth century.

Despite these discrepancies in social and cultural characteristics, an analysis of the family groupings compared to family Social Register listings and club memberships indicates a rank ordering according to status almost precisely identical to that found in Pittsburgh and Philadelphia. All of the core families were listed in the Cleveland *Social Register;* 78 percent of the non-core families were so listed, compared to 62 percent of the marginal upper-class families and only 50 percent of the elite, non-upper-class group.

Analysis of family club memberships reveals a similar rank ordering. Looking first at the six clubs which appeared to have the most prestige in the city in our prior analysis (Union, Rowfant, Tavern, Cleveland Country, Kirtland Country, and Chagrin Valley Hunt), 78 percent of the core families, on average, belonged to these clubs (compared to 47 percent of the non-core families, 36 percent of the marginal families, and only 14 percent of the elite group). Even in the six clubs of lesser stature (Roadside, Hermit, Cleveland Golf, Mayfield, Euclid and Colonial

TABLE 47

Cleveland Endogamous Marriage Patterns as Related to Other Social Factors

Family Group		% in Social Register	Percentage of Family Group in Club: Tavern	Rowfant	Roadside	Union	Hermit	Cleveland Country
Core	$N = 6$	100	100	33	83	100	38	100
Non-Core	$N = 18$	78	50	24	56	83	22	50
Marginal	$N = 13$	62	15	31	38	85	8	68
Other	$N = 24$	50	0	4	8	63	8	17
Total Ave.	60	67	28	18	37	78	15	47

Family Group	Cleveland Golf	Mayfield	Kirtland	Chagrin Valley Hunt	Euclid	Colonial
Core	67	67	67	67	50	50
Non-Core	44	50	44	28	33	11
Marginal	58	23	5	0	38	38
Other	0	25	0	0	4	21
Total Ave.	28	37	23	15	25	25

clubs), a similar rank ordering prevailed, with the core families averaging 59 percent membership; non-core, 36 percent; marginal, 34 percent; and elite, 11 percent. The overall averages of club memberships were also similar, with the core families averaging 67 percent; non-core, 41 percent; marginal, 35 percent; and elite, 13 percent.

How does one explain the seeming dichotomy of generally less preferred social, cultural and economic origins of the core families with the remarkably high status accorded them by marriage, the Social Register and the clubs? In large measure, the race for social status in Cleveland appeared to go by default to those families who persevered over time. Evidently many of those old New England families who had migrated to the Western Reserve in the early nineteenth century found the wanderlust stirring their souls again a century later. Most of these families left Cleveland in the early twentieth century, either returning to their eastern roots, or striking out for greener pastures in the West or South.

This phenomenon was reflected in an analysis of iron and steel families retaining residence in Cleveland from 1931 to 1968. As is made clear in Table 48, the core families had by far the greatest staying power in Cleveland, followed by the non-core, marginal and elite families. Thus, almost regardless of social and cultural origins, if a family made money and could stick it out in Cleveland for several generations, they could move into the very core of the upper-class system. Since so many others had considered the maintenance and preservation of their upper-class system of such little interest, however, one wonders how much the final price of upper-class status was actually worth.

This appears to be the most seminal fact about the upper-class system in Cleveland, compared to those in Pittsburgh and Philadelphia. On neither the club level nor the neighborhood and marital levels did the indigenous upper-class system in Cleveland ever fully congeal. The families who could have been expected to provide the social leadership in the city (those New England eminences), appeared to disdain the Cleveland social scene, forsaking it for what they considered more important social ventures.

This abandonment of Cleveland by its old families was perhaps caught most poignantly in 1964 by Donald S. Carmichael, president of the Cleveland City Club:

TABLE 48
Residential Persistence in Cleveland by Endogamous Marital Groups

		Percentage of Family Groups Residing in Cleveland in Given Year				
Family Group		1931	1942	1948	1958	1968
Core	*N*=6	100	83	83	83	83
Non-Core	*N*=18	72	50	44	28	33
Marginal	*N*=13	62	38	15	15	15
Elite	*N*=24	25	17	8	8	4

"There is a crying need for the old families of the town—the aristocracy if you please—to recommit and dedicate themselves to a deep concern about the government and welfare of greater Cleveland."[25] Yet, by this time few of these old families remained in Cleveland to hear his call, with only twelve of the sixty iron and steel families still having members who maintained residence there. Of these, five were core families, six were non-core, and one was elite.

LOCALS AND COSMOPOLITANS IN CLEVELAND

Implicit in the above analysis is the idea that the Cleveland iron and steel elite had a high incidence of contact with other areas—through business, schooling, clubs and marriages. This more cosmopolitan aspect of the Cleveland iron and steel elite undoubtedly caused much of the diffusion in local upper-class institutions.

Cleveland's iron and steel elite had extensive social ties to other cities through their educational patterns, membership in social clubs, and marriages. The core families of Cleveland allow a detailed analysis of their cosmopolitan relationships. Two-thirds of the six core families maintained memberships in prestigious clubs in New York City, Pittsburgh, Chicago, and Washington, D.C.. As far as prep schools are concerned, the core families sent their sons to Cleveland public schools during the nineteenth century. Only the Chisholms, who sent a son to Exeter, deviated from this pattern. By the twentieth century all were sending their sons to private schools. The information on this is a little uneven; but there seemed to be a less definite pattern of prep school attendance among Cleveland core families, as compared to those in Pittsburgh and Philadelphia. None sent sons to St. Paul's; instead they sent them to assorted private schools in Cleveland and the East. Although no single school became the special preserve of the Cleveland core families, the families did become more cosmopolitan in the twentieth century, generally sending their sons east to mingle with young men from upper-class families in other cities.

On the college level, Yale University was the overwhelming choice of the Cleveland core families, with all sending sons there in the late nineteenth and early twentieth centuries. Since most of the core families were well connected in the East, especially with old Connecticut families, Yale was a logical choice for them. The Cleveland core families seemed to fit in well at Yale, with only a few attending Sheffield Scientific School. Several also sent sons to other schools.

The cosmopolitan marriages of the Cleveland core families with upper-class families in other cities were higher than was the case in either Pittsburgh or Philadelphia. Of the 150 core marriages on which information could be found, 18 percent were cosmopolitan. And this is a rather minimal figure, since at least ten to twenty other marriages existed where the information was not clear (as to whether the marriage partner was originally a Clevelander or not). At any rate, the figure for Cleveland core families was quite high. Part of the reason for this was due to their continuing strong ties to old New England families, with whom they continued to marry. The end result of the more cosmopolitan marriage pattern for Cleveland core families was to reaffirm the more diffuse nature of the Cleveland upper classes. Even the core families in this city did not seem to view themselves as a local upper class, or to have a sense of local upper-class community (as was true with the Pittsburgh and Philadelphia core families). As with clubs and neighborhood, the marriage patterns of the Cleveland core families reveal a far less compact and precise upper-class core group in the city, with a lowered sense of local orientation.

The pattern for the non-core upper-class families in Cleveland was similar to that of the core families. The prep school attendance of these families was identical, though fewer went away to prep schools in the East and many sent their sons to Cleveland public schools. In the twentieth century, the trend toward eastern prep schools did not seem to accelerate greatly. Several of the families switched from the public schools to University School in Cleveland; but there was little evidence of larger numbers going to the more famous eastern prep schools. As with the core families, Yale was the preferred school for the non-core families; but the general choice of college was more diffuse for the non-core group. This seemed to increase rather than decrease during the twentieth century, although Yale remained the marginally preferred school.

The cosmopolitan marriage patterns of the non-core families was similar to the pattern of that family group in Pittsburgh and Philadelphia: many more of non-core family marriages than core family marriages were to upper-class families in other cities. But, again, the figure for Cleveland families was quite high when compared to non-core families in these other two cities. Twenty-seven percent of the 256 non-core marriages on which information could be found were to recognizable upper-class families in other areas. This figure probably represents something of an understatement, with the actual total probably some 10-15 points higher. Again, the high percentage of cosmopolitan marriages for the non-core group adds to the growing body of evidence pointing to the weakness of the Cleveland upper-class structure.

Since the category of marginal families was partially defined by their marriages to recognized upper classes in other cities, it is natural that the percentage of these marriages would be high. With 34 percent of the ninety-one recorded marriages to upper-class families in other cities, the marginal family totals reflected this. Due to the generally more cosmopolitan nature of Cleveland's upper classes, however, the figure is only slightly above that of the non-core families in the city. On the other hand, the marginal family cosmopolitan marriage percentage was much higher than those for marginal families in Pittsburgh or Philadelphia. The figures on schooling patterns for Cleveland's marginal families were rather fragmented. Only the Bartol family sent sons away to eastern prep schools. All the other families sent their sons to public or private schools in Cleveland. On the college level, the diffuse pattern that was the case with other Cleveland family groups held true for the marginal families. The marginal families in Cleveland, then, though fairly provincial in their educational patterns, were highly cosmopolitan in marital choices.

The figures for the remaining twenty-three elite families were too incomplete to be of much value. A few bits and pieces of information will be related to fill out the picture. There was no record of any members of these families having attended eastern prep schools. All attended public schools in their home town, except for Samuel Sague, who attended University School in Cleveland. At the college level, only six families had any record of attendance, and the pattern was very diffuse. Twenty-seven percent of the seventy-three recorded marriages of elite families were of a cosmopolitan nature. On only a few of these families, however, was the data complete enough to even hazard a guess that the outside families involved were upper-class families in their areas.

Cleveland thus had a fluctuating and imprecise upper-class system, one in which the institutions were constantly shifting and the neighborhoods changing. This was reflected in the intermarriage patterns, where the ties of local community were often not strong enough to create a web of intermarriage among its local upper-class families. Cleveland had a more cosmopolitan upper class; but at the same time, it was less stable on the local scene than those in Pittsburgh and Philadelphia.

CLEVELAND'S UPPER-CLASS SOCIAL NETWORK

Because of the diffuse nature of the upper-class system in Cleveland, it was virtually impossible to reconstruct a meaningful upper-class social network, as was done for Pittsburgh and Philadelphia. On the one hand, the points of intermarriage were so few (only 8 percent of the total) that no significant kinship network emerged: the connections were occasional and largely idiosyncratic. On the other hand, the upper-class social clubs in Cleveland (especially the Union Club) were so inclusive in their membership as to establish a network in which virtually all families are included. For example, the Browns, a core family, had interlocking club memberships with all but thirteen of the sixty iron and steel families—with all of the core families; all but one of the non-core; two of the marginal; and ten of the elite families. They had at least one interlocking membership with each of forty-seven families, and as high as ten interlocks with one of the families, giving them a total of 197 club membership interlocks. The same was true generally of the other core families, of most of the non-core, of two-thirds of the marginal families and of at least one-quarter of the elite families. Thus, a "network" emerged in which all families were connected with nearly all others in an extensive fashion in terms of club membership; but the network was almost totally lacking in marital interlocks.

CONCLUSIONS

Cleveland, then, differed substantially from both Pittsburgh and Philadelphia. Unlike those two cities, Cleveland was not able to create a functioning, stable upper-class system. Few Cleveland elite families married with one another. The clubs differentiated little in terms of membership selection. Neighborhoods were short-lived, and the Cleveland iron and steel elite deserted the city in large numbers during the twentieth century. Those elements of tradition and continuity provided by the upper classes in Pittsburgh and Philadelphia were absent in Cleveland.

YOUNGSTOWN

Youngstown, a much smaller city than Pittsburgh, Philadelphia or Cleveland in the nineteenth and twentieth centuries, did not develop the opulent, distinctly upper-class suburbs with palatial homes, or the highly exclusive upper-class clubs as in these other cities. On the surface, it seemed to be a more egalitarian society. Yet this appearance was deceiving. The situation was much closer to what Robert Wiebe has called the "small town life norm" in nineteenth-century America.

> From a distance the towns exemplified a leveled democracy, sustaining neither an aristocracy of name nor an aristocracy of occupation . . . But beneath that flat surface, each community was divided by innumerable fine gradations. Distinctions that would have eluded an outsider—the precise location of a home, the amount of hired help, the quality of a buggy or a dress—held great importance in an otherwise undifferentiated society.[26]

That characteristic of Youngstown in the nineteenth century made the task of investigating its upper-class structure quite difficult. Nevertheless, analysis of social institutions revealed Youngstown to have had a tightly knit, highly cohesive and well-stratified local upper class. It also demonstrated the high level of prestige accorded this local upper class by their cohorts in other cities.

During the late nineteenth century, most of Youngstown's iron and steel elite lived in the city, near the downtown area. They preferred Wick Avenue, along with adjoining and intersecting streets, comprising an area seven blocks long and nine blocks wide. Perhaps no other city in this study had such a nearly complete concentration of the local upper class in a single area. Since 84 percent of the iron and steel elite living in Youngstown in 1880 resided in this area, there was apparently little social differentiation by neighborhood in the city. Yet, a closer investigation of the data reveals some important distinctions in residential propinquity.

An analysis of the social and cultural backgrounds of those persons not living in the Wick Avenue area demonstrates their social inferiority, according to the cultural standards of the time and area. Of these nine men, there was no information available on three of them (indicating their transiency in Youngstown). For the rest, 40 percent were Welsh, and the remainder were evenly divided among the English, Scotch-Irish and Irish. None were pre-Civil War elites. One-third were from the native American middle classes and two-thirds were from immigrant

TABLE 49

Iron and Steel Elite Residences in Youngstown, 1890s

Wick Avenue

No.	Family
305	W. S. Bonnell
310	J. V. & W. L. Wilder
314	J. Neilson
315	J. F. & H. W. Bonnell
407	T. H. Wells
410	W. F. Bonnell & J. C. Wick
416	H. Wick, Jr. & Hugh Wick
423	B. Ford
429	T. Ford & W. Arms
505	J. H. Brown
509	G. D. Wick
519	W. Baldwin
524	C. B. Wick
525	J. G. Butler & J. G., Jr.
547	E. L. Ford & P. Wick
606	M. I. Arms
613	J. M. & J. D. McCurdy
626	C. D. Arms & M. I. Arms, Jr.
655	W. J. Hitchcock & W. J., Jr.
664	J. L. Botsford, J. L., Jr. & F. H. Wick
669	G. M. McKelvey
678	E. L. Brown
679	Wm. & Martyn Bonnell
682	Myron Wick
689	H. O. Bonnell
726	R. McCurdy
728	U. A. Andrews
733	F. D. Wick
737	W. H. Wick
750	C. H. Andrews
753	F. O. & Warner Arms
773	John D. Wick
789	F. B. Williams

Bryson Street

No.	Family
534	J. E. Taylor & E. M. Wick
543	Ralph J. Wick
615	J. B. Wilder
619	Harry Bonnell
714	J. I. Williams & J. I., Jr.
722	J. A. Campbell
728	Frank Hitchcock

Lincoln Avenue

No.	Family
23	Paul Jones & E. A. Cochran
133	Charles J. Wick
138	George Tod
152	Henry & Harry Tod
215	Mason & F. G. Evans
231	G. D. Wick
249	H. W. Heedy
272	Hugh B. Wick
331	J. Stambaugh

Rayen Street

No.	Family
129	D. B. Stambaugh
147	A. W. Jones
632	J. Cartwright

Wood Street

No.	Family
230	W. E. Taylor
254	G. F. Stambaugh
322	H. Baldwin
334	D. Tod & W. Tod

Federal Street

No.	Family
446	Alexander Adams

working-class and middle-class stock. Half were Methodists; the rest were divided equally among Presbyterians, Episcopalians and unspecified Protestants. Finally, all of those for whom information was available came to America during the early nineteenth century. None were members of older colonial families—a critical distinction in the Western Reserve.

Those living in the Wick Avenue area were of significantly more preferred social and cultural origins. Nearly two-thirds were of English ancestry, while the rest were Scottish, Scotch-Irish, German, and Welsh. Fully 78 percent were members of pre-Civil War elite families, with 13 percent from the native American middle classes and 9 percent from immigrant middle-class and working-class stock. The great majority were Presbyterian. Fully 87 percent were members of colonial families which had arrived in America before 1800, while 55 percent were of seventeenth-century origins. Thus, in every respect, the iron and steel men living in the Wick Avenue area displayed social and economic origins of a more preferred nature than did the minority living outside the area.

Yet, even within the relatively small and compact Wick Avenue area, social differences may be discerned. Generally, the largest estates were on Wick Avenue itself, while smaller homes and plots were scattered on its satellite streets. Thus, if one divides the Wick Avenue neighborhood between those who lived on Wick Avenue itself and those who resided on adjoining streets, some interesting trends emerge.

Of the twenty-one families residing on Wick Avenue, 86 percent were of English ancestry and three-quarters were members of pre-Civil War elite families. Almost all were Presbyterian, with the remainder Episcopalian. Again, three-quarters were members of families who had come to America during the seventeenth century. Thus, the vast majority of the families living on Wick Avenue in the late nineteenth century represented Youngstown's oldest and most prestigious families: they were of English ancestry and Presbyterian religious affiliation; their families had immigrated to America with the earliest seventeenth-century settlers; and they had dominated the city's economic scene since before the Civil War. A minority were newer men. Although they had immigrated to America in the early nineteenth century and had not been part of the pre-Civil War economic elite, most were of English background, and all but one were Presbyterian. Thus, although newer to America and to Youngstown, they reflected the cultural and social bias of the earlier settlers.

Those residing on the streets adjoining Wick Avenue were more diverse and heterogenous. Although the largest single group were of English ancestry, there were also minorities of Scottish and Scotch-Irish, German, and Welsh. Similarly, though 48 percent were Presbyterian, the majority were rather evenly divided among Episcopalians, Methodists and unspecified Protestants. Although all were from colonial families who had come to America prior to 1800, only about a third had immigrated during the seventeenth century. Fully 80 percent, however, were members of Youngstown's pre-Civil War economic elite. Thus, although of relatively old families in

America, and despite the fact that most had been involved in Youngstown's economic expansion prior to the Civil War, most were from less preferred cultural origins than the Wick Avenue group.

By the turn of the century the configuration of upper-class neighborhoods in Youngstown had altered only slightly. Similar to 1880, only 18 percent of the seventy-three iron and steel elite families residing in Youngstown in 1898 lived outside the Wick Avenue area. Again, they generally represented men from more diverse and less preferred social and cultural origins. Of the thirteen families outside the Wick area, only 17 percent were of English ancestry, while 42 percent were Scottish or Scotch-Irish and one-third were Welsh. Only 23 percent were members of pre-Civil War economic elites. They were equally divided between Presbyterians and Methodists, with 46 percent in each group. Finally, 60 percent immigrated to America in the nineteenth century.

The social and cultural profile of these men contrasts graphically with the sixty families living in the Wick Avenue area. Sixty-one percent of the latter were of English ancestry, while 20 percent were Scottish or Scotch-Irish. Nearly two-thirds were from pre-Civil War economic elite families, with 15 percent from the native American middle class and 22 percent from immigrant middle-class or working-class stock. Similarly, 63 percent were Presbyterian in their religious heritage. Being members of old families, only 26 percent had immigrated to America during the nineteenth century: a far larger number had come to America during the seventeenth century.

Although slightly less homogeneous culturally in 1898 than in 1880, Wick Avenue itself continued to reflect the most preferred social and cultural origins in Youngstown. Fully 82 percent of its twenty-eight iron and steel families were of English stock. A like number were Presbyterian, with 52 percent derived from seventeenth-century American families. Though cultural origins remained similar, it was clear that newer men of complementary backgrounds were moving onto Wick Avenue. By 1898, only 61 percent were from pre-Civil War elite families, compared to 78 percent in 1880. In like measure, only 63 percent were now of colonial stock, compared to 86 percent in this category in 1880. Thus, Wick Avenue in 1898 reflected the rise to status of new elites in the late nineteenth century—but only those elites of the "correct" social and cultural backgrounds similar to the neighborhood inhabitants of 1880.

The iron and steel families living on the streets adjoining Wick Avenue in 1898 were also old families of established economic position, though with less preferred cultural origins. While two-thirds were members of pre-Civil War elite families, and 85 percent were of pre-1800 origins in America, only 41 percent were English; the rest were Scotch-Irish, Scottish, Welsh and German. In like manner, only 44 percent were Presbyterian, with 22 percent Episcopalian and 16 percent Methodist. These old elite families, then, remained culturally distinct from other elite families of predominantly English and Presbyterian heritage, despite living in close proximity to one another.

That those iron and steel families in the Wick Avenue area—particularly those living on Wick Avenue itself—represented families of higher social prestige receives additional support when the Cleveland Social Directory of 1885 was consulted. A listing of the prominent families of both Cleveland and Youngstown, the Directory listed a total of two-thirds of the iron and steel families who were also listed in the 1898 Youngstown City Directory. Fully 89 percent of those living on Wick Avenue were listed in the Social Directory: 59 percent of those living on streets adjoining Wick were listed, and only 38 percent of those living outside the area were so honored. Thus, despite a seeming lack of differentiation on the surface, Youngstown's elite neighborhoods were actually more homogenous and selective than those in the other cities studied.

As Table 49 indicates, Wick Avenue was a highly compact and homogeneous area, similar to the Allegheny section of Pittsburgh. Several of the homes were extended family units with more than one conjugal unit of the family living under the same roof; and the rest of the area represented an excellent example of the expanded family structure, with families living, at most, only a few doors from one another.

By 1918 the Wick Avenue area had undergone extensive change. Although most of the large estates on Wick Avenue itself remained intact, the surrounding streets were being given over more and more extensively to housing subdivisions and commercial activities. Of the sixty-nine iron and steel families listed in the Youngstown City Directory of 1918, nearly one-third continued to live on Wick Avenue itself. The surrounding streets had experienced a severe depopulation of its elite families, however, as only 7 percent continued to live there. By this time, fully 60 percent of the iron and steel elite families lived outside of the Wick Avenue area, a few of them in the newly developed suburbs.

Those remaining on Wick Avenue generally retained their earlier cultural orientation and prestige. Of the twenty-two families living on that street in 1918, nearly three-quarters were of English ancestry, and 83 percent were Presbyterian. Seventy-three percent were members of colonial families. Finally, 70 percent were members of pre-Civil War elite families. Thus, the changes over twenty years time had relatively little impact upon the homogeneity and status of Wick Avenue, which stood as a seemingly impregnable bastion of tradition and familial dominance.

The streets adjoining Wick Avenue, however, suffered a dramatic decline in their elite population over these same years. Of the five iron and steel family members remaining, four were members of the Stambaugh family—old German Methodist iron makers. They chose to remain in this area, on Wood Street, because of the existence of a German ethnic community in the area (a German Lutheran and a German Catholic church now within a few blocks of their home are indicative of this) and the location of the warehouse for their family business.

Those families who had formerly lived around Wick Avenue now lived in outlying areas, most of them in a development directly north of their old domicile, a development which covered an extensive area around Crandall Park, Wick Park and Crab Creek. The social and cultural origins of these families reflected those of the families who had earlier lived around Wick Avenue. Only 29 percent of this group of forty-one families were of English ancestry, with 36 percent Scottish and Scotch-Irish. Fifty-nine percent were Presbyterian. Fifty-four percent were members of pre-Civil War elite families, and a majority were members of families which had come to America prior to 1800. Thus, in large measure, this group represented the outward movement of a group of families which had formerly lived in the Wick Avenue area. Although the majority were of old family, and had been economic elites since before the Civil War, they were culturally distinct from the old Wick Avenue families.

By 1938, Wick Avenue had declined substantially as an elite area, and the streets surrounding it were virtually abandoned to other development. Most elite families, however, continued to live in North Youngstown, resisting the siren call of the suburbs. Of importance, however, is the fact that at least nine Youngstown iron and steel families now made their permanent homes in Cleveland, and several more had moved to the east coast—especially to Greenwich, Connecticut. Of the thirty-seven iron and steel families living in Youngstown in 1938, only 16 percent now lived on Wick Avenue, and only one other family, the Stambaugh's, continued to live on the streets surrounding Wick. Two-thirds of the families now lived in the elite area north of the old Wick Avenue area. Just 13 percent lived in the suburbs, only one family in the newly developed Mill Creek area to the south.

Of those who remained on Wick Avenue, two-thirds were English and Presbyterian, and all but one was a member of the pre-Civil War economic elite. All were members of families which had come to America prior to 1750. Of those in the northern area of Youngstown, nearly two-thirds were English and one-third Scottish or Scotch-Irish. Seventy-six percent of this group were Presbyterian, with most of the rest Episcopalian. Fully 80 percent were from pre-Civil War elite families, and an equal number arrived in America prior to 1800. Thus, the north Youngstown area, by 1938, had supplanted Wick Avenue as the area of greatest popularity among elite families—while, at the same time, attracting families of the most preferred social origins.

Those living in the suburbs in 1938 were a diverse group. None were English, but 60 percent were Scotch-Irish or Scottish, with Germans and Welsh comprising the remainder. Forty percent each were Presbyterian and Methodist, and 20 percent were Episcopalian. Only 20 percent were members of pre-Civil War economic elite families, and most were of recent arrival in America. The suburbs by 1938 had not yet become truly attractive living areas for the iron and steel elite in Youngstown. It is apparent that most of those who longed to escape the city went to suburban areas in other cities—either to Cleveland or to the east coast.

By 1958, the old iron and steel elite families had virtually forsaken Youngstown. Only eighteen families remained in the city or surrounding suburbs; and these comprised only eight separate conjugal units. Two-thirds of these families continued to reside in the elite area in north Youngstown, while one family still lived on Wick Avenue, and 28 percent lived in the suburbs. In 1968, the situation was generally static from ten years earlier for the descendants of the iron and steel elite. Sixteen of these families continued to live in the Youngstown area, with 63 percent of them living in Youngstown proper—in the area of north Youngstown. The remaining 37 percent were scattered in Poland, Girard, Mill Creek and elsewhere.

Thus, it seems evident that Youngstown developed a closely knit set of upper-class residential areas in the nineteenth century similar to the Allegheny area in Pittsburgh. It is also clear that these areas generally had impressive staying power as elite areas, lasting until well into the twentieth century. When the old Wick Avenue area began to decline as an elite domicile in the 1920s, it was replaced by a somewhat more heterogeneous and dispersed area to the north—which continued to attract upper-class families well into the mid-twentieth century. In this manner, Youngstown much resembled Pittsburgh, with its compact and homogeneous Allegheny and its more sprawling and diverse East End. Unlike any of the other cities studied, however, suburbs never held much attraction for the iron and steel elite in Youngstown. When they decided to leave the city limits, it was to leave the entire area behind. The exodus was so complete that by 1968, only 16 percent of the original thirty-seven iron and steel families still remained in the area.

SOCIAL CLUBS

Although Youngstown developed a highly articulated, homogeneous and stable series of elite residential areas, the social club structure was less precise. In town, the Youngstown Club was the only one of any real significance for the iron and steel men (although several men also belonged to more middle-class organizations such as the Elks, Knights of Pythias and Odd Fellows). Although there was a certain inclination toward social selectivity in the Youngstown Club, the tendency of the clubs in Youngstown was to hew more closely to the small-town model as set forth by Vidich and Bensman in their classic study, *Small Town in Mass Society.*

> It is the policy of the Community Club to be open to "everyone, whether dues are paid or not" and hardly a meeting passes without a repetition of this statement. Those who are leaders of the community take pride in this organization specifically because it excludes no one, and this fact is emphasized time and again in public situations.[28]

Of course, Youngstown was a small city, not a small town, and not everyone was included in the clubs—especially not the newer immigrant groups. Compared to the larger cities in the study, however, there was a small-town tendency in Youngstown.

Suburban clubs included: the Mahoning Golf Club, founded in 1898, which later became the Youngstown Country Club; the Poland Club, which later became the Boardman Country Club; the Mahoning Valley Country Club; the Mill Creek Riding Club, organized in 1928; and, finally, the Squaw Creek Country Club for wealthy Jewish citizens. These clubs did not provide a good index for delineating class standing among the iron and steel elites of Youngstown. Distinctions between the upper and middle classes appeared to be much more blurred in Youngstown than in larger cities. Several citizens of old, seemingly upper-class families, belonged to distinctly middle-class clubs like the Elks and the Knights of Pythias. Similarly, the somewhat more prestigious clubs seemed to have a broader elite rather than upper-class appeal. Added to the difficulty of determining club memberships for Youngstown families was the fact that large numbers of them chose to hold memberships in social clubs in Cleveland and other cities. These families may have been the more cosmopolitan of the breed; but the Cleveland clubs in particular seemed to function as more exclusively upper-class clubs for many Youngstown citizens.

Despite these inherent difficulties, an analysis of club memberships for the Youngstown iron and steel elite reveals some interesting patterns and nuances. The Youngstown Club, with 43 percent of the thirty-seven families as members, was the most popular of the clubs for the city's iron and steel elite. In addition, since club information could not be found on nearly half of the families, the totals for Youngstown Club could conceivably be extrapolated to 85 or 90 percent. The Youngstown Club had been organized in 1902 with eight charter members, four of whom were local iron and steel men. Never having a separate club house, it met in the Dollar Bank Building until 1926—when it switched to the top three floors of the Union National Bank Building. When organized, membership in the club was limited to 150; but by 1962, there were 800 members.[29]

The most popular of the suburban clubs, Youngstown Country Club, counted 30 percent of the iron and steel families as members. It had been organized in 1897 as the Mahoning Country Club, with a clubhouse in the area north of the old Wick Avenue residences. The charter members included seven men from iron and steel families. Membership was limited to 250 members.[30] Only one of the iron and steel families ever held a membership in the Poland Country Club, located in a suburb where several iron and steel families lived. It had a curious history, since in 1937 it had been purchased by the reputed head of the numbers racket in Youngstown, and was thenceforth used as a gambling casino. Finally, in 1951, now called the Boardman Country Club, it was ordered closed by Judge John W. Ford, son of a Youngstown steel man.[31] For these and other reasons the club held little attraction for iron and steel elites.

Besides these clubs of a seemingly elite nature, several distinctly middle-class clubs were also popular with the iron and steel families. The Elks Club, with 22 percent of the families as members, was the third most popular club for them in the city. Nor did these men represent a different, or lesser, group of men among the iron and steel elite (than those who were members of the Youngstown Club or Youngstown Country Club), since 75 percent of the iron and steel members of the Elks were also members in one or both of the other two clubs. Similarly, the Knights of Pythias enrolled 11 percent of these families as members, and the Odd Fellows attracted 5 percent.

It is difficult to reconstruct the social and cultural backgrounds of the members of the various clubs, since we are dealing with such obviously incomplete data.

Nevertheless, an analysis of the data which is available generally reflects the rather amorphous nature of the club structure in the city. All clubs displayed a marked heterogeneity in their ethnic backgrounds of iron and steel members. None reflected the ethnic homogeneity of Wick Avenue. Similarly, although all clubs were dominated by men of Presbyterian religious heritage, each also had significant minorities of men from other Protestant denominations. Further, at least one-half of the iron and steel members in each club were from families which had come to America prior to 1800, and none contained over 64 percent in this category. Only in economic origins of members was there some slight differentiation. Whereas over 60 percent of the iron and steel members of the Youngstown Club and Youngstown Country Club were from pre-Civil War elite families (and one-half of those in the Elks were also from these origins), only one-quarter of the families in the Knights of Pythias and none of those in the Odd Fellows were from such families.

When Social Register listings from other cities are examined in relation to Youngstown Club memberships, the same scattered picture emerges, although the results are a bit surprising. Again, it should be emphasized that Social Register listings for Youngstown elites is a rather moot point, since there was no indigenous index for the city. Thirty-eight percent of the families in the Youngstown Club were listed in various Social Registers, while 36 percent of the families in the Youngstown Country Club were so listed; a fairly consistent figure. The surprising fact, however, is that 38 percent of the families holding memberships in the Elks Club were also listed in various Social Registers. Even more surprising 75 percent of the families holding memberships in the Knights of Pythias were so listed, along with both of the families belonging to the Odd Fellows. More than any other single fact, this should point to the basically small-town nature of the Youngstown social system at the upper levels.

Examination of neighborhoods and social clubs in Youngstown, then, yields a somewhat confused picture. In most respects, Youngstown appeared to be the exact opposite of Cleveland. Where the latter city failed to develop a lasting, cohesive series of elite, city neighborhoods, Youngstown had a strong, stable, highly articulated structure. On the other hand, Cleveland's club structure, if not perfectly ranked according to status, was well organized and well developed. The club structure in Youngstown appeared essentially truncated when compared to Cleveland, and even more so when compared to Pittsburgh or Philadelphia.

MARRIAGE PATTERNS

With the conflicting structure of clubs and neighborhoods in Youngstown, it was necessary to turn to marriage patterns in order to determine social rankings and gradation. A study of Youngstown's iron and steel family intermarriage patterns stratified the families into our four familiar layers. Six families (16 percent of the total) were core families with four or more endogamous marriages. In fact, they married so extensively with one another that they appeared to be almost one large extended family unit—another phenomenon typical of small towns.[32] The Arms family had sixteen endogamous marriages; the Bonnells had ten; J. H. Ford, eight; the Stambaugh family, seven; the Tods, nine; and the Wicks, fifteen. There were no other Youngstown families which even came close to them in the frequency of endogamous marriage. The density of endogamous marriage for these core families was also dramatic. Thirty-three percent of the 198 recorded marriages were endogamous, ranging from 67 percent for the Arms family to 19 percent in the Stambaugh family. These families truly represented the marital hub of the city's upper class, with no other families in the city approaching them on this level.

The non-core upper-class families had at least one, but less than four, marriages into the core families. Fourteen families (38 percent of the total) fell into this group. The non-core families were quite prestigious in Youngstown and did marry into the core families at least once; but the bulk of their marriages and social relations were outside the core group—although the density of endogamous marriage was high, standing at 26 percent of the seventy-seven recorded marriages.

There were eight marginal upper-class families (22 percent of the total). They were either married into the non-core families or to upper-class families outside the city, but had no marriage ties to the more prestigious core families. There were nine elite families in the city (24 percent of the total) who did not have a significant marriage pattern. With one exception, they were all of marginal or recent immigrant background, and thus would seem to fall rather naturally into this category.

Analysis of the social and cultural backgrounds of these family groups derived from marital patterns was only marginally useful. Sixty percent of the core families were of English origin, compared to 42 percent of the non-core, 33 percent of the marginal and 20 percent of the elite. A majority, or a large minority, of the families in the three latter groups were Scottish or Scotch-Irish. Also, all of the Welsh iron and steel families were either marginal or elite in their marriage patterns. Eighty-three percent of the core families were members of pre-Civil War economic elite, compared to only 36 percent of the non-core families. Seventy-one percent of the marginal families however were prewar elites. Only 14 percent of the elite families were in this category, with the rest evenly divided between native and immigrant background, and thus would seem to fall rather naturally into this category. four family groups, all being dominated by Presbyterians.

In terms of family arrival in America, 83 percent of the core families came before 1800, one-third in the seventeenth century. Conversely, 60 percent of the noncore families arrived after that time, with only 10 percent immigrating during the seventeenth century. Again, the marginal upper-class families, with all of them coming to America before 1800 and 40 percent coming during the seventeenth century, were not consistent to expected patterns. The non-core families, then, were clearly emergent families in the late nineteenth and early twentieth centuries. The marginal families were of prior status, but for some reason chose not to engage in marital relations in Youngstown. Most moved away in the early twentieth century, marrying with upper-class families in other cities.

Comparing the marriage patterns to other social variables in Youngstown is rather difficult. Social Register listing was a somewhat random variable for Youngstown, as was membership in upper-class clubs in other cities. Also, the Youngstown clubs were so all-inconclusive as to have little utility for social separation. Nevertheless, an examination of marriage patterns in relation to these other variables does seem to have some utility. As indicated in Table 50, a status pattern emerges in Youngstown, similar to that in Pittsburgh and Philadelphia. The core family Social Register listing, although only 67 percent, was much higher than that for any of the other marriage groups. The only variation in the pattern established in Pittsburgh and Philadelphia was in the case of the marginal families, who show a higher percentage of listing than do the non-core families: but this was due to their larger number of cosmopolitan marriages, which gave them social connections in cities having indigenous Social Registers. The same was true with the elite families, but to a lesser degree. The non-core families were still primarily local in orientation, with their prestige on the local level (if marriages into core families are a valid criterion) being higher than that of the marginal or elite families.

Similarly, there was a rank ordering of the family group memberships in the Youngstown Club and Youngstown Country Club—from 83 percent for the core families to only 11 percent for the elite families in the Youngstown Club, and from 67 percent to 11 percent in Youngstown Country Club. The average membership in the two elite clubs for core families was 75 percent; for non-core, 40 percent; for marginal, 31 percent; and for elite families, 11 percent. With the three middle-class clubs, the rank ordering is generally inverted, with the marginal families having a 17 percent average membership in these clubs; non-core, 12 percent; and core and elite families each averaging 11 percent. Thus, despite the seemingly unstratified nature of the club structure in Youngstown, when viewed through the perspective of endogamous marriages a much clearer rank ordering emerges according to status.

Comparing the marital groupings to residence reveals similar results. Since Wick Avenue was so highly homogeneous, and seemingly exclusive in its residents, an examination was made of its family groupings in 1898 and 1918. In the former year—two-thirds of the core families lived on Wick Avenue, as compared to 29 percent of the non-core and 38 percent of the marginal families. Only 11 percent of the elite families maintained residences there. Of the twelve separate iron and steel kinship groups who lived on Wick Avenue in 1898, one-third each were core and non-core, 25 percent were marginal and 8 percent were elite.

In 1918, 83 percent of the core families lived on Wick Avenue, compared to only 14 percent of the non-core families, 38 percent of the marginal and none of the elite families. Of the ten kinship groups living there in that year, one-half were core families, 20 percent non-core and 30 percent marginal. Thus, the core families continued to emerge as the group of highest status in the city, and the elite families as the group with the lowest status, although the relative status differential between non-core and marginal upper-class families remained imprecise.

TABLE 50

Youngstown Endogamous Marriage Groups as Related to Other Social Factors

Group		Percentage of Groups in Youngstown Clubs					
		% in Social Register	Youngstown	Youngstown C.C.	Elks	Knights Pythias	Odd Fellows
Core	*N*=6	67	83	67	17	17	0
Non-Core	*N*=14	14	50	29	21	7	7
Marginal	*N*=8	38	38	25	25	13	13
Elite	*N*=9	22	11	11	22	11	0
Totals	*N*=37						

	Percentage of Groups in Cleveland Clubs										
	Poland C.C.	Union	Cleveland C.C.	Roadside	Tavern	Kirtland	CVH	Mayfield	Hermit	Cleveland Athletic	Pittsburgh Duquesne
Core	17	50	33	33	33	17	17	17	17	17	33
Non-Core	0	15	0	0	0	0	0	0	0	0	23
Marginal	0	0	0	0	0	0	0	0	0	0	22
Elite	0	11	0	0	0	0	0	0	0	0	0

LOCALS AND COSMOPOLITANS

In their social connections, the Youngstown iron and steel elite seemed fairly cosmopolitan. The core families, like nearly everyone else in Youngstown, sent their children to the city's public schools throughout most of the nineteenth and early twentieth centuries. The public high school, Rayen High, was located on Wick Avenue in the center of the large upper-class estates. When most of these families began moving to the north, Rayen High moved with them to the new upper-class domicile in North Youngstown. All six core families sent their sons to at least elementary school in Youngstown, though by the 1920s many were sending sons away to eastern prep schools. There was no clear pattern to prep school choices: Harvard Prep in Chicago; Lawrenceville Prep; Exeter; Greylock Institute; and Andover. No more than one or two sons went to each of these schools; and there seemed to be no inclination to become attached to one of the more prestigious schools, such as St. Paul's.

On the college level, the Youngstown families were much more cosmopolitan. There were no prestigious local colleges; so all six families sent their sons away to college in the late nineteenth and early twentieth centuries. Yale was the preferred school, and Cornell was second. The rest were scattered at Williams, Oberlin, M.I.T., Case Tech., and Western Reserve.

In their marriages, Youngstown core families displayed a more cosmopolitan appearance. Out of 198 recorded marriages, thirty-nine (20 percent) were to recognizable upper-class families in other cities. This figure was even higher than that for the Cleveland core families. It was somewhat inflated, however, by the Wick family—who had a branch in Cleveland as well as Youngstown. Even without the Wick family marriages, however, the cosmopolitan marriages were 13 percent. Therefore, Youngstown core families generally reverse the core family patterns of Pittsburgh and Cleveland, if not Philadelphia. They were quite provincial in school attendance, but cosmopolitan in marriage patterns, despite an extraordinarily heavy pattern of endogamous marriage at home.

All the non-core upper-class families sent their children to public schools in Youngstown during the nineteenth century. A few (four of the thirteen), also sent their sons to eastern prep schools. All the families sent their sons away to college, but the results were even more mixed. Two of the families sent their sons to Yale; two to Harvard; and one each to Western Reserve, Williams and M.I.T. As far as marriages to elites in other cities were concerned, the non-core families had 13 percent of their seventy-seven recorded marriages in this category. This figure is quite a bit lower than the core families of the city, and probably reflected their more provincial nature. The non-core families of Youngstown, unlike those in Pittsburgh and Philadelphia, were more locally oriented and less likely to develop cosmopolitan relationships.

There was less information on school attendance patterns for marginal families, but all seemed to have sent their sons to public school in Youngstown during the nineteenth century. Only two sent their sons away to prep schools in the twentieth century. Only three of the families had any record of college attendance—two to Case Tech and one each to Yale and Harvard. Twenty percent of the forty-seven recorded marriages of this group were to elite families in other cities—about the same percentage as for the core families, but well below the percentage for marginal families in Pittsburgh and Philadelphia. The elite families were the most provincial of the Youngstown groups. None sent sons away to prep schools: all attended public schools in the city. Only two of the nine families sent sons away to prep schools. Only two of the nine families sent sons to college—one to Penn and one to Wabash College. Their marriage patterns also bore out this localism, with none of their fifteen recorded marriages to elites in other cities.

Although the rate of Youngstown cosmopolitan marriage was rather high, their outside social relations as a whole were very provincial. There were fewer ties to eastern prep schools, and no particular university was *the* place to go for wealthy young Youngstown boys. Similarly, few belonged to clubs in other cities, and most of these were in nearby Cleveland. Most of the cosmopolitan marriages were also to Clevelanders. What appeared at first to be a cosmopolitan elite, on closer analysis revealed a group quite reluctant to venture far beyond the Western Reserve area in its social relations. It was, indeed, the city as a small town.

SOCIAL NETWORK

This small-town aspect of Youngstown may be seen by creating a social network. Although a large number of families left the city, those who remained—principally core and non-core families—created a tightly knit and highly interactive social network. With a total of eighty-eight endogamous marriages and 491 club interlocks, the resulting network at the upper-class level was quite intricate and dense. If residential propinquity would have been added to this network, the resulting web of affiliation would have been even more highly interconnected. As Table 52 shows, the core families were particularly highly interconnected by the kinship web; and when social club memberships were added, core and particularly non-core families had extensive interlocks. Viewed in this manner, twenty-two families had highly extensive club and marital connections with one another (all of the core families, plus eleven non-core, three marginal and two elite families).

Youngstown, then, at least until well into the twentieth century, appeared to have a highly functional and well articulated upper-class system. Despite the absence of a Social Register and high-status clubs and suburbs, the neighborhoods, clubs and marriages of the city functioned in such a manner as to provide a clear rank ordering of the iron and steel elite within the city.

WHEELING

It is difficult to be sure of the social nature of Wheeling at the upper levels. The general impression one has of the city, however, is that it failed to develop a local upper class, in the fullest sense, in the nineteenth century, and that most of its illustrious citizens moved on to other locales in the late nineteenth and ealry twentieth centuries.

In the early nineteenth century, Wheeling was a "new" city, like Youngstown and Cleveland. But unlike them, it did not have an old, established group of families, settled there as pioneers at its founding. To a large extent, everyone started at the same level in Wheeling—nail workers, men from prominent New England families, farmers and immigrants. From there on the race was to the swift, rather than to the prestigious. In Wheeling, more than in any of the other cities under study, one can sense a certain fulfillment of the "American Dream" of the nineteenth century—the "Horatio Alger" ideal of rags to riches opportunities abounding for ambitious men from common backgrounds.

This openness in her social structure at the upper levels made it possible for a larger number of workmen and sons of workingmen to rise to wealth and power here than in any of the other cities under study. But this social fact may have also accounted for the seeming inability to stratify that society and the subsequent loss of many of its wealthiest and most prominent citizens: the Oglebay family moved to Cleveland; the Culbertsons and Laughlins to Pittsburgh; the Woodwards to Alabama, and the Toppings and Hearnes to New York City. A few, however, such as the Hubbard, Glass, Scott, Vance and Whitaker families, did stay on in Wheeling for several generations, serving as pillars of a small upper class which functioned partially within the Pittsburgh orbit. An analysis of the institutions of this small and rather weak Wheeling upper class will serve to more clearly delineate the nature of its society.

NEIGHBORHOOD

Neighborhood played only a minor role in Wheeling. The city never developed a series of homogeneous upper-class neighborhoods, either in the city or in the suburbs (as was true to some extent of the rest of the cities in the study). Part of the problem here lay in the fact that the present researcher was unable to obtain Wheeling city directories between 1860 and 1928; but examination of available evidence would support dispersion as opposed to homogeneous concentrations. The year 1860 was a bit early for separate upper-class areas, and, by 1928, many of the wealthy old families had left Wheeling for other cities. But for those who remained, it is possible to reconstruct the extent to which elite residential areas were functional in Wheeling.

In 1860, of the twenty-six iron and steel families living in Wheeling, there appeared to be no clear pattern of stratified housing by class. Most lived in the old, or north, section of the city, with little seeming differentiation between those who were steel mill laborers and those who were now steel mill owners. They seemed to reside virtually cheek by jowl, differentiated only by quality of residence.

Of the thirty-six iron and steel families living in Wheeling in 1928, 47 percent lived in the Woodsdale suburban area, northeast of Wheeling proper. Another 28 percent lived in the Elm Grove area, directly east of Wheeling, 22 percent lived in Wheeling proper (most in hotels, apartments or the Fort Henry Club), and 3 percent lived in the area around Oglebay Park—once the home of several iron and steel families, including the Oglebays. There appeared, even at this late date, to be some social and cultural distinctions between those living in the three main areas around Wheeling. For those who resided in Woodsdale, the majority were Scotch-Irish, with a large minority of English. Conversely, Elm Grove was dominated by those of English ancestry, with a minority of Scotch-Irish. Wheeling proper was more heterogeneous, with large groups of Scotch-Irish and German (38 percent each), and a smaller group of men of English origin (25 percent).

In religious heritage, Woodsdale and Elm Grove were nearly identical, with the largest minority being Presbyterian in each area, followed by Episcopalians and Methodists. It was in the area of religion, however, that the iron and steel families living in Wheeling proper were most distinctive. Although 38 percent were Presbyterian and a total of 63 percent were Protestant, the remaining 38 percent were Roman Catholic. Thus, the only Catholic iron and steel families remaining in the Wheeling area did not live in the more oppulent suburban retreats.

All of the iron and steel residents of Woodsdale and Elm Grove were from pre-Civil War elite families; and 63 percent of those in Wheeling proper were similarly categorized. But 38 percent (all of whom were German Catholic), were from the pre-Civil War immigrant middle and working classes. In terms of family arrival in America, there were some important differences between the three areas. Eighty-nine percent of those living in Woodsdale came from families who had come to America prior to 1800; only 11 percent had immigrated during the nineteenth century. In Elm Grove, one-half came after 1800, while in Wheeling proper, nearly all were new families, with 83 percent having immigrated during the nineteenth century.

Thus, Wheeling's three main elite residential areas in 1928 each retained a rather clear cultural orientation. In Woodsdale there were the Scotch-Irish and English families who had come to America prior to 1800, all of whom were economic elites before the Civil War. Religious heritage, as long as it was Protestant, made little difference here. Elm Grove, on the other hand, catered primarily to men of English ancestry, whose families had also been economic elites prior to the Civil War. Whereas 55 percent of the families in Woodsdale had come to America before 1750, only 11 percent of those in Elm Grove had done so. In that sense, the Elm Grove area was for newer families of the proper religious pedigree. Wheeling city was heterogeneous. The city itself continued to be a haven for ethnic (German) and religious (Catholic) groups of inferior status in the area. It was likewise dominated by men whose families had come to America after 1800. Wheeling proper was the holding area for those families not yet acceptable for assimilation into the British, Protestant suburbs.

SOCIAL CLUBS

The Fort Henry and Wheeling Country Clubs formed the major locus for Wheeling's small upper class. Apparently only a small portion of Wheeling's nineteenth-century iron and steel families held memberships in two clubs during the twentieth century. Of the thirty-nine iron and steel families in Wheeling, only seven (Glass, Hubbard, Holloway, Scott, Wheat, Whitaker and Woods) were members of the Fort Henry club for any extended period in the twentieth century. The Oglebay and Laughlin families were members of the club for a short period before leaving the city. Membership in the Wheeling Country Club was held by only five families for any length of time, although the Oglebay and Laughlin families also belonged to this club for a short time.

The middle-class clubs, such as the Elks, Odd Fellows and Knights of Pythias had some attraction for the Wheeling iron and steel elite, as they did in Youngstown. Belonging to the Elks Club were the Hearne, Reister, and Whitaker families. While the Reisters were a German immigrant family, the Hearnes were of marginal native American background, and the Whitakers were an old prestigious family. No pattern in this membership was apparent. Belonging to the Odd Fellows Club were members of the Priest and Robinson families, both of recent working-class origin. The Woods family belonged to the Knights of Pythias and the Fort Henry Club. The Reister family also belonged to the Knights of Columbus, as did, perhaps, other Catholic iron and steel families in Wheeling.

The social and cultural backgrounds of the iron and steel family members of these clubs betrayed no clear pattern. Since all members of the Wheeling Country Club were also members of Fort Henry Club, each was identical—nearly evenly split between English and Scotch-Irish. All were Protestant, dominated by Episcopalians. All but one were members of pre-Civil War elite families, and most came to America during the eighteenth century. The Elks, although two of its iron and steel members were similar to those in Fort Henry and Wheeling Country, also had one German Catholic member, whose family had come to America in the early nineteenth century, and who was not a member of the pre-Civil War economic elite. The Odd Fellows were distinguished by men who were Protestant, but not of pre-Civil War elite origins; and the Knights of Pythias membership was similar.

It is difficult to compare club membership and social class, since only those Wheeling families who moved out of the city were listed in a Social Register. None of the local families, even those of seemingly high prestige, were ever listed in any Social Register. The only members of the Fort Henry and Wheeling Country Clubs to be listed were the Oglebay and Laughlin families, both of whom moved out of Wheeling early in the twentieth century.

WHEELING MARRIAGES

The families with memberships in the Fort Henry and Wheeling Country Clubs were apparently the hub of Wheeling's local upper class; but there was no convenient local index or listing to determine this. As in Youngstown, only marriage patterns would seem to provide a logical means to define the nature of Wheeling's upper-class social system. Intermarriages among the Wheeling iron and steel families were far fewer than among the families of other cities. In general, however, families belonging to the Fort Henry and Wheeling Country clubs tended to intermarry with one another—though not with great frequency. In the rapid social flux of Wheeling, with families coming and going with such rapidity, this is about all that seemed to be needed to solidify a familial relationship.

Thus, it was necessary to establish a different criteria for core families in Wheeling than was used in the other cities. Using the previous criteria, only two families would qualify. Reducing the required number of marriages to two creates a group of six families who may be considered core families in the Wheeling environment. Non-core upper-class families remain as those with one marriage to a core family: there were six families in this category. The marginal families numbered fifteen, being composed primarily of families which left Wheeling at an early date and married with Social Register families in other cities. Finally, there were twelve elite, non-upper-class families with no significant marriage patterns.

Although the endogamic marriage construct used for the other cities in the study was far less satisfactory in Wheeling, an analysis of the cultural and social backgrounds of each of the present family groupings revealed some important characteristics. The majority of the core families were English, and nearly two-thirds came to America prior to 1800. The non-core families differed in some important cultural respects from the core families. Two-thirds of the non-core families were Scotch-Irish and Presbyterian, and only 17 percent were English and Episcopalian. Just two-thirds were of pre-Civil War economic elite stock; but about the same number had come to America prior to 1800. This appeared to indicate that the Wheeling social environment at the upper levels was less than congenial to men of Scotch-Irish, Presbyterian origins: English and Episcopalian were the most preferred backgrounds. As a result, most of these non-core families left Wheeling by the early twentieth century, several migrating to Pittsburgh—the cradle of Scotch-Irish culture.

The marginal families were also dominated by those who left Wheeling at an early date. They were nearly evenly divided between those of English and Scotch-Irish origins. A majority were Presbyterian, while the rest were Episcopalians and unspecified Protestants. Nearly all were of pre-Civil War economic elite stock, with only one family each from the native and the immigrant working and middle classes. Although a slight majority arrived in America prior to 1800, a larger minority than was the case with the previous family groups had nineteenth-century origins in America. Generally, those of Scotch-Irish and Presbyterian heritage arrived before 1800, while those of English and Episcopal or unspecified Protestant origins arrived after that date. Thus, it appears that this group of families may have found Wheeling uncongenial, either because of their ethnic and religious heritage (Scotch-Irish and Presbyterian), or because of their rather late arrival in America.

The elite, non-upper-class families were a rather diverse group. Sixty-three percent were English; 25 percent were German; and 13 percent were Scotch-Irish. The religious heritage of these families was fairly widely dispersed, with relatively equal numbers of Presbyterians, Episcopalians, Methodists and unspecified Protestants. Of importance, however, was the fact that 17 percent were Roman Catholic. The economic origins of these families was also dispersed, being nearly evenly divided between pre-Civil War elites and native and immigrant working and middle classes. The great majority came to America after 1800. Generally, those of English ancestry were Presbyterian and had come to America after 1800 (although two had been members of pre-Civil War elites). Except for the German Catholic families, then, the failure of these families to attain upper-class marital status remains idiosyncratic.

The relative social status of these families was rather difficult to determine, given the facts that Wheeling had no indigenous Social Register and its own social clubs did not attract large numbers of the iron and steel elite. Further, those who were listed in Social Registers or belonged to prominent clubs in other cities tended naturally to be the same ones who left Wheeling early and did not establish marital patterns in the city. An analysis of some social indicators was, nevertheless, rather enlightening.

The core families had the highest rate of membership in the two locally prestigious clubs (Fort Henry and Wheeling Country clubs), with two-thirds belonging to each. None were listed in any Social Register. One-third held memberships in New York clubs, and one family held a membership in the Duquesne Club in Pittsburgh. A local group of high status and prestige in that area, they received little recognition outside of their home community. Conversely, one-third of the non-core families were listed in various Social Registers; and while none belonged to New York City clubs, they held an average of 23 percent membership in various prominent Pittsburgh clubs. Only one family belonged to the local Wheeling clubs, and their membership was terminated in the early twentieth century. The non-core families generally had less prestige in Wheeling, but greater status in other areas—particularly Pittsburgh.

TABLE 51

Relative Social Status Among Marital Groups in Wheeling

Family Group		% in Social Register	Percentage of Groups in Clubs			
			Fort Henry	Wheeling C.C.	N.Y.C. Clubs	Pittsburgh Clubs
Core	*N*=6	0	67	67	50	17
Non-Core	*N*=6	33	17	17	0	23
Marginal	*N*=15	60	13	13	13	27
Elite	*N*=12	0	17	8	0	0

The marginal families reflected even greater cosmopolitan prestige. Sixty percent of these families were listed in the Social Registers of other cities, and 27 percent held memberships in the Duquesne Club in Pittsburgh. Cleveland and New York City clubs were also represented by these families. Only two families, however, belonged to the Wheeling elite clubs; and one of these terminated its membership after a short time. The elite families apparently lacked prestige in both Wheeling and elsewhere. Although they held an average of 12 percent membership in the two Wheeling clubs, none were listed in Social Registers or belonged to prominent clubs in other cities. For a variety of reasons, these families failed to obtain upper-class acceptance anywhere.

COSMOPOLITANS AND LOCALS

Since Wheeling was less successful in retaining its iron and steel elite families than any of the other cities studied, it would stand to reason that those families would demonstrate more cosmopolitan tendencies. With the exception of the core and elite families, this was generally true. The six core families who remained in Wheeling were fairly cosmopolitan in club memberships: the Glass family belonged to the Union League in New York and the Duquesne Club in Pittsburgh; the Holloway family, to the Lotos Club of New York and the Duquesne Club; and the Whitaker family to the New York Yacht Club and the Union League Club in Philadelphia. The cosmopolitan club memberships of the non-core families was about equal to that of the core families. The marginal families, on the other hand, retained membership in a large number of clubs in Pittsburgh, New York, and Cleveland.

Information on secondary schooling for the Wheeling iron and steel families was woefully incomplete. But from fragmentary records it is possible to partially reconstruct the pattern. Only one-third of the core families apparently sent sons east to prep schools. The tendency, until well into the twentieth century, was to send their sons to local Wheeling public schools. Information was found on only one non-core family, the Laughlins, who sent a son to Hill School in the East. Secondary school data was obtained for six of the marginal upper-class families; and of these, 75 percent sent their sons to eastern prep schools. Information was obtained on six elite families. Of these, one-third sent their sons to prep schools, but none attended the more prestigious ones. The rest were educated in Wheeling public schools.

There was only limited information available on college attendance patterns. Of the core families, the Holloways sent a son to Yale, the Hubbards sent one to Wesleyan, and the Whitakers sent theirs to Cornell and Princeton. Among the non-core families, the Laughlins sent a son to Yale. The marginal upper-class families had a somewhat larger number of sons going away to prestigious colleges—with the Oglebays and Scotts at Yale, and the Wrights at Brown University. None of the elite families sent sons to these schools, although they did send them to the University of Wisconsin, Bethany College, Morgantown University, and St. Vincent's College outside of Pittsburgh.

Although the results were speculative at best, as far as schools are concerned, there seems to be no great difference between the pattern of the local Wheeling upper-class families and those who had joined upper classes in other cities (except for a slightly stronger preference for St. Paul's among the latter group). The Wheeling elite responded to the national trend of sending boys away to eastern prep schools with upper-class boys from other cities: moving out of Wheeling did not alter this trend in either direction.

As to marriages with upper-class families in other cities, a fairly clear distinction emerges between the local upper-class families and those who moved to other areas. Of the local families, only the Whitakers and Woodwards married with upper-class families of other areas. Of those who moved away, marriages to upper-class families in other cities were naturally numerous. This may not mean that the group was necessarily more cosmopolitan, however, since they simply seem to have changed their allegiance from one local, upper-class system to another. Thus, it was difficult to analyze the Wheeling upper-class system. Without greater stratification, it was nearly impossible either to gather coherent evidence or to make firm conclusions on the evidence in hand.

THE UPPER-CLASS SOCIAL NETWORK IN WHEELING

Table 52 indicates the degree to which an upper-class kinship network did *not* exist in Wheeling. Similar to Cleveland, the points of interconnection between families are of low frequency; and although the density is relatively high, with 19 percent of the 175 recorded marriages being endogamous, the overall picture is one of infrequent and less consequential contact in marital terms.

When interlocking memberships in social clubs in Wheeling and elsewhere were added to the marriages, the extent of network affiliation becomes more significant. Although fourteen families have multiple kinship and club interlocks with other families, the intensity of the resulting network was far less than for any of the cities under study. Since many of these clubs lay outside of Wheeling, it made the degree of connection between some of the families in the network even more tenuous.

In summary, it appears that Wheeling in large measure failed to establish and maintain a viable, functioning upper-class system. Although there were some tendencies towards this on the residential and local club level, the points of interconnection between all but a few families were sporadic and of limited consequence. Most iron and steel elite families left Wheeling quite early; and those who remained seemed truncated and incomplete in their social relationships at the upper-class level. A nineteenth-century town whose lack of a clear stratification system allowed the rise of a large number of workingmen to capitalist status, Wheeling evidently could not overcome this diffusion in the twentieth century in order to establish a workable upper-class system for those who had attained wealth. Whether the points of contention were ethnic, religious, old family or purely personal, Wheeling's elite could not seem to agree upon the ingredients for inclusion and exclusion in an upper-class system.

CONCLUSIONS

As the foregoing analysis indicates, the Pittsburgh model was generally validated in the other four cities. Despite some local variations, the institutional context of neighborhood, social clubs and marriages made it possible to identify, classify and rank order the iron and steel elites into relative status categories. Each city developed some sort of stratification system at its upper levels (whatever its degree of articulation and sophistication) which separated the more socially acceptable among the economic elite from those who enjoyed only marginal acceptance.

Despite the similarities, each of the cities was characterized by its local distinctiveness, and each upper-class stratification system varied in some respects from all of the others. In broad terms, there seemed to be four major elements which caused this differentiation: (1) the size of the city; (2) the "age" of the upper-class social system; (3) the cultural background of the area; and (4) and the degree of independence of the community in economic and social terms from other areas.

Generally, the strength and viability of the upper-class stratification system could be rank ordered according to the size of the city. The largest city, Philadelphia, had the most well-articulated and complete upper-class system, followed in descending order by Pittsburgh, Cleveland, Youngstown, Wheeling and Bethlehem. Yet, to some degree, the size of the city must be correlated to the age of the social system—particularly at the upper levels. Again, those cities whose upper-class system was the oldest also appeared to be the most well developed. This differential is particularly evident in the distinction between Pittsburgh and Cleveland. Although of similar size, Pittsburgh had an older, better developed system at the upper-class level. Cleveland appeared to have more difficulty in establishing a similar system at a later date.

The cultural background of the area was also important for providing variations. In Philadelphia, the orientation toward English ancestry and the Episcopal religion colored the nature of its class system. Pittsburgh, on the other hand, was dominated by Scotch-Irish Presbyterians. Cleveland and Youngstown were affected by both groups. But in Youngstown the preferred religion was Presbyterianism. Wheeling's heterogeneous cultural background was reflected in the confusing structure of its upper-class system, unable to identify a dominant group among its elite.

Finally, the degree of economic and social independence of a community was important. This factor had little impact upon the larger cities in the study, but was critical for the smaller ones. Wheeling and Bethlehem tended to operate within the economic and social orbits of Pittsburgh and Philadelphia, respectively. This tended to aid in the retardation of their upper-class social systems. For Youngstown, the situation was a bit different, at least for a time. Although of similar size to Bethlehem, it remained independent of economic and social domination of larger cities until well into the twentieth century. Then, as the economic and social orbit of Cleveland began to make itself felt, the once strong and highly articulated Youngstown upper-class system began to deteriorate. Thus, although correlated to city size, community independence had its own separate and important effect on the formation of the upper-class systems.

Of course there were other, more idiosyncratic factors that entered the picture to give each city a somewhat distinctive upper-class social system. But generally, the Pittsburgh model was validated. With some variations as to size, age, cultural background and community independence, each of the cities studied created, or attempted to create, remarkably similar systems of upper-class status selection.

NOTES

1. E. Digby Baltzell, *Philadelphia Gentlemen* (New York: Free Press, 1958), p. 33.
2. *Ibid.,* pp. 386-387.
3. *Ibid.,* p. 203.
4. The chart is adapted from Baltzell, *Philadelphia Gentlemen.* Baltzell compared *Who's Who in America in 1940* with neighborhood and Philadelphia Social Register listings in 1940.
5. Sam Bass Warner, *The Private City* (Philadelphia: University of Pennsylvania Press, 1968), pp. 178, 188-190.
6. Stephen J. Brobeck, "Changes in the Composition and Structure of Philadelphia Elite Groups, 1756-1790," (Ph.D. Dissertation, University of Pennsylvania, 1972).
7. Baltzell, *Philadelphia Gentlemen,* Chapter 2.
8. Nathaniel Burt, *The Perennial Philadelphians* (Boston: Little, Brown, 1963), p. 87.
9. Baltzell, *Philadelphia Gentlemen,* p. 337.
10. Burt, *Perennial Philadelphians,* p. 17.
11. William G. Rose, *Cleveland: The Making of a City* (Cleveland: World Publishing Co., 1950), p. 364.
12. *Ibid.,* p. 384.
13. George E. Condon, *Cleveland: The Best Kept Secret* (New York: Doubleday, 1967), p. 187.
14. Rose, *Cleveland,* p. 540.
15. *Cleveland Plain Dealer,* February 21, 1965.
16. *About the Rowfant Club* (Cleveland: privately printed, 1960).
17. *Cleveland Press,* January 20, 1951.
18. *Ibid.,* April 21, 1951.
19. The Colonial Club of Cleveland, *Yearbook* (Cleveland: privately printed, 1898).
20. Rose, *Cleveland,* p. 563.
21. *Ibid.,* p. 387.
22. Nathaniel R. Howard, *The First 100 Years: A History of the Union Club of Cleveland* (Cleveland: Union Club Company, 1972).
23. *The Union Club of Cleveland* (Cleveland: privately printed, 1973).
24. *Cleveland Press,* February 10, 1951. See also the *Cleveland Plain Dealer,* June 22, 1964; February 2, 1964.

25. *Cleveland Plain Dealer,* February 6, 1964.

26. Robert Wiebe, *The Search For Order, 1877-1920* (New York: Hall and Wang, 1967), pp. 2-3.

27. Herland Hatcher, *The Western Reserve: The Story of New Connecticut in Ohio* (Indianapolis: Bobbs-Merrill, 1950), p. 288.

28. Arthur I. Vidich and Joseph Bensman, *Small Town in Mass Society: Class, Power and Religion in a Rural Community* (Princeton: Princeton University Press, 1958), p. 39.

29. *Youngstown Vindicator,* March 27, 1938; March 29, 1932; OCtober 14, 1962; February 13, 1964.

30. *Youngstown Vindicator,* June 29, 1939; November 5, 1965.

31. *Youngstown Vindicator,* May 30, 1951; July 20, 1951; January 13, 1955.

32. Robert Doherty, in a paper entitled: "Industrialization and Social Change: Northampton, Mass., 1800-1850," (unpublished paper, presented to the Seminar on Comparative Economic History, March 14, 1967), makes this point concerning the "core families" of Northampton in the early nineteenth century.

Conclusions

The present study has spanned a broad scope. Beginning with the social origins of the late nineteenth-century steel entrepreneurs, it analyzed them within the context of their own city's social and cultural environment. It examined a complex of urban upper-class institutional affiliations—clubs, schools, family marriages and neighborhoods. What do we make of all this? Four conclusions emerge from the study.

First, the role of a businessman was not confined to his activities in the business corporation alone. Without denying the importance of business affairs for these businessmen, it is imperative to emphasize that they were, above all, social animals. It is ironic that historians and other analysts seem quite willing to accept this fundamental social fact about the "average" man, yet are reticent to apply it to businessmen: this, despite the fact that certain clubs and other social organizations have generally been known to have great importance for the business community and the upper classes. A strange kind of double vision occurs. While everyone knows that upper-class businessmen frequent certain social clubs, live in particular neighborhoods, and cultivate marriage and friendship cliques, somehow these are never deemed relevant to an analysis of their business activities.

This study emphasizes, however, that businessmen, like all men, function within a variety of interrelated social contexts. These range from family and cultural background, to a series of social institutions—residence, schools, clubs, marriage and community. Perhaps the most fundamental of these was the family and cultural background of the businessman. If a man came from a poor family, with a cultural background generally downgraded by the established sectors of society, it made success in the business world that much more difficult. Acceptance at the social level was even less certain. Some did achieve approval, but usually only after two or three generations of slow and careful cultivation of the establishment—until such time as the stain of undesirable origins was overcome. Most of those men from disadvantaged backgrounds never attained this status. A good example was the Carnegie family. With origins in poverty, they had also been tainted with religious and political radicalism in Scotland. Though Carnegie achieved great economic success, he was never fully accepted by the social upper class of Pittsburgh. Even more poignant was the case of Charles Schwab. A poor boy of Roman Catholic background, Schwab died insolvent in the twentieth century. He had never been accepted by the older, Protestant, upper-class families. He stood as one of the very few wealthy nineteenth-century steel makers to lose his fortune. Whereas the social ties of other, more socially acceptable steel makers shielded them from financial disaster, Schwab was a man alone, with no one to turn to in an hour of crisis. There were others from poor families with marginal cultural backgrounds who suffered a similar fate—William E. Corey, Andrew Kloman, and Charles J. Harrah. These men from disadvantaged backgrounds found the road to lasting social prestige strewn with insurmountable barriers.

On the other hand, those from the "proper" sort of family and cultural background found their path to fortune and social acceptance well paved. Not only was it easier to secure a good position in the family-oriented firms of the nineteenth century, but their social position allowed them continued good fortune and prosperity in the twentieth century. There was not a single instance of a steel family heir from a good family slipping into permanent insolvency. Instead, incorporating their own personal fortunes with those of other old family members, they built large permanent nest eggs which would guarantee upper-class standing for their respective heirs. Although it is often comforting to think of the "rags to riches" millionaires, the fact remains that the vast majority of those who held executive positions in the nineteenth century, and who continued as part of a wealthy and powerful upper class in the twentieth century, were those who were originally from the proper kinds of family and cultural backgrounds.

What were the "wrong" kinds of family and cultural backgrounds? This varied somewhat by city; but several of them can be isolated. Poverty itself was important, though not as an independent variable. If a man had the other requisites of social position, poverty was not a major drawback. More important were religion and ethnic background. Generally, one had to be Protestant to be accepted. Catholicism and Judaism were enormous disadvantages to be overcome by the person seeking social acceptance. Ethnic tensions complemented religious differences. Though a German Catholic or German Jew would suffer more severe impediments, the German Protestant would not find immediate acceptance either. He might expect eventual inclusion in the social upper class if he cultivated his human relationships properly; but it almost always took two or three generations. The immediate and long-range success of businessmen depended, in large measure, on their familial and cultural backgrounds.

These iron and steel masters functioned within a series of social institutions which did a great deal to shape their total world. The place of residence, social clubs, marriages, and the type of city in which they resided, all played important roles. Though the iron masters had lived close to their mills in the early nineteenth century, without much thought to social homogeneity or the number of surrounding commercial and industrial establishments, the later decades of the century saw the emergence of socially distinct neighborhoods. Increasingly, the acquisition of a fine home in the proper neighborhood formed a principal goal of the businessman's life. Although it is difficult to calculate the effect of this on business decision making in total, one example may demonstrate its importance. Henry Oliver of Pittsburgh, desirous of increased social status, purchased a stately home on Ridge Avenue in Allegheny in the 1880s. This was a very expensive venture, and had come at a point when the Oliver steel firm was facing severe challenges. At the very time when money was needed for plant innovation and expansion, during a period when Oliver's mill failed three times, he spent a fortune on the "right" home in the "right" neighborhood. In other words, he was willing to sacrifice more rapid business expansion in order to obtain social acceptance. How many other businessmen reacted in a similar fashion is difficult to judge; but it is significant that the growth of lavish, new, upper-class neighborhoods came at a time when business was demanding great amounts of capital. Many businessmen, it would seem, were willing to divert some of this capital into immediate social gratification.

At about the same time, a series of social clubs, graded on the order of exclusivity, were founded in these cities. Although there was usually one club in each city which was open to nearly all businessmen (except perhaps Jews, and sometimes Catholics), it became a principal preoccupation of these iron and steel manufacturers to gain acceptance to the more exclusive ones. Whereas those from old families with respectable backgrounds could expect nearly automatic admission to these upper-class clubs, nothing was taken for granted, and much time and effort was spent on cultivating their relationships. Cleveland Amory tells the story of four Boston bluebloods, all of importance in the business community, who gathered at the Somerset Club on April 12, 1945. They lunched together, played cards, ate dinner, then played more cards. Late that night they went home. The next morning they heard for the first time of the death of President Roosevelt—some twenty-four hours before.[1] This is an extreme example; yet it does demonstrate the centrality of the club structure in the lives of most businessmen, often even to the exclusion of pressing business and political events.

For those from more marginal circumstances, the struggle for acceptance into these clubs was even more time consuming. Many newer elite families in the twentieth century spent more time and effort cultivating social acceptance than they had spent in acquiring business success in the nineteenth century. The classic case in this regard was that of Edward T. Stotesbury of Philadelphia. The head of Drexel and Morgan in Philadelphia, he was from a middle-class Quaker family. During the first two decades of the twentieth century he and his family became the most reknowned party-givers in the city (and at their resort in Bar Harbor). Much time, money and energy was spent on this; and when the Stotesburys finally crowned their many years of striving with an invitation to Philadelphia's Assembly Ball, Stotesbury (according to legend) had the invitation encased in glass in his front hall, bathed in flood lights for all to admire. This, not business success, was the most satisfactory achievement in his life.

Marriage choices also played a critical role in the lives of businessmen. In the nineteenth century, marriage formed such a crucial part of the business environment that, in true dynastic fashion, partnership was cemented by a marriage alliance. With the old family firms, this was the surest way to insure a mutually satisfactory arrangement. In the twentieth century, the young man from good family must be certain to marry well, lest he be considered improvident. Several young men from "good" families had been separated from their inheritances for marrying the wrong sort of girl. Without the financial backing of family trust funds and inheritances, the young man was without power or influence in the business world of the twentieth century. Continuing as the key point of assimilation, marriage was not something to be taken lightly. Though romantic love was fine, the old families made certain to insulate their young sons and daughters—by sending them to exclusive prep schools or colleges, by living in socially homogeneous neighborhoods, and by seeking recreation at similar country clubs and resorts—in order to preselect, as far as possible, the marriage partners for their children.

For families from newer elite backgrounds, marriage into the older upper-class families became the ultimate point of assimilation. Thus the Rockefellers, Chisholms, Currys and others spent much time and money seeking the most provident marriage alliances for their children, and were willing to share large accumulations of wealth with older, less affluent families in order to bask in their social prestige. This was a key factor in the maintenance and permanence of these older upper-class families. In return for the hand of their daughter or son in marriage, they were given at least partial guardianship over vast new fortunes. This process was graphically portrayed in Philadelphia. When the Stotesbury family married their daughters with the older upper-class families of the city, their investment firm of Drexel and Morgan (long in the hands of new elites) reverted back to the older upper-class families in the person of Edward Hopkinson, Jr.

The city of residence also had an influence upon the lives of businessmen. An important cultural and economic entity, each city made its imprint upon its native businessmen. Culturally, it made a difference as to the kind of men who rose to executive positions within the local iron and steel industry. An old, seacoast city like Philadelphia drew nearly all of its top level executives from older, seacoast families. It was nearly impossible for someone from a variant background to achieve a top position, either through starting his own firm or rising within existing firms. Newer cities like Cleveland and Youngstown shared some of Philadelphia's preference for seaboard aristocrats; but being newer, they were more open, with a more heterogeneous business elite resulting. Pittsburgh was not as new as Cleveland or Youngstown, nor as old as Philadelphia. Neither did it have ties with old seacoast families. Instead, Pittsburgh represented the rise of a cultural minority of earlier times—the Scotch-Irish. Wheeling, a new city, but one without ties to older sections of the country, was heterogeneous in its makeup. Being part southern and part western, no single group dominated it culturally. The business elite in Wheeling, then, was not only more heterogeneous, but also more open—with the largest number of men from working-class origins rising to positions of leadership.

The economic viability of the city also was important. Pittsburgh, Cleveland and Philadelphia, throughout most of the twentieth century, were centers of considerable growth and opportunity. Thus, one finds large numbers of their upper-class families remaining involved and influential in these financial institutions and industries. A few did leave, to be sure, finding the opportunities in New York more attractive; but the dominant pattern in these cities was to keep a firm hold upon the local economic situation. In Youngstown this was true for the first twenty-five to thirty years of the twentieth century. After that a certain economic decline ensued, with larger numbers of the Youngstown upper class leaving for Cleveland, Pittsburgh or New York. Wheeling was less economically successful. A profound decline hit the city in the early twentieth century, with most of its upper-class businessmen leaving for greener pastures. By the mid-twentieth century, relatively few remained; and for those who did there was little of any economic consequence left to control.

All these elements of the institutional complex had a profound effect upon the lives of businessmen. Some were more intimately involved than others; but the general pattern was one of deep immersion in the social and cultural realities of their existence. The businessmen who operated outside of this context were more the exception than the rule. In order to properly analyze the role and influence of business an investigation of this wide range of involvements was required.

The second conclusion, which is closely related to the first, is that most of these business entrepreneurs were not isolated individuals, but were members of a group, a class. Although "class" refers fundamentally to economic stratification, these economic factors (like the businessmen himself) did not operate in vacuum. Milton Gordon has explained the elements of class, or social class, in a particularly cogent manner:

> They [economic factors] function within a particular political and community power context, which they, in turn, condition. They are associated with particular occupational specializations. They have the effect through time of producing a status order, and this status order in turn plays a role in determining economic rewards in the current society. These economic factors, furthermore, make for different lev-

> els of consumption and correspondingly different "ways of life" or cultural attributes. The cumulation of these phenomena produces restrictions on intimate social contracts which lead to "group life" divisions in the society. All these phenomena, set in motion basically by the operation of the economic system, in turn work back to some extent on the economic mechanism itself and affect its operation.[2]

The basic prerequisite for these iron and steel entrepreneurs was the attainment of a certain economic level, which most of them did achieve. Although there were variations in the amount of wealth, nearly all became wealthy enough to be considered for inclusion in the social upper class. All had also achieved a necessary occupational specialization—that of independent entrepreneurs or highly skilled and highly paid business executives—in order to be considered for inclusion in this class group.

As noted above, however, the mere acquisition of money or the attainment of high economic position alone was not enough to insure entrance. More important was to establish a network of interrelationships through clubs, residence and marriage. For those who could pass the tests of family and cultural background (or who were able to overcome these prior obstacles), the path was open for admission into the select circle of upper-class activities. The problem is that many analysts have seen the operations of upper-class institutions as a rather silly game, a meaningless set of honors bestowed upon bemused participants. Very often the acquisition of club membership or the striving after a "good" marriage was viewed as an infantile preoccupation of a decadent set of puerile aristocrats. What these analysts miss are the realities of power in the situation. These social achievements, these hallmarks of arrival of status, served to set the group apart from the rest of society for important political and economic reasons. Through their functioning as a group, as a class of social cohorts, they were better able to protect their common concern and interests.

The functioning of men's clubs in the various cities are a good case in point. Membership in these clubs was essential to the businessman who wished to rise above a certain point in the business hierarchy. So much business was done over lunch, or late in the afternoons in these clubs, that if a businessman did not belong he would miss out on many of the important transactions in his industry. Though membership in the elite clubs (such as the Duquesne of Pittsburgh and the Union League of Philadelphia) was more open to general elite influence, in each city there was at least one club which was highly selective in its membership.

Marriages and residence were more indirect. Residence was the least exclusive of the social characteristics of upper-class status. Correlating more closely with simple economic standing, one could usually purchase a fine home in the "best" neighborhood with little interference. Yet the process of selectivity worked in subtle ways here. There was little solace in living in a fine neighborhood if one's neighbors refused social intercourse, or moved away. This happened to Tom L.

Johnson of Cleveland. No sooner had he moved into a select neighborhood on Euclid Avenue, when his neighbors began moving further east. He followed them, and the same thing happened again. Generally, a few subtle hints were enough, and families tended to settle most often among their social equals. Fearful of being considered upstarts—and thus being denied club memberships and marriages of greater importance—the new elite families would settle in the "appropriate" neighborhood, biding their time until they received full acceptance. Thus, the upper-class neighborhoods retained an impressive social homogeneity. Not as exclusive as clubs, they nevertheless provided an environment for socialization of like peoples.

This process of residential stratification was abetted by the summer resorts. Using a similar selection process, with the same subtle social barometers in operation, they tended toward a social homogeneity. This meant that during the summers certain resorts were "the" places to go; and they were places to be achieved, not bought. If too many "outsiders" came in, the resort acquired a "bad" name, causing the older families to move on to a new place. Thus, even during the summer's leisured recreation, there was a constant interaction between social class members.

Marriage was the ultimate point of assimilation in social class, and the most important. Yet it is also the most difficult to summarize. Generally, those who managed to be accepted in the right clubs, neighborhoods, schools and resorts became candidates for marriage in the social upper classes. When this occurred, there was little question any longer of the individual's place in the group. He was no longer "on the rise": he had arrived. He now functioned within the most intimate familial and social relationships of the group.

All this would be rather meaningless social preening, were it not for the economic manifestations of class. For it is through these institutions that the social upper classes gather and express their interests. This is a complex process, but nonetheless real. Leaders of the more prominent banking and financial institutions of each city and of New York all shared common class characteristics. All, or nearly all, belonged to the same upper-class clubs, lived in similar neighborhoods, attended the same schools, and in the end, married together. The same was true of members of the leading law firms. The proper breeding, the proper schooling, the correct family background, were always more important than the scores on bar examinations. These financial and legal institutions, operating with their social cohorts on the boards of directors of the major industrial corporations, exerted a web of control and influence of great extent.

To ignore these class and familial connections is to ignore reality. Although commonality of background and class participation does not always insure mutual accord, it does imply a certain basic commonality of purpose. As Ralph Linton has noted: "the small group of individuals who control big business and banking in this country are probably more conscious of their common interests than the members of any other so called class."[3] There was a stronger tendency to recognize class over individual interests—to posit one's duty to family and class—among the upper classes than among any other group in society. These ties, including an interlocking network of marriages, served to allow the group to operate nearly as one in the economic mechanism of the twentieth century. Although, for example, one sees some friction between the Cleveland and Youngstown upper-class groups over control of Republic Steel and Youngstown Iron and Steel in the early twentieth century, by mid-century most of this had abated. This was because of the increasingly closer class connections of the two groups through common club memberships, residences, and most of all, through marriage. The most important aspect of the economic consolidation of the steel industry in the twentieth century was its social consolidation in the hands of the upper classes.

The third major conclusion is that these upper-class business entrepreneurs and their families remained, despite strong class ties, very community oriented and place oriented. There is, of course, some variation in this by individual and by city. In each city there were certain of the iron and steel entrepreneurs who appeared more rootless. The turn of the century saw them setting into nearly perpetual motion—owning homes in New York, Europe, the southern United States, and in the northern resort areas: they became early prototypes of modern day "jetsetters." Their sense of place was transient and ephemeral; they became the true cosmopolitans.

These cosmopolitan types were in a distinct minority. More common were those who were deeply rooted in their home communities. Despite attendance at schools and colleges away from home, despite economic ties and club memberships in other cities, despite summer resorts and winter retreats to Florida, they remained closely tied to their local communities. This was true particularly of those in the innermost circles of the local upper class—the core families. Although being of generally the highest prestige—both locally and nationally—of any of the family groups, they were in reality the least cosmopolitan. This was seen most clearly in their marriage choices. Whereas the other family groups felt somewhat more free to marry exogamously outside their home community, these core families felt duty-bound to their social obligations at home. Thus, they remained as the social arbiters of the local community, reserving the bulk of their marriages for their social peers on the local level.

The variations by city were also important. Generally, the Pittsburgh upper class (particularly its core families) were the most locally oriented. They were followed by Philadelphia and Youngstown. At the lower end of the scale, although in different ways, were Cleveland and Wheeling. The reasons for Pittsburgh's more local orientation are not easy to discern. Part of the reason undoubtedly was their Scotch-Irish heritage. Generally disdained in the early nineteenth century by the seacoast upper classes of English background, they developed their own defense mechanism of closure. Just as the eastern societies shut them out of their social institutions, the Pittsburgh Scotch-Irish developed their own sense of uniqueness, asserting their own moral and social superiority. However false and hollow this may have been in its inception, it could well have developed a staying power in the late nineteenth and early twentieth centuries. Now secure in wealth and position, they could posit a powerful urge to continue the comfortable home ties.

The nature of the city's residential development itself may also have had something to do with it. Pittsburgh's upper-class neighborhoods showed less decline than those of any other city in the study. Whereas the upper class of the other cities had pretty well vacated the urban environment by the mid-twentieth century, one still found large numbers of the Pittsburgh upper class living in their old urban neighborhoods. This no doubt added to the desirability of Pittsburgh in their minds. Why leave, why develop extensive outside ties, when the life at home was so comfortable? There were no doubt other factors in producing Pittsburgh's relative provincialism; but these two seem strongest.

Philadelphia, although fairly strongly community oriented, did display more cosmopolitan characteristics than the Pittsburgh upper classes. Though there was a great pride and attractiveness in the home institutions, the Philadelphia upper classes lacked some of the characteristics of the Pittsburgh group. First, as an accepted part of the seaboard upper class, they found it easier to intermarry and establish social relations with upper classes from like cities than did the Pittsburgh upper class. Thus, the Boston and New England old family members who came to Philadelphia to enter the steel industry remained there, marrying into its old families. In Pittsburgh these relationships tended to be far more transient. Philadelphia's urban, upper-class neighborhoods disappeared in the early twentieth century, scattering upper-class Philadelphians to the suburbs. Though these suburbs display much permanence, providing a certain sense of place and community, they probably had a less integrating effect than the urban, upper-class neighborhoods in Pittsburgh.

Youngstown, prior to the 1930s, was probably the most place-oriented of all the cities. The small, cohesive upper class married extensively, and nearly exclusively, with one another. In addition, they all lived within a very few blocks of one another in the Wick Avenue area of Youngstown, further promoting this sense of community. As the inner city neighborhoods deteriorated, however, the families were forced to move. Instead of moving to the Youngstown suburbs, many moved into the suburbs of Cleveland. Coterminous with this process, they began to marry exogomously at a rapid rate. By the 1960s the Youngstown upper class could no longer be considered strongly community-oriented.

Wheeling was a little perplexing in terms of cosmopolitanism. A large proportion of her upper-class families left around the turn of the century, making them appear more cosmopolitan. Yet, most simply resettled in new communities, making themselves solid pillars of their newly adopted upper-class establishments. Their marriage patterns and other social relationships in that sense, remained quite localistic: very few became rootless beings. Those upper-class members who stayed in Wheeling generally retained rather highly localistic arrangements. Due to the small size of the local upper class, there were a fair number of outward marriages; but few of these were to identifiable upper classes in other cities.

On balance there was a strong residue of localism among the Wheeling upper classes: many of them had simply transferred it to other social environments.

Cleveland appeared to be the most genuinely cosmopolitan, the least community oriented, of the cities in the study. Part of this was due to strong continuing ties with its old New England communities. A not unusual pattern was for upper-class Cleveland families to reach back to Connecticut or Massachusetts for a marriage partner. Yet it was broader than this. The Cleveland upper-class families also married with upper classes in other areas—New York, Chicago, Pittsburgh, Youngstown, Wheeling, and elsewhere—with greater frequency.

It is not easy to find reasons for this. Cleveland's constantly shifting neighborhoods certainly did little to implant a sense of community or sense of place among the upper classes. More than any city in the study, Cleveland's neighborhoods deteriorated faster, with new ones being built more quickly. Added to this was the rather unstratified nature of the club system. No social club in Cleveland quite had the prestige of the Pittsburgh Club, Philadelphia Club or Somerset Club. This may have made marriages to families from other cities—particularly cities with more highly stratified systems—more attractive for social reasons. And, finally, after having moved to a frontier environment in the early nineteenth century, then having moved one's residence so many times in succeeding years, may have made it psychologically impossible for these Cleveland upper classes to ever truly develop a sense of place. Somewhat like the children of career army men, they were not sure where "home" was.

Whatever these variations, however, the great majority of the upper-class families in all the cities were community oriented. This was especially true of those with the highest overall prestige. It is important to correct Baltzell's view of a marked break around 1880 from a local, community-oriented upper class to a national one. However many national ties are established, these generally rested firmly upon a foundation of local roots and institutions in which the relationships of community (culture, ethnicity, marriage, clubs, etc.) were powerful cementing factors.

The fourth, and final conclusion, has to do with the continuity of institutions. Previous historians have tended to emphasize the dynamics of change at the upper-class levels of American society. This has created an image of a "circulation of elites," of a "shirt sleeves to shirt sleeves" phenomenon in the American past. In the period from the War of 1812 to the coming of Andrew Jackson to the presidency, the stress has been upon the "decline of aristocracy" and the "rise of the common man." Then, again, in the period after the Civil War, following the lead of Henry and Brooks Adams, historians have stressed the rise of a new plutocracy which displaced older aristocrats. Similarly, others have seen a great change around World War I, with the seeming passage of the "Age of Innocence" dominated by genteel old families, who are replaced by the "Babbits" of the twenties. Again, at the end of the twenties, social commentators like Arthur Schlesinger Jr., A. A. Berle, Gardiner Means and Frederick Lewis Allen have observed the "Passing of the Older Order," and the emergence of a new, more democratic group of leaders. Yet this study would indicate there has been more continuity than change among the business elites and upper classes in America.

This continuity can be seen in several ways. It can be viewed first of all, in the backgrounds of the iron and steel entrepreneurs of the late nineteenth century. Although the great expansion of the industry opened the way for the rise of several men from newer elite backgrounds, the bulk of the iron and steel manufacturers came from the ranks of the upper-class and upper-middle-class families of the early nineteenth century. Not only were the great majority of them the sons of businessmen and professionals; they also represented a continuation of the dominant cultural groups of the early nineteenth century. The great majority were English, Scottish, Welsh, or Scotch-Irish in background; and there was an inordinant representation of Episcopalians and Presbyterians, the two "elite" religions of the nineteenth century. Rather than representing a new group, or any essential break with the dominant groups of the past, they instead represented a strong continuity. With only a small minority of the nineteenth-century iron and steel manufacturers from backgrounds of poverty, immigration or cultural disadvantage, there is little evidence of a great break with the past business elites and upper-class groups in the late nineteenth century.

This continuity can be seen throughout the twentieth century also. At first glance there appeared to be a momentous change in the steel industry at the turn of the century, with the rise of the new consolidations. As they absorbed most of the old family firms and installed new management—who tended increasingly toward the professional bureaucrat, with no ties to these older upper-class families—it did seem as if the "old order" had passed. Yet, upon closer investigation, the continuity become more apparent. It is true that the old families no longer participated, generally, in the running of the steel mills of the twentieth century. But their forms of involvement had merely shifted to another, more indirect type. Now they either served on the boards of directors of these consolidations or, more often, were represented on them by their financial, legal and class cohorts.

This shift to a more indirect influence in the steel industry of the twentieth century was supplemented by a much broader involvement in the economic affairs of the largest financial and non-financial institutions in America. Through trust funds invested with upper-class banking institutions, and looked after by members of "bluestocking" law firms, these nineteenth-century iron and steel families were able to posit a strong presence in some 28 percent of the 200 largest non-financial corporations in America.[4]

This strong continuity was mirrored in, and influenced by, a basic continuity in social institutions. Although most of the upper-class clubs and other barometers of upper-class standing were originated in the late nineteenth century, they represented a vaildation of the old instead of the creation of something new. Rather than demonstrating the rise to power of a new plutocracy or the emergence of a new metropolitan, cosmopolitan upper class, they more clearly and finally articulated the position of the older localistic upper classes vis-à-vis the newer groups. At the same time, they set forth the steps and procedures by which those newer elites could gain entrance, as newer families were slowly and carefully assimilated into the older upper-class structure during the twentieth century.

Through this constellation of clubs, marriages, Social Register listings, and the like, the older upper-class groups were able to exercise a control and dominance over both the political and economic world at the upper levels. Just as there was little drastic change in the personnel of these clubs and other institutions during the twentieth century, there was also little change in the reality of power in the economic sphere. These same club members and marriage cohorts continued to control the major investment and law firms and to sit on the boards of directors of the major corporations. New members were added, thus broadening and expanding the group, but never producing fundamental reorganization.

Despite the changes in wealth and upper-class membership throughout these years, a more basic continuity remained. A core of upper-class members continued, while others on the periphery either came and went, or were slowly incorporated into the long-range and persistent upper-class institutions. The upper-class institutional context stood as a bulwark of conservatism in an age of dynamic change—a conservatism which was, in turn, to temper the degree of change which was possible in the economic and political spheres.

NOTES

1. Cleveland Amory, *The Proper Bostonians,* (New York: Harper, 1932), p. 359.
2. Milton Gordon, *Social Class in American Sociology* (New York: McGraw-Hill, 1963), p. 234.
3. Ralph L. Linton, *The Study of Man* (New York: Appleton, Century, Crofts, 1938), quoted in E. Digby Baltzell, *Philadelphia Gentlemen* (New York: Fress Press), p.364.
4. Based upon preliminary analysis of these firms by the present author.

Statistical Appendix: Kinship and Club Networks in Five Cities

Table 52, following, presents in tabular form the network affiliations described in Chapters 4 and 5. Generally, the table measures the following network properties: frequency of endogamous marriage (the percentage of total marriage choices which are endogamous); the frequency of club membership; the density of club membership (the percentage of total possible upper-class social club memberships in the city held by each family); the density of total participation in the endogamous marriage and social club network (the percentage of total marriage choices and club memberships in which each family participates); the frequency of club memberships with all other families in the city (social club interlocks); and, finally, the density of these social club interlocks between the families (the percentage of family interlocks compared to the total number if all families were members of all clubs).

The only exception to the above format is with the city of Youngstown. In that city, since so many of the interlocking club memberships were in Cleveland, and elsewhere, rather than in Youngstown, it did not seem to make much sense to attempt to calculate either the density of club memberships or the density of the family club interlocks.

TABLE 52
Comparative Summary of Upper-Class Networks

City	Number	Average Number of Endogamous Marriages	Percentage of Endogamous Marriages	Average Number of Club Members	Percentage of Club Members	Percentage of Total Connections	Number of Club Interlocks	Percentage of Club Interlocks
PITTSBURGH	*N*=207	3.4	27	3.7	33	30	347	15
Core	*N*=43	10.6	33	7.0	64	42	615	27
Non-Core	*N*=61	3.0	27	4.0	36	32	386	17
Marginal	*N*=32	1.0	15	2.6	24	20	288	13
Elite	*N*=71	0.4	9	1.7	16	14	178	08
PHILADELPHIA	*N*=75	2.0	20	1.8	23	21	31	05
Core	*N*=13	7.5	23	5.5	69	32	93	16
Non-Core	*N*=13	2.5	19	1.9	24	21	34	06
Marginal	*N*=19	1.3	22	1.3	16	19	23	04
Elite	*N*=30	0.0	00	0.5	06	05	8	01
CLEVELAND	*N*=60	1.4	13	3.8	31	24	90	13
Core	*N*=6	6.5	24	8.0	67	37	174	25
Non-Core	*N*=18	2.0	14	5.0	42	27	111	16
Marginal	*N*=13	0.4	04	4.0	33	21	100	14
Elite	*N*=23	0.1	02	1.6	13	11	47	07
YOUNGSTOWN	*N*=37	2.4	26				13	
Core	*N*=6	10.8	33				26	
Non-Core	*N*=14	1.4	26				12	
Marginal	*N*=8	0.3	04				12	
Elite	*N*=9	0.0	00				5	
WHEELING	*N*=39	1.0	21	0.7	15	18	5	03
Core	*N*=6	4.2	48	1.5	30	42	12	06
Non-Core	*N*=6	1.0	20	1.0	20	20	5	03
Marginal	*N*=15	0.4	10	0.7	15	12	5	03
Elite	*N*=12	0.0	00	0.3	05	03	2	01
AVERAGE: ALL CITIES:	*N*=418	2.5	23	3.0	33	28	192	NA

Bibliographic Note

What I intend in this relatively short space is to give the reader some idea of the kinds of materials which were utilized to gather information, rather than give listings of hundreds of obscure county histories and other compendia.

The most difficult and time-consuming aspect of this study was the compiling of biographical information on the 696 iron and steel masters. For some, the information was quite extensive; for others, the task seemed almost impossible at times. The general sources used to find biographical data were national biographical and genealogical compilations. The single, most useful source here was the *National Cyclopedia of American Biography* (58 volumes, New York: J. T. White, 1892-1964). Unlike the *Dictionary of American Biography* or *Who's Who,* the *National Cyclopedia* carries a much more extensive treatment of nineteenth-century businessmen. A useful source of genealogical information was Frederick A. Virkus, ed. *The Abridged Compendium of American Genealogy* 7 volumes, (Chicago: Marquis & Co., 1925-).

The national compendiums, however, contained information on only about 10 to 15 percent of the iron and steel men. Far more useful were the more obscure publications. First of all, much biographical material was obtained from the obituary columns of trade and industrial publications. *Iron Age* (1873–) was the most useful; but a great deal of material was also found in the publications of the various engineering associations, and in other trade and industrial journals. Other fertile sources were the county and city histories published through the late nineteenth and early twentieth centuries. Most of these were multivolume works which included large biographical sections of locally prominent citizens. Despite their puffery, they were invaluable sources of information on many businessmen who had otherwise slipped from public view.

Information on social clubs, and on the neighborhood and marriage patterns for iron and steel families were obtained from a wide variety of sources. Much of the basic information was gathered from such local indices as the Social Register and Blue Book. This was supplemented in most cities by information from newspapers, especially the "society column." In Pittsburgh, I was fortunate to be able to use the *Bulletin-Index,* a "society" newspaper which provided many important insights. In addition, most of the social clubs in each of the cities published their own histories, which also provided membership lists for certain years. Records of marriage were found in newspaper clipping files and in genealogies; kinship systems were reconstructed from these cemetery records, and Social Register and Blue Book notations.

References to secondary materials, or to those primary materials which were most helpful in constructing certain sections of this work are included in the notes following each chapter of this text.

Index

ABOUT THE AUTHOR

John N. Ingham, associate professor of history at the University of Toronto, specializes in American social history and American urban history. He has published articles on business in the early twentieth century in *Mid-America,* the *Journal of American History,* the *Journal of Urban History, Pennsylvania Magazine of History and Biography,* and other journals.